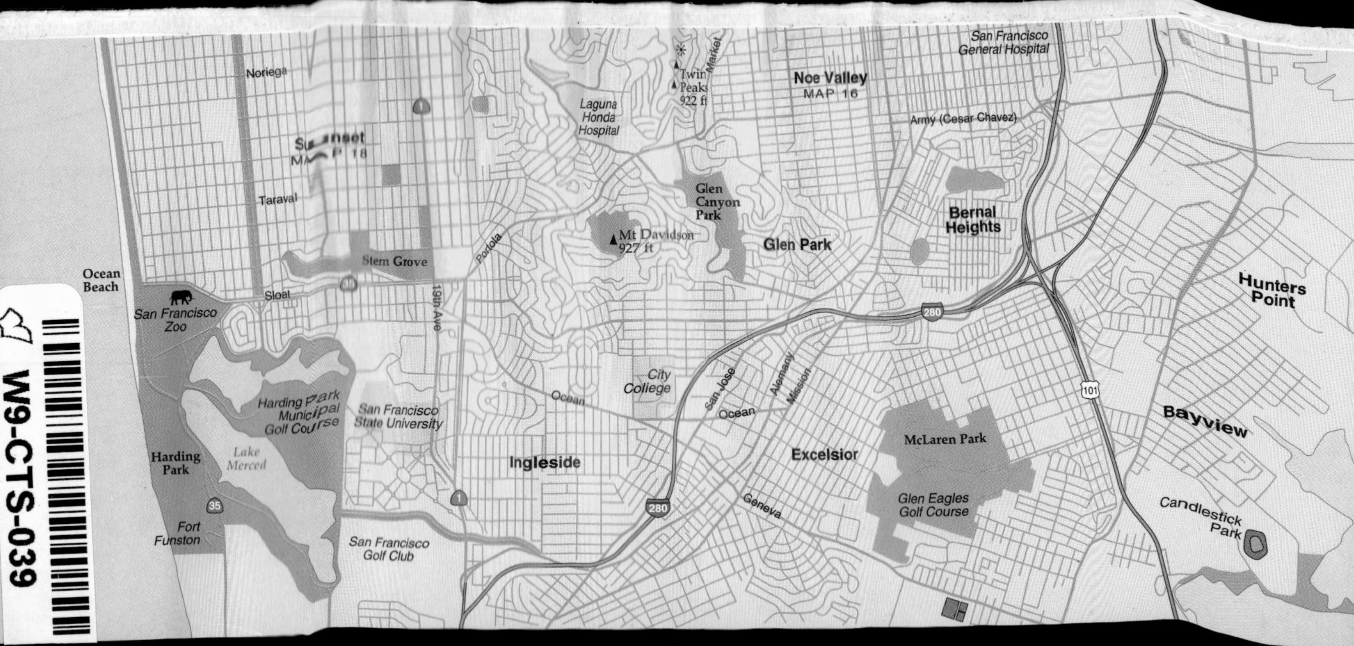

Noriega
Taraval
Sloat
Ocean Beach
San Francisco Zoo
Stern Grove
19th Ave
Portola
Laguna Honda Hospital
Twin Peaks 922 ft
Market
Mt Davidson 927 ft
Glen Canyon Park
Glen Park
Noe Valley
MAP 16
San Francisco General Hospital
Army (Cesar Chavez)
Bernal Heights
Hunters Point
Bayview
Candlestick Park
McLaren Park
Glen Eagles Golf Course
Excelsior
Geneva
Mission
Alemany
Ocean
San Jose
City College
Ingleside
San Francisco State University
Harding Park Municipal Golf Course
Lake Merced
Harding Park
Fort Funston
San Francisco Golf Club
280
101
35
1

San Francisco

a Lonely Planet city guide

by Tony Wheeler

San Francisco
1st edition

Published by
Lonely Planet Publications
Head Office: PO Box 617, Hawthorn, Vic 3122, Australia
Branches: 155 Filbert St, Suite 251, Oakland, CA 94607, USA
10 Barley Mow Passage, Chiswick, London W4 4PH, UK
71 bis rue du Cardinal Lemoine, 75005 Paris, France

Printed by
Colorcraft Ltd, Hong Kong

Photographs by
Front cover: Golden Gate Bridge, Philip Coblentz
Title page: Broadway Pier, Rick Gerharter

First Published
February 1996

Although the author and publisher have tried to make the information as accurate as possible, they accept no responsibility for any loss, injury or inconvenience sustained by any person using this book.

National Library of Australia Cataloguing in Publication Data

Wheeler, Tony, 1946-
San Francisco.

1st ed.
Includes index.
ISBN 0 86442 333 0.

1. San Francisco (Calif.) – Guidebooks.
I. Title. (Series: Lonely Planet city guide).

917.94610453

Tony Wheeler

Tony was born in England but grew up in Pakistan, the Bahamas, and the USA. He returned to England to do a degree in engineering at Warwick University, worked as an automotive design engineer, returned to university to complete an MBA in London, then dropped out on the Asian overland trail with his wife Maureen.

They've been traveling ever since, having set up Lonely Planet Publications in the mid-'70s. Travel for the Wheelers is considerably enlived by their daughter Tashi and their son Kieran.

From the Author

I left my heart in San Francisco after spending a year and a half there in the mid-'80s. I've been a regular returnee ever since and I could happily move back tomorrow. So exploring the Bay Area in detail was a real labor of love, but it's too big, too varied, and too complex a conglomeration of cities for one person to even dream of coming to grips with. Fortunately the enthusiastic band of hard-living LP-ites at the Lonely Planet office in beautiful downtown Oakland (some of them real honest-to-God native Californians) fanned out to add an insider's perspective to my outsider's viewpoint. Particular thanks to the following staffers for graciously revealing all their favorite restaurants, bars, rumors, and odd-ball places (well, almost all): Hugh D'Andrade, Michelle Gagne, Don Gates, Heather Harrison, Carolyn Hubbard, Cyndy Johnsen, Eric Kettunen, Caroline Liou, Carolyn Miller, Jen Morris, Ann Neet, Sacha Pearson, Erin Reid, Caryn Sherne, Scott Stampfli, Scott Summers, and Laini Taylor.

Other San Francisco locals who reluctantly gave away their well-guarded secrets are Howard Karel, Kathy Parnell, and Ilysse Rimalovski.

From the Publisher

This first edition was brought to life in the skylit wonderland of Lonely Planet USA in Oakland, California. Laini Taylor swung the scalpel, AnneLise Sorensen withheld anesthetic, and Michelle Gagne tied the sutures and made the monster live. The maps were drawn by Scott Summers, and Hugh D'Andrade illustrated and designed the book, despite persistent attempts by the editorial staff to thwart him. Special thanks to Don Gates for fact-checking, research, and melodrama, Kate Hoffman for her snack drawer, Jen Morris for sneaking away from the sales department to help out, and Carolyn Hubbard and Caroline Liou for editorial guidance.

Thanks also to Chris Carlsson for the sidebar on Emperor Norton, Morrissey for spiritual guidance, and J.R. Swanson for the Critical Mass illustration.

Warning & Request

Things change - prices go up, schedules change, good places go bad, and bad places go bankrupt - nothing stays the same. So if you find things better or worse, recently opened, or long since closed, please write and tell us and help make the next edition better.

Your letters will be used to help update future editions and, where possible, important changes will also be included in a Stop Press section in reprints.

We greatly appreciate all information that is sent to us by travelers. Back at Lonely Planet we employ a hardworking readers' letters team to sort through the many letters we receive. The best ones will be rewarded with a free copy of the next edition or another Lonely Planet guide if you prefer. We give away lots of books, but, unfortunately, not every letter / postcard receives one.

Contents

Introduction

Visually spectacular, historically colorful, and a regular trendsetter in everything from flower power to gay liberation, San Francisco consistently tops the polls as America's favorite city.

The city's irresistible attraction starts with the way it looks. Streets soar up and plunge down the steep hills, framing spectacular views and hiding quiet little pockets within the urban chaos. In the background there's always the Bay, crossed by not one but two of the world's best known bridges. What's more, San Francisco is a city of multiple disguises; sure there's a booming downtown business center, but there are also a host of micro cities. San Francisco's colorful, crowded, and frenetic Chinatown jostles up against ritzy Union Square. It quickly fades into the bars, cafes, and restaurants of North Beach, the Beat center of the '50s. That blends into Fisherman's Wharf, the raucous tourist center and jumping-off point for Alcatraz. There's also the Latino enclave of the Mission, the gay epicenter of the Castro, the club scene in SoMa, reminders of the flower power era in the Haight-Ashbury, and the much-loved Golden Gate Park.

Of course, there's much more to do than simply eye the scenery. In San Francisco getting there is half the fun, particularly on the city's beloved cable cars. Accommodations range from a competitive bunch of international youth-oriented backpacker hostels to glossy five-star palaces and some wonderfully romantic B&Bs. San Francisco has to be one of the world's great eating centers with everything from Mexican and Asian cheap eats to stylish restaurants serving the city's cutting edge California cuisine. After dark the city's theaters, clubs, and bars are surprisingly relaxed and welcoming; San Francisco isn't keen on the fashion police arbitrating who will and won't gain entry.

Nor is San Francisco the start and finish of the Bay Area. Head north to trendy Marin County – laid back, affluent, and on top of everything new from hot tubs to mountain bikes. Head further north to the wilds of Point Reyes National Seashore or the pleasures of the famous Wine Country, home to America's most acclaimed wine makers. Across the Bay are the East Bay centers of Berkeley and Oakland. The San Francisco Bay Area: it's quite a region.

Facts about San Francisco

HISTORY

San Francisco is a new city. It was less than 250 years ago that the first European eyes were set on the Bay. Prior to the European arrival the area was inhabited by a number of Native American tribes, the most numerous of them the Coast Miwoks who lived in present-day Marin County, and the Ohlone tribes scattered in small settlements throughout the rest of the Bay Area. Altogether, these groups probably only numbered about 15,000 people.

Remarkably the first European visitors to this area of California totally missed the San Francisco Bay, the largest bay in all of California. Sir Francis Drake stopped by in 1579, landed at Point Reyes about 35 miles north of San Francisco, claimed the area as Nova Albion and thus gave Queen Elizabeth I her second New England. He then sailed off south to engage in a little more piratical profiteering at the Spanish expense and blithely sailed straight past the Golden Gate, the entrance to the Bay, without noticing it. Not many years later, in 1595 Spanish explorer Sebastian Rodriguez Cermenho renamed the Point Reyes bay, now known as Drakes Bay, as La Bahia de San Francisco but then wrecked his ship on Point Reyes and had to crawl south to the safety of Acapulco in a vessel lashed together from the wreckage. He too failed to notice the San Francisco Bay; its European discovery had to wait nearly another 200 years.

Spanish San Francisco

The Spanish already had one California, the long peninsula now known as Baja (low) California, south of today's Mexican border, when they decided to move north into Alta (high) California in 1796. Three different Spanish groups came to Alta California: the military established their *presidios* (forts), civilians founded the *pueblos* (settlements), but the best known and longest lasting of the Spanish – and later Mexican – establishments were the religious missions.

The Spanish established their first mission in San Diego in 1769, and pressed north to build the second in Monterey. This overland party led by Gaspàr de Portola originally overshot its intended destination of Monterey and stumbled upon a bay which they took to be Cermenho's San Francisco Bay at Point Reyes. But, impressed though they were by this huge expanse of water, they turned back to set up the Monterey mission in 1770, which became the center of Spanish California.

In 1775 Juan Manuel de Ayala sailed the *San Carlos* into the Bay, the first European ship to enter the Golden Gate. He was followed in 1776 by Captain Juan Bautista de Anza, who built a presidio above the Golden Gate and the Mission Dolores, three miles south in the heart of today's Mission district. Today there are traces of that initial settlement at both sites. Five more Bay Area missions followed in Santa Clara (1777), in Santa Cruz (1791), near Fremont (1797), in San Rafael (1817), and in Sonoma (1823). An official Spanish pueblo was established in San Jose at the same time as the nearby mission but an unofficial village also sprang up between the Golden Gate presidio and the Mission Dolores. This tiny village was known as Yerba Buena, and it's the real birthplace of modern San Francisco.

The Spanish missionaries had little respect for the Native Americans, an intrinsically gentle people according to the descriptions of early settlers, but they were wiped out because of new diseases and simple neglect, rather than any deliberate policy.

The Gold Rush & Boom Years

The Spanish were kicked out of Mexico in 1821 so it was the new Mexican government to which President Andrew Jackson made an offer to buy the Bay Area in 1835. He was turned down but this was still a sparsely populated region and when the Americans did take over in 1846, as a result of victory in the Mexican-American War rather than a successful cash offer, Yerba Buena's mixed population was still only 200 to 300.

Yerba Buena was renamed San Francisco in 1847 and official American control followed in early 1848, just a week after a momentous discovery was made 120 miles east in the Sierra Nevada mountains: gold. The news was soon out and prospectors began to flood in; over 100,000 hardy "49ers" made the long overland trek or the dangerous sea voyage to San Francisco and the population exploded from 500 to 25,000 within a year. In 1850 California became the 31st state in the union and by 1854 the booming gold rush town already had more than 500 saloons and 20 theaters to entertain the hard-spending miners.

The initial gold rush fever had subsided by 1859 when a second rush took place, this time for the even richer wealth of the silver Comstock Lode near Reno in

Nevada. Extracting this fabulous hoard required capital investment rather than hard sweat, but it financed another boom cycle for the city.

The late 1870s saw the boom years of the gold and silver rushes dry up and there were ugly attacks on the substantial Chinese population which had arrived in California both for the mineral rushes and to construct the transcontinental railway. Nevertheless, the city grew steadily and at the turn of the century the population was approaching 350,000. The Spanish-American War in 1898 and the Klondike Gold Rush in Canada's Yukon in 1896 underlined the city's importance as a port while the opening of numerous banks established its continuing importance as a financial center. Then the "Big One" brought a severe shake up.

The Big One

There had been major earthquakes in 1812 and 1865 but the Big One of May 18, 1906 is estimated to have come in at around 8.3 on the Richter Scale (which had not, at that time, been invented), a magnitude still unmatched in Californian tremblor history. The quake was centered 25 miles north of San Francisco near Point Reyes but it was not the quake itself which was to devastate the city. The real damage came from the fires – lit by toppling chimneys and fed by fractured gas mains – which swept across the city. Water mains had fractured too so there was no water to fight the blaze and by the time the conflagrations had burned out three days later the city had been devastated from the waterfront all the way to Van Ness Ave. It was stopped there only by dynamiting the great buildings along the boulevard to make a fire break. In 1906, about 600 people were estimated dead as a result of the fire and its catastrophic aftermath (in con-

COURTESY OF THE BANCROFT LIBRARY

Downtown San Francisco after the 1906 quake

Earthquakes

Earthquakes are the very tangible evidence of what sounds like a dry subject: plate tectonics theory. The earth's surface is made up of a number of large plates which are gradually shifting in relationship to one another. Problems develop when one plate rubs up against another because the shift is not a gradual and gentle one. Unfortunately, the city of San Francisco straddles the San Andreas Fault, the dividing line between the Eastern Pacific and the North American plates. Half of the Bay Area is on its way north to Alaska.

Earthquakes are measured on the Richter Scale, which records the total amount of energy released in the quake. It's a logarithmic scale which means each step up the scale is 10 times as powerful. A magnitude 5 earthquake is 10 times as powerful as a magnitude 4 earthquake. The 1906 quake was approximately 8.3, the 1989 quake 7.1.

The further away from a city a quake has its epicenter the better. The Big One of 1906 had its epicenter 25 miles north of downtown San Francisco and 1989's Big One was 45 miles south. How far underground the quake takes place is another factor. The center of activity can be many miles beneath the surface and quakes do not usually result in huge chasms opening up as one side of the street moves a block north and another a block south.

The underlying strata has a big influence on the likely damage bill and if you're in an earthquake zone the number one rule is to build on rock. The 1989 quake damaged the Oakland side of the Bay Bridge, built on squishy bay bottom mud, but left the San Francisco side relatively unscathed, strung between solid San Francisco and Yerba Buena Island rock foundations. The final factor in what an earthquake can do is tied up with the buildings it shakes. When things begin to bounce, steel-reinforced concrete, which combines strength with flexibility, is far better than an unreinforced brick building. ■

trast Tokyo's 1923 Big One killed over 100,000), but later calculations boosted the number up to 3000. In addition, as many as 100,000 people were made homeless and tent cities were established in Golden Gate Park, the Presidio, and other city park land.

The Big One gave San Francisco the opportunity to rebuild the city. Just a year earlier an architect had actually come up with a plan that blended the streets into the city's roller coaster terrain, but in the race to rebuild the city this was completely ignored and San Francisco was rebuilt to the same straightforward pre-quake grid pattern, resolutely ignoring the imperatives of topography. Ten years of frantic rebuilding followed the quake and the opening of the Panama Canal in 1914 helped make San Francisco an even more important port. The 1915 Panama-Pacific International Exposition saw the city bigger and brighter than ever.

The Barbary Coast

Notorious during the latter half of the 1800s as a world-class hotbed of murder and mayhem, the district that today engulfs the northeastern edge of the Financial District, from Chinatown to Embarcadero, between Washington and Broadway Sts., was awarded its name for its resemblance to the pirate-plagued coast of North Africa, home of the Berbers. Beginning with the first gold strikes lucky prospectors had swarmed to San Francisco, worn from cheerless camps and hard days of digging. These new arrivals met with sailors, gamblers, and restless adventurers from all walks of life, all yearning to put their excess riches to use. The wild lengths of the Barbary Coast were soon lined with just their sort of burlesque attractions: casinos and cat houses, saloons and cabarets, opium dens and distilleries, each catering to vices of every taste. The drugs, gambling, and prostitution brought further lawlessness to the new red-light district and its streets began to take on ominous nicknames. The meeting of Jackson and Kearny Sts. was known as "Killer's Corner" while the black heart of the district became "Devil's Acre." It was not until 1917 that a federal decree closed the brothels once and for all and laid to rest the city's most sordid period.

Still, old habits die hard and the area had not quite danced its final jig. Largely unaffected by the traumas of WWI, San Francisco retained some its boisterous past and even during Prohibition kept its revelers reveling with a smattering of speakeasies and underground clubs, earning a front seat in the developing jazz scene. Even to this day the legacy of the 1920s juke joints keeps both sides of the Bay swinging late into the night.

The Depression & WWII

Like other cities, San Francisco suffered through the Great Depression and, like other cities, gigantic public works projects were one of the attempts to yank the economy out of the doldrums. The Bay Area certainly got its money's worth from these 1930s projects; the Bay Bridge of 1936 and the Golden Gate Bridge of 1937 are still magnificent symbols of the city and for the millions of commuters, they're also damned useful.

The distant thunder of WWI may have had little impact on San Francisco but WWII was a different story. The Bay Area became a major launching pad for military operations in the Pacific and gigantic shipyards soon sprang up around the bay. The Kaiser Shipyard in Richmond employed over 100,000 people while the workers at Marinship of Sausalito turned out 93 ships during the war.

Other wartime industries sucked huge numbers of workers into the Bay Area and the city's population jumped by nearly 140,000 to reach its highest level ever (more than 775,000) by the early 1950s.

1950s – The Beat Generation

From the days of the Gold Rush, San Francisco has always been a freewheeling city. Artists, musicians, and writers often sang its praises in their works, but it wasn't until the mid-1950s that national attention was first focused on "the City" as the birthplace of a scene of its own. When Jack Kerouac and Allen Ginsberg, upstart students at Columbia University, and Gregory Corso, 17 years old and fresh out of jail, fled the indifference of New York City and joined forces with the San Francisco Renaissance, a poets' movement begun by poet and literary critic Kenneth Rexroth, the Beat Generation was given a voice. Kerouac became their author, Ginsberg their poet, and jazz the cool sound of North Beach, hub of the new Bohemia.

City Lights Bookstore, Tosca Cafe, and Vesuvio Cafe were at the center of the Beat gatherings, crowded with "hipsters" rallying around their search for the "real" America. The Beats spoke of a life unbound by social conventions, motivated by spontaneous creativity rather than greed and ambition. Even the term "beat" (associated with the rhythm of bongo drums that were a common element to their poetry readings) was taken from the jazz-speak of the day meaning a state of finished exhaustion and alluding to the supreme happiness preached in the Beatitudes of Jesus. The term *beatnik* came along later; created, it is claimed, by *San Francisco Chronicle* columnist Herb Caen fusing the "far out" Beats with the just-launched Sputnik satellite.

1960s – Drugs & Revolution

The Beats spearheaded '50s counterculture and the hippies followed in the '60s. The Haight-Ashbury was the new North Beach, a suburb in transition where living was comparatively cheap. If marijuana was the drug of choice for the '50s then LSD was the '60s trip. Long hair and the new wave of rock music were adopted from England and in 1966 San Francisco promoter Bill Graham was packing them into the Fillmore and Winterland Auditoriums with local bands like the Grateful Dead and Jefferson Airplane. When 20,000 people congregated in Golden Gate Park for a free concert in 1967 the "Summer of Love" kicked off and "flower power" and "free love" became San Francisco passwords.

Across the Bay, however, peace and love was not the order of the day. While hippies in the Haight were dropping acid and wearing flowers in their hair, the Berkeley revolutionaries were leading the worldwide student upheavals of the late '60s, slugging it out with the cops and the university administration over civil rights.

The dreary badlands of neighboring Oakland were the scene for yet more revolution when Eldridge Cleaver, Huey Newton, and Bobby Seale founded the Black Panthers, the most militant and extreme of the groups involved in Black emancipation in the era.

1970s – The Next Revolution

After a decade of realignments and upheavals the '70s were comparatively relaxed. The '60s hippies had led a sexual revolution but it was a predominantly heterosexual one; a homosexual one followed in the '70s as San Francisco's gays stepped decisively out of the closet and slammed the door shut behind them. Gay Pride became a rallying call and the previously underground homosexual community "came out" in all its glory. With the 1977 election of gay activist Harvey Milk to the Board of Supervisors, recognition of the gay rights movement reached a new peak, but the euphoria was to be short-lived. The following year, Milk and Mayor George Moscone were assassinated by Dan White, an avowedly anti-gay former police officer.

Their deaths marked the beginning of the end of the heyday, the opulence of which further faded when the first cases of AIDS – at the time known as GRID, Gay-Related Immune Deficiency – were reported in San Francisco in 1981. From these events a new era of information and protection was born. The rainbow banners and lavender triangles, signifying the community's pride and resilience, are as common today as they were 20 years ago but the extravagance of the '70s now resurfaces mainly at the Castro and Folsom St. Fairs and the annual Gay & Lesbian Freedom Day parade.

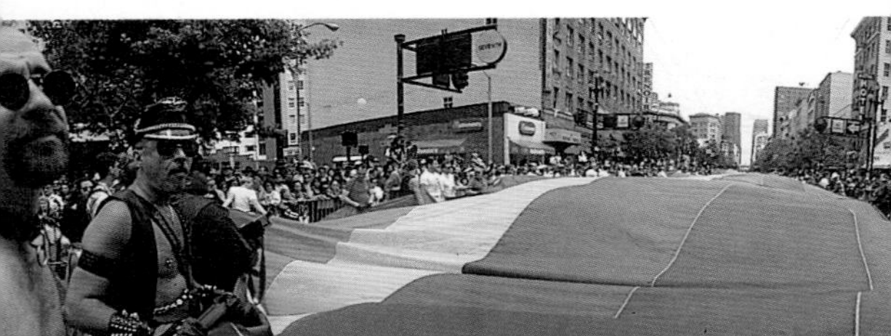

RICK GERHARTER

Gay San Francisco

From its earliest days as a seaport, through the riotous Gold Rush years to the present, San Francisco has been a liberal city with a tradition of tolerance for alternative lifestyles. It was here, appropriately enough, that a gay community began to form during WWII and its aftermath. San Francisco served as a gateway to the Pacific, with arriving and departing naval fleets mooring at the harbor. When the armed forces conducted purges and dishonorably discharged scores of gay servicemen, it was in San Francisco that they found themselves. Unwilling to head home, many stayed, forming the foundation of the world's largest and strongest gay community.

In the early '50s, a chapter of the Mattachine Society, the first serious homosexual rights organization in the USA, sprang up in San Francisco, and in 1955 the Daughters of Bilitis (DOB), the nation's first lesbian organization, was founded in San Francisco. These were the beginnings of what is known as the homophile movement, a non-confrontational, non-conformist gay movement that distanced itself from bar culture.

During the 1959 mayoral campaign, challenger Russell Wolden accused incumbent mayor George Christopher of turning San Francisco into "the national headquarters of the organized homosexuals in the United States." Christopher was reelected, but was not about to be accused of being soft on queers. He responded with a massive police crackdown of gay male cruising areas, raids which resulted in a public blacklist of gay citizens.

Resistance to this persecution did not come out of the homophile movement but from the bars, and one in particular, the Black Cat, which was dubbed by Allen Ginsberg as "the greatest gay bar in America." Jose Sarria, a drag performer at the Black Cat, ran for city supervisor in 1961, becoming the first openly gay person to run for public office in the USA.

The age of tolerance had not yet arrived, however. In 1965 a dance sponsored by the Council on Religion & the Homosexual was raided by the police, and everyone in attendance was arrested and photographed. The city was outraged and even the media denounced the behavior of the police. This event helped to turn the tide in the city's perception of the gay community. The crackdown on gay bars stopped, and a gay person was appointed to sit on the police community relations board.

The Stonewall Riots in New York in June of 1969 marked the beginning of modern gay liberation and Gay Pride, a movement definitely going strong in modern San Francisco. ■

Dykes on Bikes,a popular group at the Gay Pride Parade

RICK GERHARTER

1980s & '90s – Another Big One

The 20th-century's second Big One for San Francisco, the Loma Prieta earthquake, came at 5:04 pm on October 17, 1989, and measured 7.1. A section of the upper level of the Bay Bridge slumped on to the lower deck and fires fed by fractured gas mains burned down many homes in the affluent Marina district but the worst disaster was when a double-decker section of I-880 in Oakland collapsed, killing 42 people who were crushed in their vehicles. In all, 67 people died but the damage would have been far worse were it not for a baseball game.

In 1989 the baseball World Series was a local affair between the National League's San Francisco Giants and the American League's Oakland As. When the quake struck the third game was about to start at Candlestick Park and a large chunk of the Bay Area population was at home watching it on TV, not out on the freeways stuck in rush hour traffic.

As after the 1906 quake, since 1989 San Francisco has experienced a period of urban renewal with a building boom that is sprucing up neighborhoods and historic buildings all over the city.

CLIMATE

Mark Twain summed up the San Francisco climate a century ago: "The coldest winter I ever spent was summer in San Francisco." There's more than a hint of truth to that throwaway line; it can get surprisingly chilly in summer. The cause is that famous fog; a hot day inland sucks the fog in from the sea and as it rolls across the city the temperature plummets and the wind picks up. In winter, when the contrast between land and sea temperatures is less extreme, the fog is less frequent and the weather is more consistent.

The Bay Area has an unusual collection of micro climates, a result of the famous fog meeting the famous hills. A convenient hill can neatly redirect the fog as it rolls across the city and one area may consistently be fog-free and sunny while the next block is in the mist. Basically, Twin Peaks to the ocean gets most of the fog, while the bay side of the city stays sunny, but still windy.

You can expect afternoon temperatures to range between the mid-50°s F and high 60°s most of the year, with highs in the 80°s occurring unpredictably from spring through fall. San Francisco receives the most rain from December to March. The key is to always dress in layers and never venture out without a sweatshirt – or you'll probably end up buying one.

ECONOMY

Although WWII saw enormous wartime production operations the Bay Area is not a major industrial center. There are plenty of other key activities, however. From San Francisco's early boomtown days, with all the gold rush wealth pouring into the city, banking found a friendly environment. Later A.P. Giannini's visionary mission to extend banking to ordinary people led to the foundation and extraordinary growth of the Bank of America. Today Montgomery St. is known as the Wall St. of the West.

To the north of the Bay Area the Napa and Sonoma Valleys only turn out a small portion of America's annual wine production but what they do produce is the absolute best. When you talk about fine American wines you mean wines from the Napa and Sonoma Valleys.

The Bay Area is also home to two of America's best universities: the University of California at Berkeley and Stanford University. Their muscular scientific reputation has spearheaded the region's strength as a research center, particularly in nuclear science. If you want to smash atomic particles this is the place to do it. Electronics are another Bay Area specialty. Hewlett Packard, Apple, and Intel all call Silicon Valley, home and garage start-up companies have become part of the industrial mythology of the Santa Clara Valley (the area from Palo Alto to San Jose and beyond).

The Bay Area started as a trading port, even before the Gold Rush, and it remains one of the West Coast's most important ports today. The Bay bridges in the '30s and container shipping in the '70s killed off San Francisco's working waterfront but the business has simply shifted across the Bay to the huge new container ports at Oakland. The rapid growth in Pacific Rim business ensures that shipping will remain a key business.

POPULATION & PEOPLE

The bare figures lie; San Francisco's population is technically only about 700,000 but to think of San Francisco in isolation is a major mistake. In reality the city of San Francisco is just one part of the whole San Francisco Bay Area, a continuous conurbation with a total population of about 5.6 million. The major cities of the Bay Area are San Francisco (population 753,400), Oakland (380,000), Berkeley (140,000), and San Jose (835,500).

Like the rest of the state the Bay Area is a major focus for US immigration and the population is growing and rapidly evolving. A born and bred San Franciscan often seems like a rare species. Although San Francisco started as a Spanish and then Mexican settlement it's only in recent years that the city has hosted a large Hispanic community. Centered in the Mission district Hispanics now constitute about 14% of the city's population, many of them refugees from the political unrest in Central America during the 1970s and '80s. Chinese started to flood into the Bay Area with the Gold Rush and a strong Japanese community also developed before WWII. In recent years there has been more Chinese immigration along with influxes of Koreans, Vietnamese, and other Asian groups so that today they constitute nearly 30% of the population.

ARTS & CULTURE

The Bay Area is very culture conscious: a lot of books get written and read, the proliferation of art galleries around the city shows an avid interest in art, and the city's orchestra, opera, and ballet are world-class.

Literature

With its many excellent booksellers and a reputation as the principal US publishing center after New York, it's hardly surprising to learn how much has been written about the San Francisco Bay Area. To visit the sites of all that literary history grab a copy of *The Literary World of San Francisco & its Environs* (1990) by Don Herron, which shows you where the writers lived and worked and the places they wrote about.

Gold Rush to the 1920s The colorful mining era of the 1850s and 1860s attracted writers to chronicle San Francisco's frontier history. Mark Twain made his journalistic debut in the Bay Area reporting on pioneering life at the Comstock Lode silver mines. His *Roughing It,* published in 1872, covered his westward stagecoach journey and the mining days.

Bret Harte, a contemporary of Twain (and some say editor of *Jim Smiley and his Jumping Frog,* Twain's first published short story), was also one of the most popular writers of the era. Harte's distinctly Western flavor gave rise to the "local color" movement, putting the Pacific coast on the map with a bonafide regional identity.

Best known today for his *Devil's Dictionary* (1911), Ambrose Bierce was the world's first newspaper columnist. Penning the *Sunday Examiner's* "Prattles," his rapier wit and unfailing eye for controversy afforded him the nickname "Bitter Bierce."

TONY WHEELER

North Beach's City Lights Books is the last bastion of the Beat Generation.

Scottish-born Robert Louis Stevenson lived briefly in Monterey and San Francisco and honeymooned by an abandoned silver mine in nearby Calistoga. This stay led to his book *The Silverado Squatters* (1872).

While Stevenson, Bierce, and Twain were imports, professional hell-raiser Jack London was San Francisco-born and Oakland-bred. London turned out a massive volume of writings including his own, suitably fictionalized story under the title *Martin Eden* (1909) and is remembered in Oakland with a Jack London Square and museum. Another Oakland-raised author, Gertrude Stein, recalls her stay in *The Making of Americans* (1925) and is herself remembered by a sculpture of the very quality she found Oakland to be lacking. "There is no there there," Stein quipped; the sculpture *There* at Oakland's City Center now proves her wrong.

The Modern Era San Francisco in the '30s often reads like a vision from a Dashiell Hammett detective novel, with Sam Spade and Nick Charles as his classic private eyes and *The Maltese Falcon* (1930) and *The Thin Man* (1932) his classic books. Retracing Hammett sites in San Francisco is a popular pastime.

Poet Kenneth Rexroth began his Bay Area tenure of literary prominence with his first collection entitled *In What Hour* (1940). Also an influential critic, Rexroth was instrumental in jump-starting the careers of several Bay Area artists, notably those of the Beat Generation. Another of that scene's fixtures, Michael McClure – an

Literary Streets of San Francisco

TOM SMALLMAN

In January 1988, the San Francisco Board of Supervisors approved Lawrence Ferlinghetti's proposal to rename 12 city streets in honor of famous artistic figures from the city's past. All but two were authors. The signs were unveiled outside of City Lights Bookstore, at the corner of what that day became Jack Kerouac St., and for these artists a new era of recognition was born. The 11 other recipients were Mark Twain, Jack London, Richard Henry Dana, Dashiell Hammett, Isadora Duncan (dancer), William Saroyan, Benjamino Bufano (sculptor), Frank Norris, Ambrose Bierce, Bob Kaufman, and Kenneth Rexroth. ■

original member of Rexroth's San Francisco Renaissance and one of the earliest Beats – is famed for his scandalous play *The Beard* (1965).

After the chaos of WWII, the Beat Generation engaged in a new style of writing: short, sharp, and alive. Their bible was Jack Kerouac's *On the Road* (1957), a pseudo-documentary in "spontaneous prose." Allen Ginsberg was their premier poet and his *Howl & Other Poems* (1956) their angry anthem. A writer himself, Lawrence Ferlinghetti became the Beats' patron and publisher and today their era lives on at his City Lights Bookstore, still churning out the hipsters after 40 years in North Beach.

The '60s Essayist Joan Didion captures the '60s sense of upheaval in *Slouching Towards Bethlehem* (1968), casting a caustic look at flower power and the Haight-Ashbury. Tom Wolfe also puts the Bay Area during the '60s in perspective with *The Electric Kool-Aid Acid Test* (1968), blending tales of the Grateful Dead, Hell's Angels, and Ken Kesey's band of Merry Pranksters. A precursor to the spirit of the era, Kesey's own *One Flew Over the Cuckoo's Nest* (1962) pits a free-thinker against stifling authority, drawing from his own experiences at a local psychiatric ward for its setting.

Richard Brautigan's curious novels haven't aged too well but had a major cult following in their time. *Trout Fishing in America* (1967) is one of the best. East Bay writer Philip K. Dick is chiefly remembered for his science fiction, notably *Do Androids Dream of Electric Sheep?* (1968), which under the title *Blade Runner* became a classic sci-fi film. Dick's *The Man in the High Castle* (1962) envisions a Japanese-dominated San Francisco after Japan and Germany have won WWII and divided the USA between them. Frank Herbert of *Dune* fame was also a local during these years, as was Thomas Pynchon, whose *The Crying of Lot 49* (1966) takes place in '60s Berkeley.

The '70s & '80s No writer watched San Francisco's gay fraternity emerge from the closet with clearer vision than Armistead Maupin with his *Tales of the City* series. Starting, like the best Victorian potboilers, as newspaper serials in 1979 they became a smash hit collection of literary soap operas, light as a feather but a great-to-read romp through the heady days of pre-AIDS excess. *Tales of the City, Further Tales of the City, More Tales of the City, Babycakes,* and *Significant Others* bring that period back to life. The late Randy Shilts, local author of *And the Band Played On* (1987), a moving account of the early years of AIDS awareness, also wrote for the *Examiner* and *Chronicle.*

Contemporary Writers Today the San Francisco literary community is stronger than ever, with many prominent writers making their homes here, including Alice Walker, Pulitzer Prize-winning author of *The Color Purple* (1988), Chilean novelist Isabel Allende, author of *The House of the Spirits* (1985), and romance novelist Danielle Steele, who bought the ostentatious Spreckles Mansion in 1990.

Amy Tan's best-selling *The Joy Luck Club* (1989), looks back on the lives of four Chinese women and their American-born daughters in Chinatown. Another Chinese-American, Maxine Hong Kingston's award-winning *Woman Warrior: Memoir of a Girlhood Among Ghosts* (1976) is a lyrical account of a Chinatown girlhood. Local favorite Anne Lamott sets her poignant and witty novels in Marin County; her autobiographical *Operating Instructions* (1993), written in diary form, recounts the joys and horrors of motherhood. Postmodernist author Kathy Acker teaches at the Art Institute and Dorothy Alison, whose novel *Bastard Out of Carolina* (1992) won the National Book Award, lives in Sonoma County.

The list of Bay Area writers would not be complete without mentioning Wallace Stegner, whose prize-winning novels and nonfiction qualify him as one of the great writers of the American West. Stegner died in 1993, but his legacy lives on at Stanford University, whose Creative Writing Program is named after him.

There's an impressive group of poets as well. US poet laureate Robert Hass, whose works include *Human*

Wishes (1990), is a professor at the University of California at Berkeley. Czech Nobel laureate Czeslaw Milosz also teaches at Berkeley, and the two have teamed up on translations of Milosz's poetry.

Art

The Bay Area's small Native American population was disappearing even before the Spanish and Mexican eras ended. Nevertheless, traces of their artwork survive, blended with Spanish colonial design in the murals on the walls and ceilings of mission churches. Gold rush fortunes soon financed gold rush art collections and painters quickly followed, inspired by the state's dramatic scenery and financed by San Francisco's nouveau riche art collectors. The San Francisco Art Institute and the M.H. de Young Museum were both in operation before the turn of the century and homeless artists, dispossesed by the 1906 earthquake, moved south to establish Carmel as an artist's colony, a role it continues to play in a rather exclusive fashion.

A Californian version of the impressionist Plein-Air movement celebrated the state's natural scenery and clear light early in the century. The social realist school had a major impact on San Francisco and the Diego Rivera gallery at the Art Institute shows the Mexican muralist at his best. The depression-era Work Projects Administration (WPA) continued the mural tradition; there are fine examples at Coit Tower and in the Rincon Annex near the Embarcadero.

The Bay Area also played an important part in the elevation of photography to an art form, particularly with the work of Edward Weston and Ansel Adams.

In the late 1950s and early '60s, local painters were among the first to reject the orthodoxy of Abstract Expressionism in favor of a loose, painterly, representational art. Known as Bay Area Figurative painting, its chief practitioners were Richard Diebenkorn, David Park, and Elmer Bischoff. The superb San Francisco Museum of Modern Art is a worthy home for the city's collection, and the Oakland Museum across the Bay (see the Excursions chapter) has a permanent exhibition featuring most of the area's styles and movements.

Film

San Francisco has made a great backdrop for an amazing number of movies. Many are available on video, or for an intensive San Francisco movie experience simply stay at the Phoenix Motel (see the Places to Stay chapter)

PHILLIP COBLENTZ

Victorians

San Francisco's rich collection of Victorian houses were built in a wide variety of styles. Early Victorians were often in the simple and rather severe Italianate style of the 1870s, flat-fronted with no visible roof line but with a deep cornice around the top of the building. Gothic Revival houses were popular at the same time; gable roofs, pointed arches over the windows, and verandas or porches running the width of the house are all gothic giveaways.

Increasing ornamentation and a wider variety of wooden flourishes produced the Stick Style, named for its vertical stick-like patterning. This style was also known as Eastlake, after English furniture designer Charles Eastlake. In the 1880s and '90s the exuberant Queen Anne style produced the most ornate and picturesque Victorians, replete with balconies, towers, turrets, chimneys, bay windows, and gables. The Haas-Lilienthal house in Pacific Heights is a fine example of this period's design. The Haight-Ashbury is another good area to go hunting for Victorians. ■

with a library of San Francisco films for their guests' enjoyment.

A number of big production companies are based locally, including Francis Ford Coppola's Zoetrope Studios and, most famously, in Marin County, George Lucas's Lucasfilm and Industrial Light & Magic, the high-tech company which produces computer-generated special effects for Hollywood's biggest releases.

You can relive San Francisco history in period pieces like David Niven's *The Barbary Coast* (1935), Clark Gable's *San Francisco* (1936; catch the quake of 1906), or Jack Nicholson's *Psyche-out* (1968; relive the hippie era in Haight-Ashbury). More recent chronicles of the city's history include *Patty Hearst* (1988), a surprisingly long-time-in-coming recap of the weird '70s kidnapping case. The Oscar-winning *The Life & Times of Harvey Milk* (1986) tells the story of the murder of Mayor Moscone and his openly gay city supervisor. Dustin Hoffman narrates the story behind the AIDS quilt and the city's AIDS battle in *Common Threads* (1989).

Alcatraz Island was a natural for prison movies; John Frankenheimer's 1961 *Birdman of Alcatraz* with Burt Lancaster was filmed there, although the Alcatraz tour goes to great pains to tell you the movie has little connection with reality.

We've all hurtled up and down San Francisco's streets with Steve McQueen in *Bullitt*, the 1968 thriller which serves as the benchmark for a good car chase, but Clint Eastwood's Dirty Harry character also found San Francisco familiar territory. The maverick cop started his film career there with the 1971 *Dirty Harry*, loosely based on the real life Zodiac killer who sniped his random victims. The suspenseful 1974 Francis Ford Coppola film *The Conversation* stars Gene Hackman as a surveillance expert who does his spying from the St. Francis Hotel. Paul Verhoeven's raunchy 1992 thriller *Basic Instinct* ran fast and furiously through its Bay Area locations. The club scenes in the film were filmed at Rawhide in the SoMa district.

Alfred Hitchcock's movies often made use of San Francisco locales. You can stay in the York Hotel on Sutter St., famous for its 1958 *Vertigo* stairway sequences. The most famous San Francisco private eye was Dashiell Hammett's Sam Spade. His screen double, Humphrey Bogart, appears in *The Maltese Falcon* (1941), a classic murder mystery.

Comedies are just as at home here as thrillers. The 1967 hit *The Graduate* pays several visits to Berkeley and is notable for Dustin Hoffman's unique ability to head toward Berkeley by crossing the Bay Bridge in the San

Francisco direction. Speeding across the Bay Bridge in a red Alfa Romeo simply looks better on the top deck – never mind that it's going in the wrong direction. In *Foul Play* (1978), Chevy Chase and Goldie Hawn combine thriller with comedy and throw in more car chases and some great scenes at the San Francisco Opera House.

Architecture

The Bay Area is architecturally diverse with buildings reflecting the region's Spanish and Mexican heritage, its strong links with Asia, and its own homegrown style.

Spanish and later Mexican settlers left a much more permanent reminder with their missions and associated civil settlements. They built using adobe (mud-brick), an easy material to construct with but remarkably unsuited to the earthquake-prone Bay Area.

The American takeover of California and the Gold Rush brought a rapid change in building styles and techniques. Sawn timber arrived from Australia and the East Coast together with ready-made components and even complete, pre-fabricated houses. As San Francisco changed from a temporary settlement to a permanent town, rows of Victorians were built, similar in general design and usually made of wood but remarkably varied in their appearance and embellishments.

New techniques and styles developed towards the turn of the century. Led by architect Daniel Burnham, the classical Beaux Arts or City Beautiful style was adopted for the Civic Center buildings while at the same time the folksy Arts & Crafts movement was adapted to California in the many private homes designed by Berkeley-based architect Bernard Maybeck.

Steel frame construction also started to appear at this time and the successful performance of these new buildings in the 1906 earthquake led to larger and higher steel framed buildings in the city's reconstruction. Willis Polk was one of the city's busiest architects, one of his best known buildings was the pioneering glass-curtain-walled Hallidie Building on Sutter St. Population growth and the movement to the suburbs inspired the California bungalow, small and simple single story designs that were soon popping up all around the world. The 1920s brought the Mission Revival style, a nostalgic look back at the state's Spanish heritage. San Francisco architects played with Art Deco and Streamline Moderne styles but the depression years of the 1930s and then WWII were relatively static and the city skyline scarcely changed for almost 30 years, until the early '60s when San Francisco's downtown suddenly started to soar skywards.

Performing Arts

San Franciscans have been keen on entertainment ever since the Gold Rush days. Today the city supports acclaimed opera and ballet companies and a symphony orchestra. (See Entertainment for more details.)

Music

Though the Bay Area's reputation as a rock & roll capital may never shake its association with psychedelia and the late '60s, that music is hardly the full extent of the area's contribution. The flower-power sound *was*

The Living Dead

With the death of Jerry Garcia on August 9, 1995, the Grateful Dead's long, strange chapter in the history of San Francisco came to an end. After some 30 years of performing, the Grateful Dead leave behind a legacy of music that will live on in the hearts of their fans – as well as on innumerable bootleg tapes.

The Dead began their fabled career in a pizza parlor in Palo Alto in 1965. Playing as The Warlocks, the band became associated with Ken Kesey and his Merry Pranksters. Performing up and down the California coast at Kesey's Acid Tests, The Warlocks came to symbolize the era's ideal of freedom through drugs and music.

With the Summer of Love of 1967, the nation focused on San Francisco as the eye of the hippie hurricane. Making their communal home at 710 Ashbury St, the Grateful Dead, with their haunting new name, played free concerts on Haight St and in Golden Gate Park for their growing mass of fans. The Monterey Pops Festival in June 1969, and Woodstock in August of that summer brought the Dead national recognition.

Unlike other bands of the time, the Dead flourished through four decades of musical growth. And along for the ride were millions of so-called "Deadheads," a dedicated throng of followers ranging from construction workers to nuclear physicists, baby-boomers to today's teenagers. Even into the 1990s, the band continued to fill venues all over the country.

The appeal of the Grateful Dead has long remained elusive to some, and the difficulty of describing the magic of their live performances adds to the mystique. As legendary rock promoter Bill Graham once said, "They're not the best at what they do, but they're the only ones that do it." ■

Jerry Garcia (left) and Phil Lesh (right) in groovier times

PHOTO 20/20 - TED STRESHINSKY

contagious, prompting a massive artistic influx into San Francisco. Apart from big-name acts like the Grateful Dead and Jefferson Airplane, Bay Area names like Janis Joplin, Big Brother & the Holding Company, and Sly & the Family Stone were key players in defining the era's sound. Master-promoter Bill Graham, often referred to as the "Godfather of San Francisco rock," used these groups to revolutionize the way popular music is presented and by doing so set the stage for a new era of world-class entertainers.

Guitar legend Carlos Santana, whose music blends Latin-influenced rhythms with a rock & roll edge, calls the Bay Area home, as does bluesman John Lee Hooker. During the '70s, local sounds turned hard-core with the emergence of seminal punk rockers the Dead Kennedys. Today, the East Bay's youth is still insisting "Punk's not dead!" producing current chart-toppers Green Day and Primus to prove it.

Jazz – a Bay Area institution since the Barbary Coast days – is also thriving, with local combos like the Charlie Hunter Trio receiving international accolades. Rap artists M.C. Hammer and Too Short have brought Oakland's inner-city life to the ears of mainstream America and even schmaltz artists like Journey, Huey Lewis & the News, Sammy Hagar and Chris Isaac have their own particular stories to tell about their much-loved "city by the bay."

RELIGION

San Francisco is predominantly Christian but the Bay Area also features just about every other religion you care to mention. There are Chinese temples in Chinatown, Japanese temples in Japantown, a Hindu temple in Pacific Heights, a Zen Buddhist retreat near Muir Beach in Marin County, and a Mormon Temple overlooking the entire East Bay. If the Bay Area has a religious specialty, however, it's the bizarre. The Reverend Jim Jones, who led his followers to mass suicide in Jonestown, Guyana, was a product of San Francisco, as is Anton LaVey and his Church of Satan.

LANGUAGE

The Bay Area speaks a whole dictionary of languages apart from traditional English. You can roll out your Cantonese in Chinatown, practice your Italian in North Beach, listen for a whole range of Latin American Spanish dialects in the Mission, and hear every possible Asian language in distinct little enclaves around the city.

Facts for the Visitor

ORIENTATION

The city of San Francisco is a compact area, covering the tip of a 30-mile-long peninsula with the Pacific Ocean on one side and the San Francisco Bay on the other. The city can be neatly divided into three sections. The central part resembles a slice of pie, with Van Ness Ave. and Market St. marking the two sides and the Embarcadero the rounded edge of the pie. Squeezed into this compact slice are the Union Square area, the Financial District, the Civic Center area, Chinatown, North Beach, Nob Hill, Russian Hill, and Fisherman's Wharf.

To the south of Market St. lies SoMa, an upwardly mobile warehouse zone. SoMa fades into the Mission, the city's Latino quarter, and then the Castro, the city's gay quarter.

The third and final part of the city is also physically the largest, the long sweep from Van Ness Ave. all the way to the Pacific Ocean. It's a varied area encompassing upscale neighborhoods like the Marina and Pacific Heights, less pricey zones like the Richmond and Sunset districts, as well as areas with a flavor all their own, like Japantown and the Haight-Ashbury. The city's three great park lands – the Presidio, Lincoln Park, and Golden Gate Park – are also in this area.

MAPS

Good quality maps of San Francisco are available from bookstores but giveaway maps from a variety of sources are generally adequate for most visitors. Rent-a-car firms have heaps of maps but the best of the free maps is the excellent *San Francisco Street Map & Visitor Guide*, available at many of the city's hotels. If you're going to be exploring the city by public transportation the Muni *Street & Transit Map* is an excellent $2 investment. Get a copy at the Visitors Information Center or any large bookstore. The Rand McNally Map Store (☎ 777-3131), 595 Market St. at 2nd, is a good place to pick up maps.

For convenience, nothing beats the *Streetwise San Francisco* map, close to pocket size yet still legible, and laminated for durability. Several detailed street atlases to the Bay Area are put out by Thomas Bros. Maps; you can pick one up at their store (☎ 981-7520), 550 Jackson St. at Columbus, or at just about any bookstore.

TOURIST OFFICES

Local Tourist Offices

Right in the heart of the city, a stone's throw from Union Square and right by the most popular cable car turnaround, the San Francisco Visitors Information Center (☎ 391-2000) is at the lower level of Hallidie Plaza at Market and Powell. The center is open weekdays from 9 am to 5:30 pm, Saturday from 9 am to 3 pm, and Sunday from 10 am to 2 pm.

The center has a 24-hour phone service offering recorded "what's on" information. It operates in English (☎ 391-2001), French (☎ 391-2003), German (☎ 391-2004), Spanish (☎ 391-2122), and Japanese (☎ 391-2101).

Advance Tourist Information

Overseas visitors should contact their local US diplomatic office concerning information from the US Travel & Tourism Administration (USTTA). Information on Californian tourism can be obtained by mail from the California Division of Tourism (☎ (916) 322-1396, (800) 862-2543), PO Box 1499, Sacramento, CA 95812. The San Francisco Convention & Visitors Bureau (☎ (415) 974-6900), 201 3rd St., San Francisco, CA 94103, is better for information on the Bay Area. They publish an excellent information booklet on the city entitled *The San Francisco Book*.

DOCUMENTS

With the exception of Canadians, who need only proper proof of Canadian citizenship, all foreign visitors to the USA must have a valid passport and most also require a US visa. It's a good idea to keep photocopies of these documents; in case of theft, they'll be a lot easier to replace.

Visas

A reciprocal visa-waiver program applies to citizens of certain countries who may enter the USA for stays of 90 days or less without having to obtain a visa. Currently these countries are: Andorra, Austria, Belgium, Brunei, Denmark, Finland, France, Germany, Iceland, Italy, Japan, Liechtenstein, Luxembourg, Monaco, the Netherlands, New Zealand, Norway, San Marino, Spain, Sweden, Switzerland, and the UK. Under this program you must have a roundtrip ticket on an airline that is participating in the visa-waiver program; you must have proof of financial solvency and sign a form waiving the

PHILLIP COBLENTZ

The Bay Bridge and the city skyline from Yerba Buena Island

right to a hearing of deportation and you will not be allowed to extend your stay beyond the 90 days. Consult with your travel agent or contact the airlines directly for more information.

Other travelers will need to obtain a visa from a US consulate or embassy. In most countries the process can be done by mail.

Your passport should be valid for at least six months longer than your intended stay in the USA and you'll need to submit a recent photo with the application. Documents of financial stability and / or guarantees from a US resident are sometimes required, particularly for those from Third World countries.

Visa applicants may be required to "demonstrate binding obligations" that will insure their return back home. Because of this requirement, those planning to travel through other countries before arriving in the USA are generally better off applying for their US visa while they are still in their home country, rather than while on the road.

The validity period for US visitor visas depends on what country you're from. The length of time you'll be allowed to stay in the USA is ultimately determined by US immigration authorities at the port of entry.

Visa Extensions

Tourist visitors are usually granted a six-month stay on first arrival. If you try to extend that time the first assumption will be that you are working illegally so come prepared with concrete evidence that you've been traveling extensively and will continue to be a model tourist. A wad of traveler's checks looks much better than a solid and unmoving bank account. Extensions are handled by the US government's Justice Department's Immigration & Naturalization Service (INS; ☎ 705-4411), 630 Sansome St. They're open weekdays 8 am to 4 pm.

Other Documents

Bring your driver's license if you intend to rent a car; visitors from some countries may find it wise to back up their national license with an International Driving Permit, available from their local auto club. A comprehensive travel or health insurance policy is very important for overseas visitors and they should bring a membership card or documentation.

EMBASSIES & CONSULATES

US Embassies Abroad

US diplomatic offices abroad include the following:

Australia
21 Moonah Place, Yarralumla ACT 2600 (☎ (06) 270 5900)

Austria
Boltzmanngasse 16, A-1091, Vienna (☎ (1) 313-39)

Belgium
Blvd. du Régent 27, B-1000, Brussels (☎ (2) 513 38 30)

Canada
100 Wellington St., Ottawa, Ontario 1P 5T1 (☎ (613) 238-5335)

Denmark
Dag Hammarskjolds Allé 24, Copenhagen (☎ 31 42 31 44)

France
2 rue Saint Florentin, 75001 Paris (☎ (1) 42 96 12 02)

Germany
Deichmanns Aue 29, 53179 Bonn (☎ (228) 33 91)

Greece
91 Vasilissis Sophias Blvd, 10160 Athens (☎ (1)721-2951)

India
Shanti Path, Chanakyapuri 110021, New Delhi (☎ (11) 60-0651)

Ireland
42 Elgin Rd., Ballsbridge, Dublin (☎ (1) 687 122)

Israel
71 Hayarkon St., Tel Aviv (☎ (3) 517-4338)

Italy
Via Vittorio Veneto 119a-121, Rome (☎ (6) 46 741)

Japan
1-10-5 Akasaka chome, Minato-ku, Tokyo (☎ (3) 224-5000)

Korea
82 Sejong-Ro, Chongro-ku, Seoul (☎ (2) 397-4114)

Mexico
Paseo de la Reforma 305, Cuauhtémoc, 06500 Mexico City (☎ (5) 211-00-42)

Netherlands
Lange Voorhout 102, 2514 EJ, The Hague (☎ (70) 310 92 09)

New Zealand
29 Fitzherbert Terrace, Thorndon, Wellington (☎ (4) 722 068)

Norway
Drammensvein 18, Oslo (☎ (22) 44 85 50)

Russia
Novinskiy Bul'var 19/23, Moscow (☎ (095) 252-2451)

Singapore
30 Hill St., Singapore 0617 (☎ 338-0251)

South Africa
877 Pretorius St., Box 9536, Pretoria 0001 (☎ (12) 342-1048)

Spain
Calle Serrano 75, 28006 Madrid (☎ (1) 577 4000)

Sweden
Strandvagen 101, S-115 89 Stockholm (☎ (8) 783 5300)

Switzerland
Jubilaumsstrasse 93, 3005 Berne (☎ (31) 357 70 11)

Thailand
95 Wireless Rd., Bangkok (☎ (2) 252-5040)

UK
5 Upper Grosvenor St., London W1 (☎ (0171) 499 9000)

Foreign Consulates in San Francisco

Check the White Pages under Consulates for diplomatic representation in San Francisco. Canada does not have a consulate in San Francisco; the nearest is in Los Angeles (☎ (213) 346-2700). Other consulates include:

Australia
Australian Consulate-General 1 Bush St. (☎ 362-6160)

Denmark
Danish Consulate, Suite 1440, 601 Montgomery St. (☎ 391-0100)

France
Consulate-General of France, 540 Bush St. (☎ 397-4330)

Germany
German Consulate-General, 1960 Jackson St. (☎ 775-1061)

Ireland
Consulate-General of Ireland 655 Montgomery St. (☎ 392-4214)

Israel
Consulate-General of Israel, 456 Montgomery St. (☎ 398-8885)

Italy
Consulate-General of Italy, 2590 Webster St. (☎ 931-4924)

Japan
Consulate-General of Japan, 50 Fremont St. (☎ 777-3533)

Netherlands
Consulate-General of the Netherlands, 1 Maritime Plaza (☎ 981-6454)

New Zealand
Consulate-General of New Zealand, 1 Maritime Plaza, Suite 700 (☎ 399-1455)

Norway
Consulate-General of Norway, 20 California St. (☎ 986-0766)

Sweden
Consulate-General of Sweden, 120 Montgomery St., (☎ 788-2631)

Switzerland
Consulate-General of Switzerland, 456 Montgomery St. (☎ 788-2272)

UK
British Consulate-General, 1 Sansome St. (☎ 981-3030)

CUSTOMS

US Customs allows each person over the age of 21 to bring one liter of liquor and 200 cigarettes duty-free into the USA.

HIV & Entering the USA

Anyone entering the USA who is not a US citizen is subject to the authority of the Immigration & Naturalization Service (INS), who can keep someone from entering or staying in the USA by *excluding* or *deporting* them, meaning they have the power to prevent entrance or to return a visitor from whence they came. Travelers with HIV can and will be excluded from entering if the INS discovers they carry the virus.

Although the INS does not test people for HIV when they try to enter the USA, the form for the non-immigrant visa asks: "Have you ever been afflicted with a communicable disease of public health significance . . . " The INS will try to exclude anyone who answers "yes" to this question.

For legal immigration information and referrals to immigration advocates, visitors may contact the National Immigration Project of the National Lawyers Guild (☎ (617) 227-9727), 14 Bacon St., Suite 506, Boston, MA 02108; and the Immigrant HIV Assistance Project, Bar Association of San Francisco (☎ (415) 267-0795), 685 Market St., Suite 700, San Francisco, CA 94105. ■

MONEY

Currency

US dollars are the only accepted currency in San Francisco. The dollar is divided into 100 cents with coins of one cent (penny), five cents (nickel), 10 cents (dime), 25 cents (quarter), and the relatively rare 50 cents (half dollar). Bills can be confusing to foreign visitors, as they're all the same size and color: get used to checking the corners for amounts. They come in denominations of $1, $2, $5, $10, $20, $50, $100, and up. There are also two different one-dollar coins that the government has tried unsuccessfully to bring into mass circulation.

There are three straightforward ways to handle money in the USA: cash, US dollar traveler's checks, and credit cards, with the proliferation of ATMs facilitating the process.

Currency Regulations US law permits you to bring in, or take out, as much as US$5000 in US or foreign currency without formality. Larger amounts must be declared to customs. There are no such limits on the import or export of traveler's checks or letters of credit.

Traveler's Checks Traveler's checks are virtually as good as cash in the USA; you do not have to go to a bank to cash a traveler's check, as most establishments will accept them just like cash. The major advantage of traveler's checks over cash is that they can be replaced if lost or stolen. In the USA, however, the convenience of traveler's checks applies only if they are in US dollars.

If you're bringing your money in the form of traveler's checks bring it in larger denomination US$100 checks. Having to change small US$10 or US$20 checks is inconvenient especially as you may be charged service fees when cashing them at banks.

Credit Cards Major credit cards are widely accepted by car rental agencies and most hotels, restaurants, gas stations, shops, and larger grocery stores. The most commonly accepted cards are Visa, MasterCard, and American Express. However, Discover and Diners Club cards are also accepted by a fair number of businesses.

In fact, you'll find it hard to perform certain transactions without a credit card. Ticket buying services, for example, won't reserve tickets over the phone unless you offer a credit card number, and it's virtually impossible to rent a car without a credit card. Even if you loathe credit cards and prefer to rely on traveler's checks and ATMs, it's a good idea to carry one (Visa or MasterCard are your best bets) for emergencies.

American Express card holders can obtain cash advances from Amex Travel Services offices (there are five in San Francisco; see the White Pages under American Express) or from Amex check dispensers at major airports.

Automated Teller Machines (ATMs) With a Visa or MasterCard and a PIN (personal identification number) you can easily obtain cash from bank ATMs all over the Bay Area. The advantage of using ATMs is that you do not need to buy traveler's checks in advance, you do not get charged the usual 1% commission on the checks, and if you're from a foreign country you get a better exchange rate to US dollars. The disadvantage is that you are charged interest on the withdrawal until you pay it back. In some cases you may also be charged a fee for each withdrawal.

With increasing interstate and international linking of cards you can often withdraw money straight from your bank account at home.

Exchange Rates

The best rates are most often obtained at banks. San Francisco International Airport has a currency exchange office at the Bank of America International Terminal

RICK GERHARTER

Flower Market, Chinatown

RICK GERHARTER

Flamboyant San Francisco nightlife

branch and in Boarding Area D; hours are 7 am to 11 pm.

At press time exchange rates were:

Australian dollars	A$1	=	US$0.78
Canadian dollars	C$1	=	US$0.75
Deutsche marks	DM1	=	US$0.73
French francs	FF1	=	US$0.21
Hong Kong dollars	HK$10	=	US$1.30
Japanese yen	¥100	=	US$1.15
New Zealand dollars	NZ$1	=	US$0.68
Singapore dollars	S$1	=	US$0.72
UK pounds sterling	£1	=	US$1.60

Costs

The cost of living in San Francisco is high, but how much money you need depends on your traveling style. You can sleep cheap in a backpacker hostel and eat cheap at the bargain-priced Mexican cantinas in the Mission, or you can quickly run up impressive balances on your gold card at palatial Nob Hill hotels and the Bay Area's swanky California cuisine restaurants.

Getting to San Francisco may take the biggest bite out of your budget; once you have arrived, how much you spend depends upon you. Car rental typically starts from around $40 a day but in San Francisco a car is sometimes more of a handicap than a help. Public transportation is cheap and convenient while parking a car is an expensive headache. A car is, however, nearly essential for traveling further afield in the Bay Area, particularly along the coast or up to the Wine Country.

Tipping

Tipping is an American practice which can, initially, be a little confusing for foreign visitors. Tipping is not really an option – the service has to be absolutely appalling before you should consider not tipping. In a bar or restaurant tip your server at least 15% of the bill. (Hint: and easy way to figure it out is to double the amount of tax.) Add about 10% to taxi fares. Hotel porters who carry bags a long way expect $3 to $5 or add it up at $1 per bag; smaller services (holding the taxi door open for you) might just justify $1. Valet parking is worth about $2, to be given when your car is returned to you.

Consumer Taxes

San Francisco's 8.5% sales tax is tacked on to virtually everything including meals, groceries, accommodations, and car rentals. Additionally, there's a 12% hotel room tax to take into consideration when booking a hotel room.

WHEN TO GO

San Francisco is a popular location any time of the year but it is best to avoid visiting during the summer. This is the prime tourist season so prices are higher, lines are longer, and parking is more difficult, though weatherwise it's not even the best time of year. In terms of weather, summer in San Francisco can be foggy (see Climate for details) while inland or north in the Wine Country it is often too hot and dusty for comfort. You're more likely to find the Bay Area's climate hospitable at other times of the year.

WHAT TO BRING

The Bay Area's climate is fairly mild, rarely getting too hot or too cold so you don't need to come prepared for extremes. Be ready for surprisingly sudden changes, however, and always carry a sweatshirt.

San Francisco is a much more casual place than the East Coast; only a handful of snooty Nob Hill restaurants require jackets and ties for male visitors and that aside, casual clothing is quite OK in even the classiest Bay Area restaurants. Don't plan to make much use of your swimsuit in San Francisco apart from at a hotel pool. The Pacific Ocean here is a cold, gray, current-plagued, and uninviting stretch of water.

COMMUNICATIONS

Mail

The main San Francisco post office (☎ 441-8329) is the Civic Center Post Office, 101 Hyde St. Mail can be sent to you here marked c/o General Delivery, San Francisco, CA 94142, USA. Post offices are generally open weekdays 9 am to 5 pm and Saturday 9 am to 1 pm. There's a post office (☎ 956-3570) in the basement of Macy's on Union Square, open Monday to Saturday from 10 am to 5:30 pm and Sunday 11 am to 5 pm.

Postal Rates Postal rates for 1st-class mail within the USA are 32¢ for letters up to one ounce (23¢ for each additional ounce) and 20¢ for postcards.

International airmail rates are 50¢ for a half-ounce letter and 40¢ for a postcard to any foreign country with the exception of Canada (40¢ for a one-ounce letter and 30¢ for a postcard) and Mexico (35¢ for a half-ounce letter and 30¢ for a postcard). Be aware that stamp-dispensing machines can be a rip-off, charging you more than face value and sometimes not giving change.

The cost for parcels airmailed anywhere within the USA is $3 for two pounds or less, and $6 for five pounds.

Telephone

The Pacific Bell Smart Yellow Pages, referred to throughout the text as the Yellow Pages, is the comprehensive telephone directory, organized alphabetically by subject.

Bay Area area codes are:

San Francisco, Peninsula & Marin County	415
East Bay	510
Wine Country	707
San Jose	408

When dialing another area code the code must be preceded by a 1. For example, to dial an Oakland number from San Francisco the number will start with 1-510. Local calls usually start at 20¢ but there are "non-local" calls even within the same area code and costs rapidly jump upwards once you call to another area code.

Hotel telephones will often have heavy surcharges. Toll free numbers start with 1-800. Dial ☎ 411 for local directory assistance, ☎ 1 (Area Code) 555-1212 for long distance directory information, ☎ 1 (800) 555-1212 for toll free number information or ☎ 0 for the operator.

International Calls If you're calling from abroad the international country code for the USA (and Canada) is "1." To call a San Francisco number you simply dial your local international access code + 1 + 415 + number.

To dial an international call direct from the Bay Area dial 011 + country code + area code + number. Treat Canada as part of the USA; there's no need to dial the international access code 011. For international operator assistance dial ☎ 00.

As a general rule it's cheaper to make international calls at night, but this varies with the country you're calling. The exact cost for making an overseas call from a pay phone will depend on the long-distance company and the country in question. For calls to Australia and Europe, typically the cost should be about $1.50 for the first minute and $1 for each subsequent minute. Other continents usually cost about twice that.

Fax & Telegram

Fax machines are easy to find in the USA, at packaging outlets like Mail Boxes, Etc., photocopy services, and hotel business service centers, but be prepared to pay high prices (over $1 a page). Telegrams can be sent by Western Union (☎ (800) 325-6000).

Email & Internet Access

When carrying your own laptop, one of the easiest ways to log on or send email is to ask when making hotel reservations if your room is equipped with a modem line. Some, like the Mandarin Oriental (☎ (800) 526-6566) and the Pan Pacific (☎ (800) 327-8585), cater primarily to business travelers, so this won't be a problem. For those traveling without such hardware, another way to log on is to stop by any public library branch, all of which are equipped to allow Web browsing and access to chat groups, though not to send or receive email.

For access to all the online services, a group called SF Net (☎ 695-9824) has begun placing coin-operated (25¢ per five minutes) computer stations in cafes throughout the city. Among the best-suited of these sites are artsy Jumpin' Java (☎ 431-5282) at 139 Noe St., laid-back Cafe Abir (☎ 567-7654) at 1300 Fulton St., and cosmopolitan Yakety Yak (☎ 885-6908) at 679 Sutter St. The Icon Byte Bar & Grill (☎ 861-2983), 297 9th St., offers a more complete set-up than the single sites in the above cafes, and if you happen to be staying at the Green Tortoise Guest House (☎ 834-1000), 490 Broadway, you're in luck there, too.

BOOKS

If you're interested in finding out more about the city, Booksmith in the Haight-Ashbury and City Lights Bookstore in North Beach have good selections of local travel and history, and the Rand McNally store downtown has maps and guidebooks. (See the Shopping chapter for bookstores.)

The Knopf and Eyewitness guides to San Francisco, full of photographs and illustrations, make good supplementary guidebooks, but are slim on practical information. *A Guide to Mysterious San Francisco* by Doctor Weirde (Barrett-James Books, 1994) will help you find the city's haunted houses, murder sites, and strange museums; *Access to San Francisco* (Access, 1994) is particularly good for shoppers; and *San Francisco & the Bay Area* by Barry Parr (Compass American Guides, 1992) has pretty good coverage of the environs.

Historic San Francisco by Rand Richards (Heritage House, 1991) is an interesting and comprehensive history of the city from its early days, and *The Haight-Ashbury: A History* by Charles Perry (Random House, 1984) is a fascinating look at the Haight in the '60s.

MEDIA

Newspapers & Magazines

The Bay Area's number-one daily, the *San Francisco Chronicle*, is definitely not one of the USA's great newspapers. It's supplemented by the evening *San Francisco Examiner.* On Sundays they get together to produce the *San Francisco Examiner-Chronicle,* which includes the popular "pink section" entertainment supplement.

A journalistic highlight is the amazing assortment of free papers. The leaders in this field are the *San Francisco Bay Guardian,* the *SF Weekly,* and the *East Bay Express,* all with intelligent coverage of local events and politics plus superb restaurant, film, and other arts reviews. They also have extremely colorful personal ads and the *Guardian*'s "Ask Isadora" sex advice column is a not-to-be-missed insight into just how weird the Bay Area can be.

San Francisco is no competitor for New York in the magazine field but is home to *Wired,* the hit magazine of the computer culture, and a stack of small cutting-edge "zines" found in comic book shops and bookstores around the Mission.

TV & Radio

There are no Bay Area TV surprises; you'll simply find the usual network stations and proliferation of cable stations. KQED, the PBS affiliate, is found on channel 9.

Bay Area radio is much more varied and interesting. You can probably pick up 70 or 80 different stations from rap music, through rock of any decade, country & western, jazz, classical, news, talk, sports, different languages and, of course, fire breathing Christianity.

Here's a small selection of interesting listening:

88.5 FM	KQED	national public radio, news & talk
90.3 FM	KUSF	University of San Francisco radio
90.7 FM	KALX	UC Berkeley radio
103.7 FM	KKSF	smooth jazz
104.5 FM	KFOG	wonderfully laid-back classic rock
105.3 FM	KITS	alternative & modern rock
106.1 FM	KMEL	current chart hits, rap & the like

PHOTOGRAPHY & VIDEO

See the Shopping chapter for information on camera stores and repair and developing services.

Overseas visitors who are thinking of purchasing videos should remember that the USA uses National Television Systems Committee (NTSC) color TV standard, which is not compatible with other standards like Phase Alternation Line (PAL). It's best to keep those seemingly cheap movie purchases until you get home.

TIME

San Francisco is on Pacific Standard Time, three hours behind the east coast's Eastern Standard Time and eight hours behind GMT. In the summer there's Summer Time in Britain and Daylight Saving Time in the USA so the eight hour difference is usually maintained.

ELECTRICITY

Electric current in the USA is 110-115 volts, 60 Hz AC. Outlets may be suited for flat two-prong or three-prong plugs. If your appliance is made for another electrical system, you will need a transformer or adapter; if you didn't bring one along, check Radio Shack (several locations) or another consumer electronics store.

LAUNDRY

Fancier hotels will do laundry but it isn't cheap. Laundries are very common and very cheap; typical costs are around $1.25 to $1.50 for washing and 25¢ per 10-minute drying cycle. To liven up the drudgery of wash day, try Brain Wash (☎ 255-4866), 1122 Folsom St., where you can hang out in the cafe while you wait for your clothes. At the corner of Golden Gate Park, Wash Club (☎ 681-9274), 520 Frederick St. at Stanyan, offers shoe repair, photo developing, TV, and video games in addition to washers and dryers and a dry-cleaning service.

WEIGHTS & MEASURES

Distances are in feet, yards, and miles; weights are in ounces, pounds, and tons. Gasoline is measured in US gallons, which is about 20% smaller than the imperial gallon and equivalent to 3.79 liters.

HEALTH

For most foreign visitors no immunizations are required for entry, though cholera and yellow fever vaccinations may be required of travelers from areas with a history of those diseases. There are no unexpected health dangers, excellent medical attention is readily available, and the only real health concern is that, as elsewhere in the USA, a collision with the medical system can cause severe injuries to your financial state.

Travel Insurance

No sensible visitor will arrive in the USA without the security of a good travel insurance policy. When looking for a policy, coverage for lost baggage, canceled flights and minor medical bills may be nice to have but what you're really after is coverage against a true catastrophe. Your travel agent will have suggestions about travel insurance and many policies offer higher levels of coverage for the USA. Check the fine print as some policies may exclude coverage for "dangerous" occupations which can include scuba diving, motorcycling, skiing, rock climbing, and the like. If you're likely to engage in anything like that you don't want a policy which leaves you in the cold. For young visitors, policies issued through student travel oriented organizations like STA, Travel Cuts, Campus Travel, or Council Travel are usually a good value.

If you do require medical attention be sure to save all invoices and documentation and put in a claim to your insurance company as soon as possible.

Medical Attention

Check the Yellow Pages under "Physicians & Surgeons" or "Clinics" to find a doctor. Your hotel should be able to make suggestions. Dentists can be found by calling the Dental Information Service (☎ 398-0618). In real emergencies call ☎ 911 for an ambulance. In that case you're not going to be too worried about where you end up, but San Francisco General Hospital (☎ 206-8000), 1001 Potrero Ave., has an emergency room. Be aware that the base fee for a visit to the emergency room is $125. If you have injuries or require any serious treatment the price skyrockets to above the $1000 mark. The moral: don't get hurt or sick in the USA!

WOMEN TRAVELERS

Women travelers are perhaps less likely to encounter problems in live-and-let-live San Francisco than in other US cities, although the usual precautions apply.

San Francisco's Women's Building (☎ 431-1180), 3543 18th St., is a meeting place for a number of women's organizations, including the National Organization for Women (NOW), and provides numerous resources and services for women. Some other woman-friendly centers in San Francisco are Old Wives Tales Book Store (☎ 821-4575), 1009 Valencia St. in the Mission, and the YWCA (☎ 775-6502), 620 Sutter St. The San Francisco branch of Planned Parenthood (☎ 441-5454), 815 Eddy St., Suite 200, provides healthcare services for women, including pregnancy testing and birth-control counseling.

Of course, any serious problems you encounter should be dealt with by calling the police (☎ 911). San Francisco's 24-hour rape crisis hotline is ☎ 647-7273. Check the Yellow Pages under "Women's Organizations & Services" for more local resources.

DISABLED TRAVELERS

Berkeley was a pioneer in disabled resources so there are a great deal of sources and provisions for disabled travelers in the Bay Area. The Center for Independent Living (☎ (510) 841-4776), 2539 Telegraph Ave., Berkeley, was the East Bay starting point, their office in San Francisco (☎ 863-0581) is at 70 10th St.

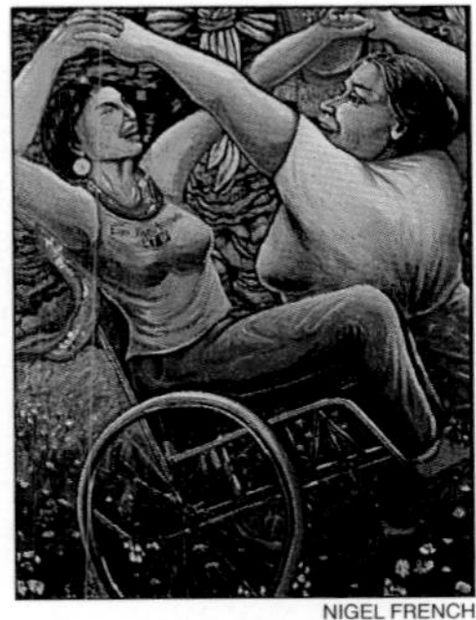

NIGEL FRENCH
Mural, the Women's Building

All the Bay Area transit companies, including BART, Muni, AC Transit, and Golden Gate Transit, offer travel discounts for the disabled and they have a jointly issued ID card to access these reductions. All Muni Metro and BART stations are wheelchair accessible. Muni's *Street & Transit Map* details which bus routes and streetcar stops are wheelchair friendly. The *San Francisco Bay Area Regional Transit Guide,* published by the Metropolitan Transit Commission, has a section on Disabled Services. The major rent-a-car companies are generally able to supply hand-controlled vehicles with one or two day's notice.

GAY & LESBIAN TRAVELERS

Locating the gay community in San Francisco doesn't require much detective work. Just head into the Castro where most businesses are gay-owned and oriented, most hangouts are gay-dominated, and most residents, obviously, are gay. A Different Light Bookstore (☎ 431-0891), 489 Castro St., is the Bay Area's number one gay bookshop and is a good place to go to start learning your way around. Pick up a copy of *Betty and Pansy's Severe Queer Review* (1995) while you're there. These two wicked queens rate bars, cruising areas, cafes, local bands, etc., and are as hilarious as they are honest.

There are also a number of gay publications such as the every-other-weekly *Bay Times* and the weekly *Bay Area Reporter* – both come out on Thursday and have articles and events listings.

Check the Yellow Pages under Gay & Lesbian Organizations for the extensive listings of community resources. Some good numbers to know are the Gay, Lesbian, Bisexual, & Transgendered Switchboard Hotline (☎ (510) 841-6224), the Gay Youth Talk Line (☎ (800) 246-7743), and the AIDS Hotline (☎ 863-2437).

SENIOR TRAVELERS

Though the age at which senior benefits begin varies, travelers from 50 years and up (though more commonly 65 and up) can expect to receive cut rates at such places as hotels, museums, and restaurants. Some national advocacy groups that can help seniors in planning their travels are the American Association of Retired Persons (☎ (202) 434-2277) 601 E St. NW, Washington, DC 20049 (for Americans 50 years or older); Elderhostel (☎ (617) 426-8056), 75 Federal St., Boston, MA 02110-1941 (for people 55 and older, and their companions); and the National Council of Senior Citizens (☎ (202) 347-8800), 1331 F St. NW, Washington, DC 20004.

SAN FRANCISCO FOR CHILDREN

San Francisco is fairly children friendly and even some of the priciest restaurants are relaxed enough to accept children. The Exploratorium was designed with children in mind and the California Academy of Sciences is great for kids, especially the Steinhart Aquarium. Around the Bay the Lawrence Hall of Science in Berkeley and the Tech Museum in San Jose both bring a child's perspective to science.

Simply getting around San Francisco can be a fun adventure for children. Every kid tall enough to hang on will want to ride outside on the cable cars and the Bay ferries will also appeal. On Muni, children under five travel free and children age five to 17 (and adults age 65 and up) travel at a discount fare. The basic adult fare is $1 which drops to 35¢ for discount travelers.

For general information (and encouragement), see Lonely Planet's *Travel With Children* by Maureen Wheeler (1995).

DANGERS & ANNOYANCES

Like any US urban area, San Francisco has its no-go zones but the places where a visitor would be most at risk are also the places where a visitor is least likely to be. The Bay Area's other dangers and annoyances are either more mundane (panhandlers) or spectacular but unlikely (the next "Big One" is still due one day).

Unsafe Areas

Like most big US cities San Francisco has its dangerous neighborhoods, more so after dark than during the daytime. Avoid deserted areas; crowds and activity are usually good safety signs. Areas in which to avoid walking alone at night are the Tenderloin, Western Addition, Market St. and SoMa, Hunters Point, and some of the city's parks, particularly Mission Dolores Park and Buena Vista Park. Stick to the well-lighted streets whenever possible. If you find yourself somewhere you would rather not be, act confident and sure of yourself; then go into a store and call a taxi. If your nightmare comes true, there's no 100% recommended policy but handing over whatever they want is much better than getting knifed or shot. Have something to hand over: drugged or otherwise, crazed muggers are not too happy to find their victims are penniless.

Panhandlers & the Homeless

Once upon a time guidebooks advised Americans venturing into the Third World how to cope with the culture shock of encountering beggars. These days you're as likely to bump into beggars on the streets of San Francisco as on the streets of Calcutta, except here they've been relabelled "panhandlers." With all the competition for your pocket change, panhandlers can get pretty imaginative. In San Francisco I saw signs proclaiming: "Let's be honest, I need a beer," "residentially challenged," and "non-aggressive panhandlers."

The official advice is "don't encourage them" – it only helps to make visitors an easy mark. Instead, you can donate to a good cause like homeless rehabilitation by buying a "Street Sheet," a newspaper that benefits a number of programs.

Earthquakes

San Franciscans are very earthquake conscious. The main danger during a really big quake is being hit by something falling, whether it's falling debris or furniture toppling over. If you're indoors try to get under shelter, a strong table or a door frame are good bets. Don't rush outside because you may be hit by falling glass or building debris. If you're outside, move away from buildings, trees, power lines, signposts, or anything else that might fall on you or shower debris on you. If you're in a car, stop if it is safe but not under bridges or overpasses or in tunnels, and be careful not to block the way of rescue vehicles.

BUSINESS HOURS & HOLIDAYS

Office hours in the Bay Area are commonly Monday to Friday, 9 am to 5 pm although there can be a variance of half an hour or so. Many shops are open longer hours and through the weekends while many supermarkets are open 24 hours.

Banks are generally open weekdays 8 am to 4 pm and on one day of the week until later in the evening. On Saturdays they are often open until noon.

When holidays fall on a weekend they are often celebrated on Friday or Monday instead. Holidays include:

New Year's Day	January 1
ML King, Jr. Day	third Monday in January
Presidents' Day	third Monday in February
Easter	a Sunday in March or April
Memorial Day	last Monday in May
Independence Day	July 4
Labor Day	first Monday in September
Columbus Day	second Monday in October
Veterans Day	November 11
Thanksgiving	fourth Thursday in November
Christmas Day	December 25

SPECIAL EVENTS

San Franciscans like to party and they're very keen on dressing up. Halloween is a surprisingly popular event in the Bay Area, when you'll spot people driving around in costume and come across unlikely people, like bank tellers, in full regalia. Even the Bay Area's premier foot race is as much a fancy dress party as a sporting event.

January & February

Chinese New Year Late January or early February. The New Year is celebrated in San Francisco's Chinatown with color and verve similar to Chinese centers in Asia. The Golden Dragon Parade, led by a 75-foot long

TOM SMALLMAN

JAMES LYON

RICK GERHARTER

Street festivals are a lively tradition in San Francisco: Chinese New Year in Chinatown (top left), Halloween in the Castro (top right) and Carnaval in the Mission (above)

dragon, is the highlight of the festivities. Check with the Chinatown Chamber of Commerce (☎ 982-3000), 730 Sacramento St., for details.

March

St. Patrick's Day March 17. The consumption of large quantities of green-colored beer precedes a downtown parade on the Sunday nearest March 17. Phone ☎ 661-2700 for details.

April

Cherry Blossom Festival Late April. The arrival of spring is celebrated in Japantown with martial arts demonstrations, tea ceremonies, and other uniquely Japanese events. Phone ☎ 563-2313 for details.

San Francisco Int'l Film Festival Two weeks in April – The country's oldest film festival is concentrated at the Kabuki cinema in Japantown with films also at other Bay Area cinemas. Phone ☎ 929-5000 for details.

May

Cinco de Mayo Weekend closest to May 5. Two days of music, dancing, and parades in the Mission mark the Mexican victory over the French at the Battle of Puebla in 1862. Phone ☎ 826-1401 for details.

Bay to Breakers Third Sunday in May. Over 100,000 Bay Area joggers make their way from the Bay (the Embarcadero) via Golden Gate Park to Breakers (the Pacific Ocean). Phone ☎ 808-5000, extension 2222, or contact the *San Francisco Examiner* for details and entry forms.

Carnaval Memorial Day weekend. If Rio and New Orleans can have a carnaval why not San Francisco? Lots of music and dancing in the streets of the Mission. Phone ☎ 826-1401 for details.

June

Gay Events June is a celebratory month for San Francisco's gay community, with the Gay & Lesbian Film Festival playing at the Castro Theater and Gay Pride Week leading up to the last Sunday in June, when the often outrageous Gay Freedom Day Parade is held. The evening before the parade is the Pink Saturday party on Castro St. Up to a half of a million people congregate down Market St. for the city's biggest annual parade, followed by a huge party and fair at the City Hall.

Street Fairs June also brings a number of street fairs including the North Beach Festival (☎ 403-0666) and the Haight St. Fair (☎ 661-8025).

Cable Car Bell-Ringing Championship Late June / early July. Cable car drivers compete to be the loudest or most tuneful bell ringer. Phone ☎ 923-6202 for details.

July

Independence Day July 4. Independence Day brings fireworks to Fisherman's Wharf and a Teddy Bear Parade & Picnic in Oakland.

Polk St. Fair Mid to late July. Another street fair, this one with a strong gay emphasis.

September

Opera in the Park First Sunday following the start of the opera season. The San Francisco Opera puts on a free show at Sharon Meadow in Golden Gate Park to mark the start of the opera season. Phone ☎ 864-3330 for details.

San Francisco Shakespeare Festival Free performances of a different play each year, starting Labor Day weekend in Golden Gate Park and other Bay Area parks. Phone ☎ 666-2222 for details.

San Francisco Blues Festival Late September. Two days of blues on Fort Mason's Great Meadow. Phone ☎ (510) 762-2277 (BASS tickets) for details.

San Francisco Chinatown Moon Festival End of September. Chinatown's celebration of the traditional Autumn Moon Festival.

Folsom St. Fair Late September. One of the funnest, most outrageous street fairs in the city, though perhaps a little too risqué for children.

October

Castro St. Fair Early October. Another popular street fair, again with the gay community as the driving force.

San Francisco Jazz Festival Mid to late October. Catch jazz performances throughout the city; call ☎ 788-7353 for details.

Halloween October 31. Fancy dress opportunities are never passed by lightly in San Francisco and this is the most crazed night of the year, with hundreds of thousands of costumed revelers taking to the streets, particularly Castro St. The Exotic-Erotic Halloween Ball (☎ 567-2255) at the Concourse Exhibition Center is one of the highlights. Halloween is also the time for the annual Pumpkin Festival at Half Moon Bay.

November

Día de los Muertos November 2. Mexico's surprisingly vivacious Day of the Dead is celebrated in the Mission. Phone ☎ 826-8009 for details.

WORK

Unemployment levels in San Francisco are above the national average, which is not helped by military base closures and the continuing decline in military employment levels. Foreign visitors are not legally allowed to work in the USA without the appropriate working visa and recent legislative changes are specifically targeting illegal immigrants, which is what you will be if you try to work while on a tourist visa. See Visa Extensions in the Visas & Embassies section for warnings on longer stays.

EMERGENCIES

Dial ☎ 911 for all police, fire, and ambulance emergencies. At the front of various Bay Area White Pages directories there's a page of 24-hour "Emergency Crisis Hotlines." In San Francisco call ☎ 781-0500 for the suicide crisis line, ☎ 362-3400 for drug treatment, or ☎ 206-3222 for rape crisis.

The phone directories also have a First Aid & Survival Guide which includes advice on surviving an earthquake and a list of steps for performing CPR.

If you have something stolen report it to the police; you'll need a police report to make a claim if you have a travel insurance policy. If your credit cards, cash cards, or traveler's checks have been taken, notify your bank or the relevant company as soon as possible. For refunds or lost or stolen traveler's checks (not credit cards) call American Express (☎ (800) 221-7282), MasterCard (☎ (800) 223-9920), Thomas Cook (☎ (800) 223-7373), or Visa (☎ (800) 227-6811). For lost American Express Cards call ☎ (800) 528-4800. To report other lost or stolen credit cards check the local Yellow Pages under "Credit Cards."

Foreign visitors who lose their passport should contact their consulate. Having a copy of the important pages of your passport will make replacement much easier.

Getting There & Away

AIR

The Bay Area has three major airports: San Francisco International Airport, on the west side of the Bay; Oakland International Airport, only a few miles across the Bay on the east side; and San Jose International Airport, at the southern end of the Bay. The majority of international flights use San Francisco; at Oakland and San Jose "international" means Mexico and Canada. All three airports are important domestic gateways. See the Getting Around chapter for airport transport information for San Francisco and Oakland.

Scan the Sunday travel section of the *San Francisco Examiner-Chronicle* or the Bay Area's free weekly papers for travel ads and discounted fares out of San Francisco. Good travel agents include STA Travel (☎ 391-8407), 51 Grant Ave, and Council Travel (☎ 421-3473), 530 Bush St., or (☎ 566-6222), 919 Irving St. These student-oriented agents also have offices in Berkeley and Palo Alto.

Within North America

The Bay Area is a major hub in North American air traffic, so there should be little trouble finding a flight or connection to just about anywhere on the continent. Locating the cheapest/most convenient flight leaves several options.

PHILLIP COBLENTZ

Two San Francisco icons: the Golden Gate Bridge and fog

Regional airlines (those serving fewer destinations than the intercontinental biggies) are a good bet as they tend to fly their routes more often than their globe-trotting competitors. Southwest Airlines (☎ (800) 435-9792) covers the western USA fairly completely. They often run specials with rates undercutting other major airlines. USAir and United are also better than average and have a wide range of destinations.

Fares change as often as the winds these days, but nearly all of the best fares come with an "advance order" stipulation, which means you must purchase them seven to 21 days in advance to get the bargain rate. "Companion fares" are also increasingly common, letting two people travel for the price of one. Roundtrip fares to the East Coast typically run around $400 (give or take $100). Roundtrip to Chicago hovers at around $300, slightly less to Denver or Dallas, and if you feel like darting down to Los Angeles to catch the sunset, it's around $100. Ditto Seattle and Portland, if you're lucky.

Continental flights outside the USA likewise vary depending upon the frequency of flights, the time of year, the distance traveled, and the whim of the industry. Some average roundtrip fares for Canada include Vancouver ($250), Edmonton ($350), Winnipeg ($400), and Montreal and Quebec ($475). Mexico City averages around $350, and the fares continue to rise the further south you go. Again, these fares are rough guidelines of what to expect. Call a travel agent or check the newspapers for specifics.

To/From Abroad

Visit USA Passes Almost all domestic carriers offer Visit USA passes to non-US citizens. The passes are actually a book of coupons redeemable for flights; high season prices average $479 for three coupons and $769 for eight. Often, the coupons can only be purchased in conjunction with an international flight (Mexico and Canada excluded). Delta, American, and Continental all have good programs; call them and other airlines for information.

Round-the-World Tickets Visitors from Australia or even from Europe may want to consider including San Francisco in a Round-the-World (RTW) itinerary. Travel agents in London can put together an itinerary using several airlines for as little as £800 either via the northern hemisphere or dipping down to Australia. Add in South Africa as well and you're looking at around £1000. Two or three airlines also group together to offer their own combination deals, typically from £1400 to

£1600 via the North Pacific and £1800 to £2200 when including Australia and/or South Africa.

In Australia fares are around A$1800 or Africa can be added to the itinerary starting from A$2200. Qantas, British Airways, and USAir offer RTW possibilities utilizing their combined routes for less than A$3000.

A variety of combinations are offered from Asia using, for example, an Asian or US airline to fly to the USA, the US airline to fly on to Europe, and the Asian airline to take you back to the starting point. Typically these cost around S$4800 from Singapore and HK$18,000 from Hong Kong.

To/From Latin America Most flights to/from Central and South America go via Los Angeles, Miami, or Houston. Most countries' major airlines, as well as US airlines like United and American, serve these destinations, with onward connections to San Francisco. Continental has flights to/from about 20 cities in Mexico and Central America.

To/From Europe British Airways, United Airlines, and Virgin Atlantic have non-stop services between London and San Francisco. Other US airlines arrive in the USA at a gateway city and continue on connecting domestic flights. Cheaper flights to San Francisco from London may involve a flight to Los Angeles or some other gateway and a connecting flight. The direct flight takes about 11 hours westbound (London to San Francisco), and nine or 10 hours eastbound because of the prevailing winds. Westbound flights usually leave London in the morning and arrive in San Francisco in the evening. Eastbound flights go overnight.

A straightforward economy roundtrip ticket is around £800 and a business class roundtrip ticket costs about £3000. Cheaper fares vary with the season; summer (June through August) and Christmas are the peak periods and weekends may also be more expensive. Apex tickets, which usually must be purchased 21 days in advance and involve cancellation penalties if you change your plans, cost from £350 to £1000 roundtrip. Bargain fares around £300 or even less can be found using one of the less popular international airlines from London to New York and continuing on a US domestic flight. Charter flights typically cost around £400 roundtrip. The business of discounting tickets is so well-developed in Britain that you can get heavily discounted first-class and business-class tickets as well as cheaper economy tickets.

PHILLIP COBLENTZ

The weekly London "what's on" magazine *Time Out*, the *Evening Standard*, and the various giveaway travel papers are all good sources of ads for cheaper fares. Good agents for low-priced tickets in London include:

Campus Travel
174 Kensington High St., London W8 (☎ (0171) 938-2188) or 28A Poland St., London W1 (☎ (0171) 437-7767)

STA
86 Old Brompton Rd., London SW7 & 117 Euston Rd., London NW1 (☎ (0171) 937-9962)

Trailfinders
194 Kensington High St., London W8 (☎ (0171) 937-5400)

Travel Cuts
95A Regent St., London W1 (☎ (0171) 637-3161)

Other airlines with services to and from Europe include Aeroflot (Moscow), Air France (Paris), Finnair (Helsinki), KLM (Amsterdam), and Lufthansa (Frankfurt). Although there are good value charter deals from European cities the general price of fares will be much higher than from London.

To/From Australia & New Zealand Neither Air New Zealand nor Qantas currently fly direct to San Francisco, their services go to Los Angeles with a connecting domestic flight, sometimes on a code-sharing flight designed to make you think it's all the same airline. United Airlines does have direct flights to San Francisco from Sydney. With the advent of long range 747-400 aircraft most services now overfly Hawaii so at least the Pacific is covered in one mighty leap. From Auckland to Los Angeles it takes 12 to 13 hours and from Sydney to Los Angeles, 13½ to 14½ hours. Typical Apex

PHILLIP COBLENTZ

roundtrip fares vary from A$1400 to A$1800 from the Australian east coast and NZ$1800 to NZ$2000 from New Zealand.

Weekend travel sections in major city newspapers in Australia or New Zealand will have ads for travel agents specializing in cheap fares. In Australia, Flight Centre, and STA travel agencies have competitively priced tickets. STA also operates in New Zealand.

To/From Asia San Francisco has a huge network of business links with Asia so there are many flights to and from Asian capitals. They include, with typical apex roundtrip fares, China (Air China, Y12,340), Hong Kong (Cathay Pacific, HK$11,000), Indonesia (Garuda, US$1300), Japan (Japan Airlines, ¥300,000), Korea (Korean Airlines, US$1400), Malaysia (MAS, M$4600), Philippines (Philippine Airlines, US$1550), Singapore (SIA, S$3400), Taiwan (China Airlines and Eva Air, NT$25,000 to NT$37,000), and Thailand (Thai International, 29,000B). United, Northwest, and American Airlines also fly Asia routes.

Airline Offices

Airline offices in San Francisco include:

Aeroflot	☎ (800) 995-5555
Air Canada	☎ (800) 776-3000
Air China	☎ (415) 392-2156
Air France	☎ (800) 237-2747
Air New Zealand	☎ (800) 262-1234
Alaska Airlines	☎ (800) 426-0333
American Airlines	☎ (800) 433-7300
America West	☎ (800) 235-9292
British Airways	☎ (800) 247-9297

Canadian Airlines Int'l	☎ (800) 426-7000
Cathay Pacific	☎ (800) 233-2742
China Airlines	☎ (800) 227-5118
Continental Airlines	☎ (800) 525-0280 domestic
	☎ (800) 231-0856 int'l
Delta Airlines	☎ (800) 221-1212 domestic
	☎ (800) 241-4141 int'l
Eva Airways	☎ (415) 781-2068
Finnair	☎ (800) 950-5000
Hawaiian Air	☎ (800) 367-5320
Japan Airlines	☎ (800) 525-3663
KLM	☎ (800) 374-7747
Lufthansa	☎ (800) 645-3880
Mexicana	☎ (800) 531-7921
Northwest Airlines	☎ (800) 225-2525 domestic
	☎ (800) 447-4747 int'l
Philippine Airlines	☎ (800) 435-9725
Qantas	☎ (800) 227-4500
SAS	☎ (800) 221-2350
Singapore Airlines	☎ (415) 781-7304
Southwest Airlines	☎ (800) 435-9792
Swissair	☎ (800) 221-4750
Thai International	☎ (800) 426-5204
TWA	☎ (800) 221-2000 domestic
	☎ (800) 892-4141 int'l
United Airlines	☎ (800) 241-6522 domestic
	☎ (800) 631-1500 int'l
US Air	☎ (800) 428-4322
Varig Brazilian Airline	☎ (800) 468-2744
Virgin Atlantic	☎ (800) 862-8621

San Francisco International Airport

San Francisco International Airport (☎ 876-7809), the fifth busiest in the USA and the seventh busiest in the world, has three terminals. The North Terminal is where American, Canadian, and United Airlines are based; the South Terminal, home to Air Canada, Alaska Airlines, America West, Continental, Delta, Southwest, TWA, and USAir; and the International Terminal is where you'll find all international airlines (except for the Canadian ones), plus the international services of Alaska Airlines, Delta, Northwest, and United.

Information Information Booths (white courtesy phone ☎ 7-0018) on the lower level of all three terminals operate daily 8 am to midnight. Travelers' Aid information booths on the upper level operate daily 9 am to 9 pm. ATMs are found in all three terminals. Bank of America branches are located on the North Terminal mezzanine and behind Air China in the International Terminal. There are lockers in the boarding areas or larger luggage can be stored in the Luggage Storage/ Travel Agency in the upper level connector between the South and International Terminals. On the lower level of the International Terminal a clinic (white courtesy phone ☎ 7-0444) operates daily, 24 hours. And forget about smoking, except in smoking rooms upstairs in the North and South Terminals and downstairs in the International Terminal.

BUS

Although there are a variety of bus services between other Bay Area communities and San Francisco, Greyhound is the only regular long distance bus company operating to the city. All these bus services arrive and depart at the Transbay bus terminal (☎ 495-1575), 425 Mission St. at 1st St, only two blocks south of Market.

Local Transit

If you're heading out to neighboring communities you can take AC Transit (☎ (510) 839-2882) buses to the East Bay, Golden Gate Transit (☎ 332-6600) buses north to Marin and Sonoma Counties, SamTrans (☎ (800) 660-4287) buses south to Palo Alto and along the Pacific coast, and Santa Clara Transit (☎ (408) 321-2300) buses to go south beyond Palo Alto and to San Jose.

Greyhound

From San Francisco there are seven morning, six afternoon, and six evening Greyhound (☎ (800) 231-2222) buses to Los Angeles. The eight- to 11-hour trip costs $35 one way, $69 roundtrip. Greyhound also operate north to Seattle (19 to 25 hours, $39/79) and inland to Lake Tahoe (five to 10 hours, $20/40).

Green Tortoise

As an alternative to Greyhound there's the funky Green Tortoise bus service (☎ 956-7500), 494 Broadway at Kearny, a favorite of backpackers because they manage to combine getting there with enjoying yourself along the way. Green Tortoise information is also available from the Green Tortoise Guest House in North Beach (see Hostels in the Places to Stay chapter). The north-south trip runs between Seattle and Los Angeles via San Francisco. From San Francisco fares are: Seattle $49, Portland or Eugene $39, and Los Angeles $30. They also have trips to the Northern California redwoods (six days, $199), Yosemite (three days, $99), and the Southwest desert (nine days, $199).

TRAIN

CalTrain

CalTrain (☎ (800) 660-4287) operates down the Peninsula, linking San Francisco with Palo Alto (Stanford University) and San Jose. It's the best means of travel along this route. The CalTrain station is at 4th and Townsend Sts., in the SoMa district.

Amtrak

Amtrak (☎ (800) 872-7245) is the US national railway system and its new Bay Area terminal is at Jack London Square in Oakland. A free shuttle bus connects with the CalTrain station and with the Ferry Building on the Embarcadero. Tickets can be purchased at all three locations. Traveling north from Los Angeles it's equally simple to transfer from Amtrak to CalTrain at San Jose and take that service to San Francisco.

Amtrak connects to cities all over the continental USA and Canada. The main services through the Bay Area are the *San Joaquin* route (Oakland – Bakersfield, four times daily), the *Three Capitols* route (San Jose – Oakland – Sacramento – Roseville, several times daily) and the *Coast Starlight* route (Seattle – Oakland – San Jose – Los Angeles, daily).

CAR & MOTORCYCLE

Freeways crisscross the Bay Area. Highway 101 runs north-south through the Bay Area, continuing south to Los Angeles and north through to Eureka and on to Oregon. The bayside stretch of Hwy 101 between San

A Free Car

Want to drive there for free? Try Auto Driveaway of San Francisco (☎ 777-3740), 350 Townsend St., between 4th and 5th in SoMa. People who want their car moved from city A to city B leave the car with this organization and so long as you're willing to drive from A to B at an average speed of 400 miles per day and pay for the gas, the car's yours. There's a $10 non-refundable application fee and a $350 security deposit and, of course, you'd better have a current license and a good driving record. ■

Francisco and San Jose is a continuous traffic jam, sometimes a stationary one, sometimes a high-speed one, but always solid. Interstate 280, parallel and slightly to the west, is much more attractive and much easier on the nerves.

Further west is Hwy 1, the much slower but much more scenic coast road. Highways 1 and 101 merge to cross the Golden Gate Bridge but soon go their separate ways north or south. Just south of San Francisco, Hwy 1 is frequently washed out by rains on the unstable Devil's Slide.

On the east side of the Bay, I-80 runs north-south through Berkeley and swings across the Oakland-Bay Bridge to San Francisco. Interstate 80 also heads inland from the East Bay, passing Sacramento (91 miles), the state capital, on its way to Reno, Nevada (226 miles). Interstate 580 swings inland from the East Bay to meet I-5, about 50 miles inland. The fastest route south to Los Angeles is via I-5; the 390-mile trip takes six or seven boring hours. The route inland to Yosemite (210 miles) starts along the I-580.

HITCHHIKING

Travelers hoping to thumb their way around California may be in for an unpleasant surprise. On the whole, hitching is much less common in modern-day America than elsewhere in the world, and for good reason. Hitching is never entirely safe, travelers who decide to do it should understand that they are taking a serious risk.

That said, for people who do choose to hitch, the advice that follows should help to make their journeys as fast and safe as possible. Officially, hitchhiking is not illegal in California, but it *is* frowned upon by the highway patrol and you can expect a hassle. Local laws may be more stringent. As signs at the on-ramps will tell you, pedestrians are not allowed on major motorways, so keep off of the on-ramps and behind these signs. Fines are stiff for breaking these laws and if you are caught twice within 24 hours, you will be arrested.

Getting Around

TO/FROM THE AIRPORTS

San Francisco International Airport

San Francisco International Airport is on the Bay side of the Peninsula 14 miles south of the city center. There is a wide variety of ways of getting to or from the airport, starting with simply driving there from downtown either via Hwy 101, via I-80 and then Hwy 101 or via I-280 then I-380 and Hwy 101. The trip between the city and airport can take as little as 20 minutes but in the morning and evening rush hours it can stretch to 45 minutes or more; give yourself an hour to be safe. Coming from San Francisco, don't be fooled by the Airport Rd. exit. That's just there to confuse visitors; wait for the San Francisco International Airport exit.

The airport operates a ground transportation information hotline (☎ (800) 736-2008), weekdays 7:30 am to 5 pm. In addition, information is posted throughout the terminals, on the lower level center islands and is available at Airport Information booths. Transport arrives and departs at the upper and lower levels and zones for each type of transport are color-coded. There will be buses going to the numerous rent-a-car lots, buses going to the scattered long-term car parking lots, buses going to other airports, and buses going to nearby hotels. Visitors may find this confusing so before you step outside know what you want and where to find it:

Taxi Taxis operate to and from the yellow zone on the lower level. A taxi to downtown San Francisco will cost around $25 to $35 (plus tip), depending on your destination.

Bus & Train Regular public bus services operate at the blue zone on the lower level.

SamTrans (☎ (800) 660-4287) express bus No. 3X ($1) takes 20 minutes to reach the Daly City BART station from where you can ride the BART to San Francisco ($1.65), or to the East Bay ($2.20 to Oakland, $2.35 to Berkeley).

Or take the free CalTrain (☎ (800) 660-4287) shuttle on its nine minute ride to the Millbrae CalTrain station. From there you can ride the CalTrain north to San Francisco ($1.75 between 10 am and 4 pm, $1.25 at other times) or south to Palo Alto ($3 between 9 am and 3 pm, $2.25 at other times) and San Jose.

SamTrans also has a 7F express service between Palo Alto and the bus terminal in San Francisco via the airport. It operates every 10 to 30 minutes between 6 am and 6 pm, takes about half an hour from the airport to the city, and costs $2 for adults, but no baggage is allowed on this bus. You might get away with a small carry-on. The SamTrans 7B bus ($1) does allow baggage but it's an all-stop service, taking about an hour.

Airport transport buses, which also operate at the lower level blue zone, include the SFO Airporter (☎ 495-8404, (800) 532-8405 in Northern California only), with three different shuttle services operating every 20 minutes to a list of major hotels in three city zones. Fares are $8 one way, $15 roundtrip. The Bay Area Shuttle (☎ 873-7771) operates a similar program from major East Bay hotels, $10 each way.

Shuttle Shuttles mostly operate to and from the blue, red, and yellow zones at the upper level. A shuttle is a minibus service operating either to specific locations or on request. There is no need to book shuttles at the airport, just wait for one to come along. For transport to the airport, however, you need to phone ahead or ask your hotel to make the booking. Discount coupons are often available for shuttle services which typically cost $9 to $11 one way (and the driver would like a tip, please) and $16 roundtrip. Competition is fierce and if two shuttles arrive simultaneously you can even bargain.

Super Shuttle (☎ 558-8500) costs $11, and to other Bay Area cities costs up to $25. Lorrie's (☎ 334-9000) and Quake City (☎ 255-4899) are $1 cheaper. There are many others including American Airporter Shuttle (☎ 546-6689), Marin Airporter (☎ 461-4222, lower level), and Wharf Airporter (☎ (800) 434-1222). The Airporter Limousine bus service (☎ 673-2432) connects with the Powell St. BART station (Route One) and the Embarcadero BART station (Route Two).

Oakland International Airport

Travelers arriving at the Oakland Airport will have a little further to go to reach San Francisco, but it's by no means difficult. Shuttle buses run between the airport and the Coliseum BART station every 10 minutes from Monday to Saturday 6 am to midnight and Sunday 9 am to midnight; fares are $2. A direct Daly City BART train can be caught to San Francisco. Super Shuttle

(☎ (510) 268-8700) operates door-to-door service to destinations in the East Bay and San Francisco for $12 to $21.

MUNI

San Francisco's principal public transport system is the Muni (Municipal Transit Agency; ☎ 673-6864) which operates nearly 100 Muni bus lines (many of them electric trolley buses), Muni Metro streetcars and, of course, the famous cable cars. Muni moves over 750,000 people a day and accounts for 25% to 30% of all the vehicle travel in the city. A free Muni Timetable is available and there is a detailed *Street & Transit Map* that costs $2. Another useful booklet is *Tours of Discovery* with details of city tours by public transport.

Muni information is also available from the Visitor Information Center (☎ 391-2000), Hallidie Plaza at Market and Powell Sts, or at City Hall Information (☎ 554-7111), 400 Van Ness Ave.

Fares & Passes

Standard Muni fares for buses or streetcars is $1; children and seniors (65 +) pay 35¢. Transfer tickets are available at the start of your journey and you can then use them for two connecting trips. They can be used for

Muni Bus Routes

Some of the most important Muni bus routes for visitors include:

No. 5 Fulton Along Market, McAllister, and Fulton Sts. along the north side of Golden Gate Park all the way to the ocean.

No. 7 Haight From the Ferry Building along Market and Haight Sts., through the Haight-Ashbury, to the southeast corner of Golden Gate Park; daytime only.

No. 14 Mission Along Mission St. through SoMa and the Mission district.

No. 15 3rd St. From 3rd St. in SoMa, through the Financial District on Kearny St., through North Beach on Columbus Ave., then along Powell St. to the Fisherman's Wharf area.

No. 18 46th Ave. Palace of the Legion of Honor to Sutro Baths along the western edge of Golden Gate Park on the Great Hwy, past San Francisco Zoo and Lake Merced.

No. 22 Fillmore From Potrero Hill, through the Mission along Fillmore St., past Japantown to Pacific Heights and the Marina.

No. 24 Divisadero Through Noe Valley, along Castro St. then Divisadero to Pacific Heights.

No. 26 Valencia Through the historic areas of the Mission,

about 90 minutes but are not transferable to cable cars. Cable car fares are $2 for adults. Children under five ride free.

A Muni Passport allows unlimited travel on all Muni transport including cable cars. Passes are available in one-day ($6), three-day ($10), or seven-day ($15) versions. The passports also offer discounts at a number of city attractions. Passports are available from the Visitor Information Center at Hallidie Plaza, from the half price tickets kiosk on Union Square, from a number of hotels, and from businesses which display the Muni Pass sign in their window. A cheaper Weekly Pass costs $9 and allows bus and railway travel and discounts on cable car trips. A monthly Fast Pass costs $35 and allows cable car as well as BART and CalTrain travel within the San Francisco city area.

Bus

Buses display their route number and final destination on the front and side. If the number is followed by a letter (A, B, EX, L, etc.) then it's a limited stop or express service. On nine lines a Night Owl service operates from midnight to 6 am. You pay the fare upon boarding the bus (change or $1 bills please) or you show your pass to the driver.

along Valencia St. to Market and Polk, and through SoMa along Mission St.

No. 28 19th Ave. From Fort Mason to the Golden Gate Bridge toll plaza and on through the Presidio, Richmond District, Golden Gate Park and south through the Sunset district all the way to Daly City BART.

No. 30 Stockton From the CalTrain Station in SoMa, along 3rd and Market Sts., then on Stockton St. through Chinatown, and Columbus Ave. through North Beach to Fisherman's Wharf, Fort Mason, and the Palace of Fine Arts.

No. 32 Embarcadero From the CalTrain Station along the Embarcadero, past the Ferry Building to Fisherman's Wharf.

No. 37 Corbett A winding route from the Haight-Ashbury via Buena Vista Park to Twin Peaks.

No. 38 Geary From the Transbay bus terminal along Market St. and then Geary Blvd. all the way to the Cliff House at the ocean.

No. 71 Haight-Noriega Along Market and Haight Sts., through the Haight-Ashbury, along the south side of Golden Gate Park and then down to Noriega St. through the Outer Sunset to the ocean.

Streetcar

Downtown Muni streetcars use the same subway tunnels as BART along Market St. from the Embarcadero to the Civic Center Station. The streetcars emerge above ground and travel on the street along six routes: J – Church, K – Ingleside, L – Taraval, M – Ocean View, and N – Judah. The routes are identical as far as Church St. The K, L and M routes then continue on past the Castro station while the N route follows Judah St. out to the ocean, paralleling the south side of Golden Gate Park, and the J bisects the Castro and the Mission and reconnects with K and M at Balboa Park.

As of September 1995, the new F line has been in service, running antique cable cars from around the world along Market St. from SoMa's Transbay Terminal to Castro St. It will eventually travel a route along the Embarcadero all the way up to Fisherman's Wharf, but at press time it was not yet completed.

The L and N lines operate 24 hours although between 1 and 5 am, buses replace the streetcars. The other lines operate from between 5 and 6 am (a bit later on weekends for the M line) to just after midnight.

Cable Car

The three cable car routes in San Francisco are tourist favorites – where else can you travel *in* a tourist attraction from one tourist highlight to another? There's sitting space for about 30 passengers but they are often outnumbered by the strap hangers who cling precariously to the outside. In this age of seat belts and air bags, taking advantage of what is clearly a very foolish means of transport makes it all the more fun.

The starting points, particularly the Hallidie Plaza/Market St. terminal for the Powell St. lines, can be very crowded, entailing a long wait for a ride. Further down

Cable Car Routes

California St. This route runs straight up California St. from the Embarcadero Terminal at Market St. through the Financial District and Chinatown then up Nob Hill before dropping down to Van Ness. There are great views of the Bay during the climb up (or drop down) Nob Hill. Although this route is just a straight shot it does have the shortest lines.

Powell-Mason From the Hallidie Plaza terminal at the junction of Market and Powell Sts. the cable car climbs up Powell St. past Union Square, and then turns along Jackson St. for one block

the route finding space can be a matter of luck. There are cable car ticket machines at the terminal and a ticket conductor on each cable car. The standard fare, irrespective of distance, is $2 but that's just for one ride; there are no transfers on cable cars. An all day cable car ticket costs $6. For more on cable cars, their history, and how they work, see the sidebar in the Things to See & Do chapter.

BART

The Bay Area Rapid Transit system or BART (☎ 788-2278) is a subway system linking San Francisco with the East Bay. The state of the art system opened in 1972 and is convenient, economical, and generally quite safe to use, although caution is required around some BART stations at night. There are four BART lines, covering a total of 71 miles, with Daly City, Richmond, Concord, and Fremont as the extremities of the service.

One-way fares vary from 90¢ to a maximum of $3.45. Popular routes like San Francisco to Oakland or Berkeley are typically $1.75 to $2.10. BART tickets are sold by machines in value from 90¢ up to $40 and are magnetically encoded so that each time you pass through a station entry and exit gate the value of your ride is deducted from the ticket. If your ticket still has value, it is returned to you and can be reused until it is exhausted. If you arrive at an exit gate and your ticket's remaining value is less than the ride, you simply put it in an Addfare machine and pay the appropriate amount. A monthly Muni Fast Pass (see Muni) includes BART travel within San Francisco.

BART services operate until at least midnight each night, starting weekdays at 4 am, Saturday at 6 am, and Sunday at 8 am. Bicycles can be carried on BART but not in the commute direction during the weekday commute hours. (See the Bicycle section for more details.)

before descending down Mason, Columbus, and Taylor towards Fisherman's Wharf. On the return trip it takes Washington instead of Jackson, and passes by the Cable Car Museum.

Powell-Hyde This route follows a similar pattern to the Powell-Mason line but follows Jackson St. for five blocks and then turns down Hyde St. to terminate at Aquatic Park, near Fisherman's Wharf. Along Hyde St. it crosses the top of the crookedest section of curvy Lombard St. Coming back, it takes Washington and runs past the Cable Car Museum.

Transfers

From San Francisco BART stations a $1 transfer is available to Muni bus and streetcar services. In the East Bay you must get an AC Transit transfer ticket before leaving the station and then pay an additional 60¢.

ADJACENT TRANSPORT SYSTEMS

If you want to go down the Peninsula, across to the East Bay, or north to Marin County there are other buses to use including AC Transit (☎ (800) 559-4636) to the East Bay; Golden Gate Transit(☎ 332-6600) to Marin and Sonoma Counties; CalTrain / SamTrans(☎ (800) 660-4287) to San Mateo County; and Santa Clara County Transit (☎ (408) 321-2300) to the southern end of the Bay.

CAR & MOTORCYCLE

A car is the last thing you want in downtown San Francisco but for traveling further afield – up to the Wine Country for example – a car can be invaluable.

Driving & Parking

Driving in San Francisco has two problems: negotiating the hills and parking. If you're driving a stick shift (manual transmission) you better have your hill-start technique well honed. Drive carefully; at some of the steepest intersections you're liable to find yourself gazing into space until the nose of your car lurches on to the street level. The city is well marked with signs to tourist zones like North Beach, Fisherman's Wharf, or Chinatown.

Finding a parking spot can often be excrutiating. Sidewalks are color coded for parking restrictions, a system not helped when the colors have long-since faded. There is not likely to be any on-site explanation of the coding so here it is:

- no parking or even stopping
- loading zone from 7 am to 6 pm
- 10-minute parking zone from 9 am to 6 pm
- for picking up / dropping off passengers
- disabled parking only; identification required

Even finding a vacant parking meter may not protect you from parking tickets. Some city meters are strictly for commercial loading, not for regular parking. During the commute hours parking is forbidden on certain busy streets and almost everywhere in the city there will be

TONY WHEELER

TONY WHEELER

In San Francisco, getting there is half the fun. Cable cars and ferries provide colorful means of transportation.

designated hours each week when parking is forbidden due to street cleaning. On hill streets (with a grade as little as 3%) you must "curb wheels" so that they ride up against the curb. This is to prevent cars from running away downhill.

Downtown parking meters typically cost $1 to $1.50 an hour. Downtown parking garages run $8 to $20 a day. Cheaper parking downtown can be found overnight at the parking garage at 123 O'Farrell St. (6 pm to 8 am for $5) or by the day at the garage at 5th and Mission Sts. (24 hours for $12). The parking garage under Portsmouth Square in Chinatown is very reasonably priced for shorter stops, and ditto the St. Mary's Square Garage on California St. near Grant. The multi-story parking garage at Sutter and Stockton Sts., just north of Union Square, is also a good value.

Mission St. in SoMa is a good place to look for meter parking. The Financial District is not bad at night or on weekends but forget it during the working day. A place to give up all hope? At Fisherman's Wharf on a sunny weekend, a legal parking place is a near impossibility.

Parking tickets run $15 to $275 (for blue zone violations). Major parking offenses can result in your car being towed away and you will then have to pay the fine to the Parking & Traffic Department (☎ 553-1200) and a hefty towing and storage fee ($144 for the first day plus $26 for every additional day) to City Tow (☎ 621-8605), 1475 Mission St. in SoMa. Phone the Police Department Towed Vehicle Information (☎ 553-1235) if you think your car has been towed.

The American Automobile Association (AAA; ☎ 565-2012) has an office at 150 Van Ness. Members can call ☎ (800) 222-4357 for emergency road service and towing.

Bridge Tolls

The Bay Area's five major bridges all have one-way tolls. The Golden Gate Bridge costs $3 southbound, except for car poolers (driver plus three passengers) weekdays 5 to 9 am and 4 to 6 pm.

The other four bridges are, north to south, the Richmond-San Rafael Bridge, the San Francisco-Oakland Bay Bridge, the San Mateo-Hayward Bridge, and the Dumbarton Bridge. They all run east-west and all have a $1 toll collected from westbound traffic. During the weekday commute hours, 5 to 10 am and 3 to 6 pm, a car pool (driver plus two passengers) crosses free. Avoiding the backup at the toll booths is a more important issue than saving the $1 toll. ■

Car Rental

All the big rent-a-car operators can be found in the Bay Area, particularly at the airports, along with a host of smaller or local operators. Rates go up and down like the stock market and it's always worth phoning around to see what's available. Booking ahead usually ensures the best rates. Typically a small car might cost $35 to $45 a day or $150 to $250 a week. In any case, airport rates are generally better than city ones. On top of that there will be 8.5% sales tax and $9 or $10 a day loss/damage-waiver or LDW, which means insurance. Some credit cards pick up the insurance tab but it's always wise to check with your card company. Overseas-issued credit cards almost certainly will not offer any insurance coverage. The rent-a-car companies won't explain these alternative insurance policies as they're in the business of selling insurance.

Most rates include unlimited mileage; if a rate looks like a real bargain it may be because you're going to get hit for a mileage charge. Even around the city it's surprising how quickly the miles mount up. Most operators requires that you be at least 25 years of age and if you don't have a suitable credit card, a large cash deposit will be required and you will be treated with great suspicion! Return the car with a full tank of fuel; if you let the operator refill the car for you the gas price will be much higher.

Some of the larger operators and their main San Francisco outlets are:

Alamo	☎ 882-9440, (800) 327-9633	687 Folsom St.
Avis	☎ 885-5011, (800) 331-1212	675, Post St.
Budget	☎ 928-7864, (800) 527-0700	321 Mason St.
Dollar	☎ 771-5300, (800) 800-4000	364 O'Farrell St.
Hertz	☎ 771-2200, (800) 654-3131	433 Mason St.
Thrifty	☎ 788-8111, (800) 367-2277	520 Mason St.

Want to rent something flashy? Sunbelt Car Rental (☎ 771-9191) rents convertibles, BMWs, Corvettes, Jaguars, Mustangs, and 4-wheel drives. A motorcycle? Dubbelju (☎ 495-2774) has BMWs and Harleys.

Buying a Car or Motorcycle

One way to possibly beat the high cost of renting a car is to buy a used vehicle upon your arrival and sell it when you depart. If you go this route, it helps to either have a bit of the auto mechanic in you, or find a mechanic you can trust; you won't get much return value on a "lemon" or a gas guzzler. Don't ask yourself "Do I feel lucky?" because even minor repairs could cost well over $100.

Once you've purchased the car, you must have its emissions smog-tested at a garage and get a certificate that verifies the vehicle meets state standards. You must then purchase a rather costly auto insurance policy and take the smog certificate and proof of insurance, along with the ownership title and bill of sale, to any office of the Department of Motor Vehicles (DMV). It normally takes a full morning or afternoon to get your auto registration, which will cost anywhere from 7% to 12% of the cost of the car.

As your departure from the USA approaches, you must set aside time to sell the car, perhaps also laying out additional money to place a classified ad in a newspaper.

If you are traveling alone and don't object to a little wind, you might consider buying a motorcycle, which is cheaper than a car and tends to be easier to sell. Be sure to buy a helmet for yourself and any potential passengers: helmets are required by law in California and the law is strictly enforced.

TAXI

Taxis are usually fairly easy to find in San Francisco although they do not cruise the streets in the same proliferation that you'll find in, say, New York. Fares start at $1.70 for the first mile and then 30¢ per ⅙ of a mile thereafter. A 10% tip should be added to the fare. Cabs can be found cruising the streets, at cab stands, or by phoning one of the taxi companies. Complaints can be made to the cab companies or to the Police Department Taxicab Complaint Line (☎ 553-1447). The main companies are:

City Cab	☎ 468-7200
De Soto Cab	☎ 673-1414
Luxor Cab	☎ 282-4141
Veteran's Taxicab	☎ 552-1300
Yellow Cab	☎ 626-2345

BICYCLE

For most visitors bicycles will not be an ideal way of getting around the city – there's too much traffic and all those hills are fearsome – but the Bay Area is a great place for recreational bike riding. A bike is the ideal way to explore the Presidio, Golden Gate Park, or to travel across the Golden Gate Bridge to Marin County, birthplace of the mountain bike. For more on city biking see the Bicycling section under Activities in Things to See & Do.

Bicycles can be rented for around $20 to $25 a day. Try the Avenue Cyclery (☎ 387-3155), 756 Stanyan St., right

J.R. SWANSON

Critical Mass

Downtown San Francisco becomes a sea of festive bicyclists on the last Friday of every month. The event is called Critical Mass, and it typically involves as many as 1000 cyclists who gather at the Bay end of Market St. and ride, bells ringing, to a different destination each time. There is no organization or committee behind the event, and the whole thing operates without leaders or security, in what the *Chronicle* has called "civilized anarchy." The event brings together all sorts of people who would never otherwise meet and talk, and the whole thing has done wonders in waking up the bureaucracy to the plight of the city's bicyclists. To take part, just show up with your bike at Justin Herman Plaza (near the Embarcadero BART station) at 5:30 pm – just in time for rush hour! ■

NIGEL FRENCH

by Golden Gate Park in the Haight-Ashbury. Nearby is the Start to Finish Biking Shop (☎ 221-7211), 672 Stanyan St., and there are two other Start to Finish shops: at 2530 Lombard St. (☎ 202-9830) in the Marina district, and at 599 2nd St. at Brannan (☎ 243-8812) in SoMa. American Bicycle Rental (☎ 931-0234), 2715 Hyde St., is at Fisherman's Wharf.

If you want to buy rather than rent the Bay Area is a terrific place for buying the very latest in high-tech bicycles. See the Shopping chapter for more on new bicycles. If you want a cheap used bike for some casual pedalling in the Bay Area (which you could even give away when you leave), try Pedal Revolution (☎ 641-1264), 3075 21st St., in the Mission.

Bicycles & Public Transport

If you want to take your bicycle further afield there are various rules and regulations. Bikes are allowed on the Golden Gate Bridge, so getting north to Marin County is no problem, but getting to or from the East Bay can be difficult since cyclists cannot use the Bay Bridge. To transport your bike between the East Bay and San Francisco you can use BART or the Caltrans bicycle shuttle service (☎ (510) 286-6444) which costs $1 and operates during commute hours between the Transbay Terminal in San Francisco and Treasure Island and the MacArthur BART station in Oakland. The Alameda/Oakland ferry (☎ (510) 522-3300) allows bikes as room permits, although this shouldn't be much of a problem.

BART Bikes cannot be taken on BART in the commute direction (in the morning, towards San Francisco, in the afternoon, towards the East Bay) during the weekday commute hours: 6:30 to 9 am and 3:30 to 6:30 pm, though you can take them in the opposite direction. At other times, you can take a bike on the last car of the train but you must have a permit which you can get for free from any BART station. Bring your ID. The permit is valid for three weeks; for longer than that you need a three-year permit which costs $3. The long-term permit is available from the Lake Merritt BART station or by calling ☎ (510) 464-7127.

CalTrain Bicycles are allowed on Peninsula trains that have a B in their number but you must apply for a free permit first; call ☎ (800) 660-4287 for information.

Golden Gate Transit Bicycles (up to 25 of them) are allowed on ferry services but bus No. 40 (San Rafael – Richmond – El Cerrito) is the only bus service permitting bikes, and only two, please.

No Luck Muni does not allow bicycles on buses or on streetcars.

WALKING

Of course you can walk around San Francisco, and much of the city is compact enough to make walking a pleasure. What other way is there to explore Chinatown? The one secret to walking the city is to be aware of the topography. Sometimes skirting around the hills can make the walk slightly longer but will avoid a lot of exhausting ups and downs. Of course sometimes you'll want to ascend those fearsome hills, just for the views.

FERRY

Ferry services on the Bay were important over a century ago and reached their peak in the 1930s. The daily flow of East Bay and Marin County commuters arriving every morning at the Ferry Building on the San Francisco Embarcadero made it one of the busiest transport interchanges in the USA. The opening of the Oakland Bay Bridge (in 1936) and the Golden Gate Bridge (in 1937) virtually killed the ferries, although in recent years they have enjoyed a modest revival for both commuters and tourists. The principal ferry operators are:

Blue & Gold Ferries From Pier 39 at Fisherman's Wharf the Alameda-Oakland Ferry (☎ (510) 522-3300) operates via the Ferry Building to Alameda and Oakland. Free transfers are available to and from Muni and AC Transit buses. Blue & Gold also operates the Vallejo Ferry (☎ 705-5444) to Vallejo, with connections to the Marine World Africa USA theme park and a variety of Bay cruises.

Golden Gate Ferry Part of Golden Gate Transit, the ferries operate regular services from the Ferry Building in San Francisco to Larkspur and Sausalito in Marin County. Free transfers are available to Muni bus services. Bicycles are permitted. Call ☎ 332-6600.

Red & White Fleet Operating from Pier 41 and Pier 43½ at Fisherman's Wharf there are services to Sausalito and Tiburon in Marin County and a less frequent weekend service to Angel Island. During commute hours services also operate between the Ferry Building and Tiburon. Call ☎ 546-2628.

Red & White also operates a daily San Francisco City Tour, a Muir Woods Tour, and a Golden Gate Bridge Cruise. The very popular Alcatraz service is operated by Red & White.

ORGANIZED TOURS

Walking tours are a great way of getting intimate with the city (see Things to See & Do), but there are other less energetic tours. Gray Lines (☎ 558-9400) has offices at the Transbay Terminal and on Union Square at Powell and Geary Sts. Their horribly fake-looking motorized cable cars trundle around the city and they have a variety of half-day and full-day tours that travel further afield. There are a variety of such tour operators in the city.

Things to See & Do

San Francisco is built on a seven-mile-wide peninsula with the Pacific Ocean on one side and the San Francisco Bay on the other. The densely populated downtown area is squeezed into the hilly northeast corner of the peninsula and the often dramatic cityscape came about because the streets were laid out as if their planners had never so much as glanced at the city's topography. They simply dropped a grid pattern on to the steeply undulating terrain, and the result is that streets often shoot up and down. It can make parking hazardous, breeds bicycle messengers of superhuman strength, and provides for a dramatic setting for movie car chase scenes.

UNION SQUARE

San Francisco's downtown tourist center, Union Square, takes its name from Civil War (1861-65) gatherings where citizens vocalized their support for the anti-slavery Union side. The center of the square is dominated by the **Dewey Monument** commemorating Admiral Dewey's 1898 defeat of the Spanish at Manila and the conversion of the Philippines from a Spanish colony to an American one. Atop this 97-foot-high granite column, erected in 1903, is a bronze statue of the Goddess of Victory.

The square, bounded by Geary and Post Sts., and Powell and Stockton Sts., is surrounded on all sides by pricey hotels, airline offices, and classy shops including the city's prime department stores. I. Magnin was the oldest department store in the city until it closed in 1995, but Macy's and Saks Fifth Avenue still cluster around the square. The 1982 **Neiman-Marcus building** is the only one of any architectural note and even then it's not a San Francisco favorite. Many still miss the 1909 City of Paris store it replaced, although its predecessor's hallmark stained glass dome was saved and reinstalled. The 1904 **St. Francis Hotel**, on the west side of the square, looks out towards the Financial District. High-speed glass elevators on the 1972 tower addition offer sweeping downtown views.

Flower vendors are a long-running part of the Union Square scene but in recent years they've been joined by the homeless, a reminder that one of the city's roughest neighborhoods, the Tenderloin, is only a few blocks west.

St. Francis Hotel
The St. Francis is one of the city's oldest and most exclusive hotels and it certainly has had a colorful history. It was in the St. Francis in 1921 that comedian Fatty Arbuckle's career came to an inglorious end after he raped an actress, with a bottle, during a drunken orgy and she subsequently died from her injuries. Arbuckle escaped conviction but his movie career went rapidly downhill.

Many of detective novelist Dashiell Hammett's books, notably *The Maltese Falcon*, were set in the St. Francis and more recently Francis Ford Coppola's industrial eavesdropping thriller, *The Conversation*, peered out on the square from the St. Francis. And it was outside the St. Francis that former FBI narc and all-around nut Sarah Jane Moore took an unsuccessful shot at President Gerald Ford in 1975. ■

Getting There & Away

For many visitors Union Square will be just a short stroll from their hotel. The Powell St. station for BART trains and Muni streetcars is two blocks south of Union Square at Powell and Market, as is the Hallidie Plaza cable car terminus, where two of the city's three cable car lines originate. Many Muni bus routes also pass this transit hub.

Around Union Square

The city's famous cable cars rumble along Powell St., on the west side of the square, to and from the Hallidie Plaza cable car terminus, named after the cable car's inventor. This is the most popular and crowded spot to watch the comings and goings of the cable car; downtown's chic, modern mall, the San Francisco Shopping Center, is just across Market St. A block over at Stockton, the Virgin Megastore (☎ 397-4525), 2 Stockton St., that opened in 1995, is the world's largest music store, and the toy store FAO Schwartz (☎ 395-8700), true kid heaven, is just around the corner.

On the east side of the square, **Maiden Lane** is crowded with pricey salons and boutiques and, at lunchtime, when the street is closed to traffic and outside tables are set up, diners enjoy al fresco meals. Maiden Lane had a previous incarnation very much at odds with its present upscale image. Before the 1906 earthquake it was Morton St., lined with bordellos and known as one of the bawdiest dives in a city renowned for racy living. During the rebuilding, the city fathers endowed it with its hopeful new name and cleaned up its image to match. The 1949 **Circle Gallery** (☎ 982-2100), 140 Maiden Lane, is the only Frank Lloyd Wright building in the city and its spiral walkway marks it as Wright's practice run for his later Guggenheim Museum in New York City; contemporary artwork is on display and for sale inside.

Post St., just north of Maiden Lane, is one of the city's prime shopping streets and here you'll find the posh gift store **Gump's**, 135 Post St., a city landmark since 1865, and noted for its Oriental art.

San Francisco's compact **Theater District** lies immediately southwest of the square, crumbling from there into the porn and prostitution quarters of the dismal Tenderloin. The American Conservatory Theater's (ACT) recently renovated Geary Theater, 415 Geary St., is the best known inhabitant, and the Curran Theater, where popular musicals are often showcased, is just down the block.

A number of the city's blank-faced but powerful social clubs are just northeast of the square. The strictly male **Bohemian Club**, on the corner of Taylor and Post Sts., is one of the best known. Turn the corner onto Taylor St. to spot the club's bronze cornerstone owl with the motto: "weaving spiders come not here."

In the Grand Hyatt plaza on Stockton St., sculptor Ruth Asawa's bronze **Children's Fountain** portrays San Francisco's history in intricate detail. Its popularity with children probably stems from the fact that children helped with its design.

Two blocks north of Union Square, Burritt St. is a tiny alley off Bush St., just a few steps west of Stockton. On the wall look for a plaque announcing that:

> On approximately this spot, Miles Archer, partner of Sam Spade, was done in by Brigid O'Shaughnessy.

"Done in" fictionally, of course, in the pages of Dashiell Hammett's classic detective novel *The Maltese Falcon*.

CIVIC CENTER

The compact Civic Center area is a study in contrasts, where the city's architectural and cultural aspirations collide head on with its human problems. Separating City Hall, the Opera House, and the Symphony Hall from the downtown Union Square district are the grubby blocks of the **Tenderloin**, and the city's pressing homeless problem has come to roost in Civic Center Plaza itself. Despite its numerous sex, drugs, and prostitution enclaves and an ever-growing homeless population, the Tenderloin is also enjoying a modest rehabilitation through the efforts of Vietnamese and

49-Mile Drive
Make some stops along the way and the 49-Mile Drive could take you all day. Devised for the 1939-40 Treasure Island Exposition, the drive has changed routes over the years but manages to cover almost all of the city's highlights. Although the drive is well signposted with instantly recognizable seagull signs, a quality map and an alert navigator are still a good idea since it's easy to miss a crucial turn.

The route should be followed counterclockwise (the signs point that way) but you can start anywhere along the circuit. Starting from the Embarcadero the route goes down Market St., up Van Ness, diverts over to Japantown, heads back to Union Square, up to Nob Hill, through Chinatown and North Beach, past Fisherman's Wharf, and through the Presidio to the Fort Point lookout on the Golden Gate. Continuing through the Presidio it passes the California Palace of the Legion of Honor, goes out to the Cliff House, and continues along Ocean Beach to the zoo. Looping around Lake Merced, the route goes north up Sunset Blvd. before embarking on an extended exploration through Golden Gate Park. The route climbs up to Twin Peaks - with the best views of the city - and then descends to Mission Dolores, returning downtown through Mission Bay, under the Bay Bridge, and back along the Embarcadero. ■

other Southeast Asian immigrants whose restaurants turn out some of the city's best cheap eats.

On the west side of Van Ness, tiny **Hayes Valley** is one of the city's newest neighborhoods. Until 1989 this area was a concrete mass of freeway overpasses, but the earthquake took care of that, and several blocks of art galleries, shops, restaurants, and quirky cafes have sprung up in its place.

Getting There & Away

The Civic Center Muni and BART station is on Market St. just south of the Civic Center. Muni bus Nos. 5, 19, and 21 travel through the area.

City Hall

The 1906 disaster destroyed the earlier city hall which was replaced in 1915 with the present Beaux Arts-style City Hall (☎ 554-4000), at 400 Van Ness Ave. Modeled after St. Peter's Basilica in Vatican City, the dome is actually higher than the US Capitol in Washington, DC. Statues depicting Wisdom, Arts, Learning, Truth, Industry, and Labor tower over the Van Ness Ave. entrance while images of Commerce, Navigation, Californian Wealth, and the city of San Francisco guard Polk St.

TONY WHEELER

The 1915 Beaux Arts-style City Hall

TONY WHEELER

Evidence of San Francisco's homeless problem

The Civic Center Plaza fronts the City Hall which is surrounded by other civic buildings. A major seismic retrofitting project is still underway following the 1989 earthquake, and looks as if it will be closed to the public for several years to come.

Around City Hall

Across from City Hall, the **War Memorial Opera House** (☎ 864-3330), 301 Van Ness Ave., built in 1932, is the site for performances by the city's acclaimed opera and ballet companies. The formal peace treaty between the USA and Japan after WWII was signed here in 1951. Adjacent to it is the **Veteran's Building**, 401 Van Ness Ave., housing the Herbst Theater (☎ 392-4400). It's a near double to the Opera House and the United Nations charter was signed here in 1945. Cross McAllister St. to the 1986 **State Building**, that mirrors the curved frontage of **Louise M. Davies Symphony Hall** (☎ 431-5400), one block south.

Facing the City Hall across the plaza are the 1916 **San Francisco Main Library** (☎ 557-5440) and the adjacent **New Public Library**. The main library was damaged in the 1989 earthquake and will be supplanted by the new library, due for completion in 1996. Across Hyde St. beyond the two library buildings is **United Nations Plaza**, built to commemorate the signing of the UN charter in San Francisco. A farmer's market is held in the plaza on Wednesday and Sunday.

On the south side of the Civic Center Plaza the **Bill Graham Civic Auditorium** (☎ 267-6400), 99 Grove St., was built in 1915 and recently renamed after the rock concert impresario who was tragically killed in a helicopter crash in 1991. The **San Francisco Art Commission Gallery** (☎ 252-2569), 155 Grove St. between Van Ness and Polk, puts on small contemporary art exhibits in their window space.

SOMA

SoMa, as the South of Market area is known, has gone through a number of transitions from prime real estate to slum and back again. Today, SoMa is a combination of office buildings spilling out of the Financial District, fancy condominiums popping up along the Embarcadero near the Bay Bridge, a busy tourist and convention precinct around Yerba Buena Gardens, and the late night entertainment scene along Folsom St. Nevertheless, there are still large empty stretches and at night the derelict zones between patches of activity can be dangerous places to linger.

Getting There & Away

Four Muni and BART stations are on Market St. along the northern edge of SoMa and the important Transbay bus terminal and the CalTrain Station are also both in SoMa.

San Francisco Museum of Modern Art

In 1995 the new San Francisco Museum of Modern Art (SFMOMA, ☎ 357-4000) opened amid much fanfare directly across from the Yerba Buena Gardens and the city's modern art collection finally had a worthy home. Swiss architect Mario Botta's design, with its half-dome central cylinder flooding light down into the interior, has pleased critics and museum goers. The superb core collection includes modern painting and sculpture, industrial and consumer design, photography, video and multi-media, and is balanced by an imaginative series of temporary exhibits and a film program.

The museum is at 151 3rd St. It's open Tuesday to Sunday, 11 am to 6 pm; Thursday until 9 pm. Entry is $7, $3.50 for students and senior citizens, free for children under 13. Thursday evening from 6 to 9 pm the museum is half price and on the first Tuesday of the month it's free. There are regular free gallery tours and the complex includes an excellent shop and an overpriced cafe.

Yerba Buena Gardens & Moscone Convention Center

Still under development, the Yerba Buena Gardens (☎ 541-0312), just north of the Moscone Convention Center and west of the SFMOMA, has already become the open-air public center of SoMa. The complex includes the **Center for the Arts** (☎ 978-2787), with permanent galleries and short-term exhibits, and a theater for performances. The gallery is open Tuesday to Sunday, 11 am to 6 pm. Entry is $3/2.50, and free on the first Thursday of the month when it is open until 8 pm. The garden includes an open-air cafe, a memorial to Doctor Martin Luther King, Jr. and statues and sculptures.

Linked to the gardens by a bridge across Howard St. is the **George R. Moscone Convention Center** (☎ 267-6400), the city's main exhibition area. The center was opened in 1981 and named after Mayor Moscone, who was murdered in 1978. Guided tours can be arranged with the public relations coordinator; call ☎ 974-4055.

There's an imaginative **children's garden & playground** atop the center.

North of the gardens is the 1872 **St. Patrick's Church**, 756 Mission St., juxtaposed with the adjacent 1989 **Marriott Hotel**, 777 Market St. at 4th. Not since the Transamerica Pyramid have San Franciscans had a building they so much love to loathe and the lumpy, mirrored hotel is regularly compared to a jukebox although it undeniably looks pretty good at sunset.

Ansel Adams Center for Photography

Next to the Moscone Center, the Ansel Adams Center (☎ 495-7000), 250 4th St., is dedicated to photography as art, with particular reference to Ansel Adams but also exhibiting works by many other photographers. The center is open Tuesday to Sunday, 11 am to 5 pm. Entry is $4, $3 for students, $2 for seniors and is open until 8 pm the first Thursday of the month.

Cartoon Art Museum

This fun museum (☎ 227-8666), 814 Mission St., features constantly changing exhibits of cartoon art, from the well-known to the esoteric. It's open Wednesday to Friday from 11 am to 5 pm, Saturday from 10 am to 5 pm, and Sunday from 1 to 5 pm. Admission is $3.50, $2.50 for students and seniors, and $1 for children.

Palace Hotel

On the corner of Market and New Montgomery Sts., the luxurious Palace Hotel opened in 1875 as the most opulent hotel in the city. Along the way, it killed its creator, William Ralston, who was driven to bankruptcy and a heart attack by financial pressures. The hotel had 800 rooms and every conceivable luxury including a fireplace and toilet for every bedroom and five hydraulic elevators. Built right after the disastrous 1868 earthquake it also featured an exotic array of fire-fighting safeguards but it nonetheless burned down in the post-earthquake fire in 1906. It was rebuilt and reopened in 1909 with the central Grand Court, where horse carriages deposited arriving guests, which later became the glass-domed Garden Court. Afternoon tea in the leafy court is the place to contemplate the 1991 renovation which cost over $100 million. A drink in the Pied Piper Bar, with its huge 1909 Maxfield Parrish painting the *Pied Piper*, is another prime relaxing spot.

RICK GERHARTER

TONY WHEELER

SCOTT SUMMERS

Classical, modern, and geometric designs of SFMOMA and Center for the Arts Theater

Jewish Museum of San Francisco

This museum (☎ 543-8880), 121 Steuart St. near the Ferry Building, has changing exhibits on Jewish life. Open hours are Monday to Wednesday from noon to 6 pm, Thursday from noon to 8 pm, Sunday from 11 am to 6 pm. The entry fee is $3/1.50, free the first Monday of the month.

Rincon Center

Close to the waterfront, the Rincon Center occupies the an entire block bounded by Mission, Howard, Steuart, and Spear. A modern complex combining a shopping center (with a notable internal rainfall fountain), an open-air plaza, and office buildings, the center is fronted on Mission St. by the wonderful Rincon Annex Post

Office, a 1939 Art Deco masterpiece (look for the dolphins), and its lobby has a series of WPA murals tracing the history of California.

Audiffred Building

Across Steuart St. from the Rincon Center, the 1889 Audiffred Building, 1-21 Mission St., is another of the city's 1906 survivors. It's said the building's bartender saved the building from the fire department's dynamite crew by bribing them with whiskey and wine. Fire finally caught up with the building in 1980 but it has been rebuilt and houses the posh Boulevard restaurant.

Rincon Hill

At the San Francisco end of the Bay Bridge it seems like you can almost reach out and touch the triangular, blue and orange Union 76 clock tower on the summit of Rincon Hill. It's hard to believe you're driving over what was once the classiest patch of real estate in the city. In the 1850s the city's gold rush wealth prompted the first batch of fine homes and – long before Russian Hill, Pacific Heights, and Nob Hill became fashionable – Rincon Hill was the address of choice. Its glory days were short-lived; the 1869 2nd St. cut effectively chopped off half the hill and by the 1880s and 1890s the fine homes were being turned into rooming houses as their owners moved on. The post-quake fire destroyed everything on the hill and the new apartments and factories that followed the quake were razed when the Bay Bridge was built straight over the top of the hill. A display panel at the Embarcadero end of 1st St. recounts the sorry story.

The only reminder of this SoMa residential enclave is **South Park**, a patch of green which, if you stumble across it, is so out of place that it's almost a shock. Only one block south of the freeway, South Park was built in 1852 in imitation of a London city square and is enjoying a modest revival as a quiet little restaurant and cafe quarter. A stone's throw away at 601 3rd St. a plaque on a Wells Fargo Bank marks **Jack London's birthplace**.

Liberty Ship Jeremiah O'Brien

During WWII over 2700 10,000-ton cargo-carrying Liberty Ships were built. At the peak of production they were being turned out at a rate of more than one a day, even faster than the German U-boats could sink them. The incredible production line process took only six to eight weeks to build a complete ship. The U.S.S. *Jeremiah O'Brien* (☎ 441-3101) is the sole surviving Liberty Ship in complete and working order and is on display at Pier 32, just south of the Bay Bridge. The ship had an illustrious history including 11 voyages as part of the D-Day landings at Normandy. On board you can explore the crew area and bridge, dive down into one of the cargo holds, and investigate the engine room with its 2700-horsepower, triple expansion steam engine. One weekend each month the engine is started up. The ship is open weekdays from 9 am to 3 pm, weekends from 9 am to 4 pm and frequently later. Entry is $5 for adults, $3 for seniors and students, and $2 for children under 18.

FINANCIAL DISTRICT

Modern development and skyscrapers have started to spill across Market St. into SoMa and the Manhattanized skyline of San Francisco now extends beyond the Financial District. This compact downtown area spreads east from Union Square and Chinatown clear to the Bay. It's the city's banking center, an important factor since this has been San Francisco's core business ever since banks started to appear in the 1850s to handle the state's gold rush fortunes. Montgomery St. continues to wear the mantle of Wall St. of the West. At one time, Montgomery St. virtually bordered the shoreline, but reclamation quickly overran the cove and by the 1880s the modern bayside at the Embarcadero had been established. Most of the modern Financial District is built on reclaimed land.

Visiting the Financial District is essentially an architectural experience. It's a frantically busy area during the day with taxis, power-dressing business people, and suicidal bike messengers all competing for street space. Come dark it's a different animal; apart from a handful of restaurants and bars, the district is serenely quiet.

Getting There & Away

Many Muni bus routes run through the Financial District as well as the California St. cable car line. The Embarcadero and Montgomery St. Muni and BART stations are both on the Market St. edge of the Financial District. Muni's new F-line encircles the southeast section of the Financial District, running along Market and Embarcadero.

Tall Buildings

Until the 1960s, San Francisco was largely skyscraper

free. Since then, the skyline has been thoroughly Manhattanized but the city's tall buildings are still concentrated entirely in the downtown area.

Transamerica Pyramid San Francisco's highest building at 853 feet, the Transamerica Pyramid, 600 Montgomery St., was completed in 1972 and quickly became a modern symbol of the city. It's the single feature that makes the San Francisco skyline instantly recognizable.

At the time of its construction, architect William Pereira was roundly reviled; the mere fact that he came from Los Angeles implied he was not to be trusted, but nobody calls it Pereira's Prick any longer. Form definitely wins the battle with function at the pyramid since the old equation that the higher the floor the higher the rent is neatly undermined by the fact that higher floors also have smaller floor areas. The 48-story structure is topped by a 212-foot spire, enclosing mechanical equipment in its lower part but hollow at the top.

The Transamerica Center includes a half-acre stand of redwood trees in Redwood Plaza where Friday lunchtime concerts take place from May through September.

Between 1853 and 1859 the Transamerica Pyramid's site was occupied by the Montgomery Block, an office block which became a favorite of journalists, artists, and poets. Bret Harte, Ambrose Bierce, and Mark Twain all passed through and it's said Sun Yat-Sen plotted the demise of the Manchu Dynasty while publishing the newspaper *Young China* here.

Bank of America Building The completion of the Bank of America building in 1969 ushered in a new era for San Francisco's previously low-rise skyline. Not only was the 52-story, 761-foot building at 555 California St. much higher than any earlier building, but its red South Dakota granite construction looked very different from the city's consistent pale coloring. Collaboratively designed by two architectural firms, the building is fronted by an open plaza on the California St. side with a sculpture by Masayuki Nagare, a 200-ton black monolith which is officially titled *Transcendence* but is more popularly known as "the banker's heart." The views from the top floor lookout are only available for those drinking or dining in the 52nd-floor Carnelian Room (see Bars in the Entertainment chapter).

The bank's founder, A.P. Giannini, was born in 1870, cut his business teeth on his stepfather's produce business, and then set out on his own in 1904 to establish the Bank of Italy. Aiming his new bank at small businessmen

TONY WHEELER

The Transamerica Pyramid and Columbus Tower, seen from North Beach

TONY WHEELER

155 Sansome St.

TONY WHEELER

101 California St.

and farmers in the Italian community, he trucked out his bank's assets ahead of the advancing flames following the 1906 earthquake. As a result, his was the first bank back in business after the disaster and he never looked back. In the 1930s he consolidated his various bank holdings to form the Bank of America, which by 1948 was the largest in America. Although Bank of America still occupies the building, they no longer own it. At the end of the 1970s they had put together a hefty collection of Third World bad debts and were forced to sell their building headquarters to shore up their balance sheet.

Russ Building Although it no longer ranks in the tallest 10, the Gothic 1928 Russ Building was the tallest from its creation until 1964. Part of the school of design which followed the Chicago Tribune Tower, it stands at 253 Montgomery St., between Pine and Bush.

101 California St. After the Transamerica Pyramid this is probably the most instantly recognizable of the city's tall buildings. The cylindrical tower, erected in 1982, is sliced off at an angle at the bottom with a sloping glass wall cutting across the spidery looking 90-foot-high supporting columns. To the amateur eye it looks remarkably unearthquake-proof but presumably it is.

Merchant's Exchange Building Now a First Interstate Bank branch, the banking lobby reveals its maritime past in the series of William A. Coulter shipping paintings on the walls. At one time, the comings and goings of ships were monitored here, their arrival spotted from a lookout tower on the roof. The 1903 building at 465 California St. burned down in the 1906 fire and was subsequently rebuilt.

Museums & Old Buildings

Wells Fargo History Museum Wells Fargo, a California institution if ever there was one, has history museums in a number of California cities. The small, colorful San Francisco Wells Fargo History Museum (☎ 396-2619) at 420 Montgomery St. traces the history of the Wells Fargo Bank, the story of the 1849 Gold Rush, and features a Wells Fargo stagecoach from around 1865.

Wells, Fargo & Company was founded in 1852 by Henry Wells and William Fargo to provide banking and express and mail delivery services to businesses in the new state of California. The mining boom was underway and the new company went where the miners went, starting up stagecoach services throughout the region, buying and selling gold and transporting mail. The banking and express businesses separated in 1905 and mergers with other California banks has made Wells Fargo one of the largest banks in California (as well as the oldest) and one of the 10 largest in the USA. The museum is open weekdays from 9 am to 5 pm and entry is free.

Pacific Heritage Museum The 1984 Bank of Canton at 555 Montgomery St. at Clay incorporates the **Old Mint Building**, tucked into the side of the modern building at 608 Commercial St. The Old Mint semi-survived the 1906 quake and has become the home for exhibits on San Francisco's Asian and Pacific connections. The museum (☎ 399-1124) is open Monday to Thursday from 10 am to 4 pm and Friday from 10 am to 5 pm. Entry is free.

Bank of California Building Corinthian columns front the temple-like 1908 Bank of California. In 1875, the bank's founder, William Ralston, either drowned in his bath after a heart attack or committed suicide, as his empire crumbled and the bank closed when he tried to simultaneously buy the famous Comstock Lode silver mines and build the opulent Palace Hotel on Market St. In the basement the **Museum of Money of the American West** (☎ 765-0400) recounts the city's long association with money and banking. Gold rush San Francisco grew so fast and was so remote from East Coast "civilization" that many private mints turned out their own coinage. The bank is at 400 California St. at Sansome and the museum is open Monday to Thursday from 10 am to 4 pm and Friday from 10 am to 5 pm. Entry is free.

Pacific Stock Exchange Built in 1930, the stock exchange (☎ 393-4000) blends classical-looking columns with the sort of solid statuary normally associated with Russian socialism. It's at 301 Pine St. at Sansome and is unfortunately not open for visitors.

Hallidie Building Named after cable car inventor Andrew Hallidie, the 1917 Hallidie Building, 130 Sutter St., was the world's first "glass-curtain-wall" building and an architect's favorite. The technique of hanging a curtain of glass in front of a building's actual structure became an everyday feature of modern office buildings but this pioneering example is still worth a look. The cool green glass contrasts nicely with the elaborate fire escapes and there's a good view of it from the upstairs of the Crocker Galleria across Sutter St.

Monuments & Markers

The deep green 1959 **Crown Zellerbach Building**, 1 Bush St., is a fine example of late '50s architecture and nearby are a number of curiosities. A few steps east on Market St. a historical landmark marker indicates where Charles August Fey paved the way for Las Vegas by inventing the Three-Reel Bell Slot Machine in 1894; Australian gamblers more accurately refer to the device as a "one-armed bandit." Set in the sidewalk here a plaque marks the old shoreline of the Yerba Buena cove, a reminder of how much of the Financial District stands on reclaimed land.

Head back up Market St., past "The Wall," to the **Lotta Fountain** on the corner of Market and Kearny. Lotta Crabtree (1847-1924) embarked on her path to fame as an actress and dancer during the Gold Rush and presented this fountain to her favorite city in 1875. For years at 5:13 am each April 18, survivors of the 1906 earthquake gathered here, but there aren't many left these days.

The Wall

Around the Sharper Image yuppie gizmo shop, at the intersection of Sansome and Market, this low wall has become the prime gathering spot for the city's bike messengers. No visitor can claim to have experienced San Francisco until they've ridden a cable car and narrowly missed being run down by a crazed bike messenger. This is where these latter-day pony express riders hang out between jobs.

Bike Messengers

Bike messengers started to appear downtown about 20 years ago and today they're a familiar sight around the Financial District, often speeding the wrong way along one-way streets or hurtling through red lights narrowly missing pedestrians and averting near-death experiences. There are probably 300 to 400 bike messengers working the city, with the biggest messenger companies employing about 40 riders and the smallest just a half dozen. An experienced rider will get through about 25 tags (deliveries) in a day. Bike messengers are a serious city subculture and they've even got their fictional hero: the high-tech (and female) Chevette in William Gibson's cyberpunk novel *Virtual Light*. See Critical Mass in the Getting Around chapter for more on downtown biking. ■

TONY WHEELER

Messengers and their ilk loitering at the Wall

Market St.

Immediately south of Market St. are a number of buildings more commonly associated with the Financial District than SoMa. At 1 Market St., the warm look of the **Southern Pacific Railroad Building** of 1916 belies the raw power this company wielded in California from its creation in 1869 until early this century. The **Federal Reserve Bank**, 101 Market St., actually occupies the entire block. The lobby area has displays explaining the role of the reserve bank and, in easy steps, clarifies the whole story of capitalism! It's open weekdays from 8:30 am to 4:30 pm.

Two wonderful old buildings, both emerging from seismic retrofitting in 1995, occupy the next block. At 215 Market St., the **Matson Building** of 1921 proudly proclaims its shipping company founders across the facade. The seafaring background is further emphasized with colorful waves, fish, and other watery motifs. The **Pacific Gas & Electric Building**, 245 Market St., dates from 1925 and features sculptured figures over the entrance.

The Embarcadero

The waterfront Embarcadero is the road that runs along the now defunct piers. Once the busiest area of the city, it was killed first by the two Bay bridges, which ended the ferry boat era, and then by the death of the old-style wharves, superseded by the container ship era. Oakland is now the Bay Area's main dock.

RICK GERHARTER
Clock tower of the Ferry Building

Completed in 1898, the **Ferry Building**, located at the bottom of California and Market Sts., had its heyday in the 1920s and '30s as the arrival and departure point for ferries shuttling across the bay before the construction of the two bridges. At that time it was one of the world's busiest transport interchanges. The landmark tower is modeled on the Moorish Giralda Tower in Seville, Spain and at 240 feet was for some time the highest building in the city.

The Embarcadero Freeway walled off the Embarcadero from the Financial District but after the 1989 quake, which brought down the similarly constructed I-880 in Oakland, the freeway was doomed and demolished in 1992. It had spoiled the view anyway and there was general rejoicing when it went. Work is underway to rejuvenate the Embarcadero, watched over outside the Ferry Building by a **statue of Capitan Juan Bautista de Anza**, the city's Spanish founder.

Embarcadero Center Four skyscrapers mark the huge Embarcadero Center which runs between Sacramento and Clay Sts., starting at the Park Hyatt and Old Federal Reserve Building, and terminating at the Justin Herman Plaza and the Hyatt Regency Hotel. The four main blocks of the center (Embarcadero 1 to 4) house a mix of shops and restaurants and incorporate two of the city's 10 highest buildings.

At the bay end of the complex, Justin Herman Plaza is a popular lunch spot for Financial District suits. The topsy-turvy Vaillancourt Fountain looks like leftovers from the demolition of the Embarcadero Freeway and, due to water shortages, frequently doesn't fountain.

Jackson Square

At the northern edge of the Financial District, where it blends into North Beach, Jackson Square is a tiny rectangular enclave that survived the 1906 earthquake and fire. The old buildings, some with cast-iron facades, along Jackson St. between Montgomery and Sansome, and on the nearby alleys, are now a heady mix of antique shops and interior decorators interspersed with some upscale restaurants. Pre-quake, this was the edge of San Francisco's infamous Barbary Coast, a raucous seafront tangle of bars and brothels with wild Pacific St. as its colorful core.

Some of the survivors include the **Ghirardelli Building** at 415-417 Jackson St., which dates from 1853 and until its 1894 shift to the Fisherman's Wharf area was the Ghirardelli chocolate factory. Many of the buildings on the reclaimed land of the Financial District were built on top of abandoned ships and it's recorded that the 1862 building at 441 Jackson St. used two ships as its foundation. The 1866 **Hotaling Building** at 451 Jackson St., has a fine cast-iron and stone facade and was one of the 1906 disaster's most famous survivors, inspiring the ditty:

> If, as they say, God spanked the town
> For being over frisky,
> Why did He burn His churches down
> And spare Hotaling's whiskey?

CHINATOWN

The most densely packed pocket of the city, and perhaps the most colorful, there's no missing Chinatown. Even its entrance arches mark it off from the rest of the city. Set in a two-block-wide compact zone, it's conveniently located just a couple of blocks north of Union Square and is fenced in by the Financial District, Nob Hill, and North Beach. Grant Ave., the street immortalized in the musical *Flower Drum Song*, is the bustling thoroughfare for this hive of activity.

There are no essential sights in Chinatown, no single place which any San Francisco visitor absolutely *must* see. However, it's a great place for casual wandering and for soaking up the atmosphere and stumbling across interesting little corners and alleys as you go. Once you get off touristy Grant Ave. look for Chinese apothecary shops and colorful overhanging balconies, and listen to the continuing background noise of the Chinese language which, linguists claim, is impossible to whisper.

Chinese started to flood into California with the 1849 Gold Rush, and more came with the construction of the transcontinental railroad in the 1870s. The immigrants certainly weren't popular and anti-Chinese sentiments in the last century probably contributed to Chinatown's almost fortress-like feel. Today Chinatown is both a hugely popular tourist attraction, packed with wonderfully tacky shops and wonderfully cheap restaurants and, with a population of 30,000, home to the largest concentration of Chinese outside of Asia.

The most colorful time to visit is during the Chinese New Year in late January/early February, with a parade and fireworks and other festivities, but the day-to-day bustle of Chinatown is reason enough to visit anytime.

Getting There & Away

The California St. cable car runs east-west through Chinatown as does Muni bus No. 1 which travels from near the Bay clear out to the ocean, passing through the "New Chinatown" Richmond District. Sensibly, no buses run north-south along jam-packed Grant Ave. but Muni bus Nos. 15, 30, and 45 pass nearby on their way between SoMa/downtown and North Beach/Fisherman's Wharf. Bus No. 45 turns off, north of Chinatown, to continue on to Pacific Heights.

Chinatown Walking Tour

Chinatown visits usually begin at the dragon-studded **Chinatown Gate** at the Bush St. entrance to Grant Ave. The gate was a 1971 gift from the Chinatown Cultural Development Committee. Packed with shops and restaurants, Grant Ave. has had a colorful history from its inception as Calle de la Fundacion, the main street of the Mexican village of Yerba Buena. Renamed Dupont St., or Du Pon Gai to the Chinese, it became synonymous with brothels, gambling dives, opium dens, and brawling *tongs* (Chinese gangs). It was renamed after president and Civil War general Ulysses S. Grant in the year of his death in 1885.

The Taoist **Ching Chung Temple** (☎ 433-2623) at 532 Grant Ave. is open daily. At the intersection with California St. is **Old St. Mary's Church** (☎ 986-4388); its 90-foot tower was the tallest building in the city when it was completed in 1854, and it's also notable as the first Roman Catholic cathedral on the West Coast. Modeled after a Gothic church in Spain, it was built on foundation stones shipped from China with bricks brought around the Horn from New England.

Continue down Grant Ave. and turn left onto Sacramento St. Walk past the First Chinese Baptist Church on

RICK GERHARTER

Looking up at the Chinatown Gate

the corner of Waverly Place to the **Chinese Playground**, a handkerchief of open space. Turn right on Stockton St.; if Grant Ave. is the tourist shopping promenade in Chinatown, then this is the local one. At the end of the block, cross to the **Kong Chow Temple** (☎ 434-2513), above the post office at 855 Stockton St. Visitors are welcome to the temple on the 4th floor where, in June 1948, Mrs. Harry Truman had her fortune told; the temple also claims perhaps the oldest Chinese altar in the USA. The **Chinese Consolidated Benevolent Building** at 843 Stockton St. looks even more temple-like and was the former home of the Six Companies, the Chinese organization which used to bring Chinese laborers to California and later fought for Chinese legal rights.

Turn right down Clay St. (the Transamerica Pyramid looms ahead) and left into colorful **Waverly Place**, with its many open balconies. The **Norras Temple** at No. 109, the 1852 **Tin Hou Temple** dedicated to the Queen of Heaven at No. 125, and the **Jeng Sen Temple**, above The Pot Sticker restaurant at No. 150, are all upstairs temples along Waverly Place, but the open hours are erratic and there's not that much to be seen. Just to the right, when you emerge on to Washington St., is **Sam Wo's**, a well-known hole-in-the-wall Chinese restaurant that was a haunt of the Beat poets and is renowned for its famously rude waiters. A few steps in the opposite direction along

RICK GERHARTER

Chinatown flags on Grant Ave.

Washington St., take the right turn into narrow Ross Alley. This has been a favorite of moviemakers, featured in films like *Big Trouble in Little China*. Known at one time as Gau Leuie Sung Hong or Old Spanish Alley it was wall-to-wall gambling dens and brothels in the late 1870s. At 56 Ross Alley the signless **Golden Gate Cookie Company** (☎ 781-3956) turns out fortune cookies (spice up your day with their "sexy " fortunes). You can peer in and see how they're made. Curiously, fortune cookies are a San Francisco invention, not a Chinese one; they were dreamed up for the Japanese Tea Garden in Golden Gate Park.

From Ross Alley turn right onto Jackson St. and then right again back onto Grant Ave. At the end of the block are two of Chinatown's rare bars, **Li Po's** at 916 Jackson St. and, across the road, the curiously named **Buddha Lounge**. Turn left onto Washington St. to the **Bank of Canton** at No. 743, a colorful pagoda-like building which was built in 1909 and once housed the Chinatown telephone exchange. Further down Washington St. at No. 720 is the 1960 **Buddha's Universal Church**.

Portsmouth Square is one of the few open spaces in Chinatown and almost always has a crowd of young and old people, sitting around and talking or playing checkers, chess, or mah jong. The modern square is built over one of San Francisco's best priced car parks but it has a far more eloquent story to tell. It was originally the plaza for the Mexican settlement of Yerba Buena, and its name comes from John B. Montgomery's sloop, the *Portsmouth*. Montgomery arrived in 1846 to claim the city for the USA and a plaque commemorates that it was here that the stars & stripes was first raised in San Francisco. Two years later, by which time the city's population had already tripled from 100 to 300, and then tripled again to 1000, a real population explosion was sparked when Sam Brannan announced, in the square, the discovery of gold in the Sierra foothills.

A pedestrian bridge crosses Kearny to the **Chinese Cultural Center** (☎ 986-1822) in the Holiday Inn at 750 Kearny St. It has changing exhibits on Chinese art and culture, particularly in relation to San Francisco, and is open Tuesday to Saturday from 10 am to 4 pm, Sunday from noon to 4 pm. Admission is free.

Turn down Kearny St. and left onto Commercial St. to the **Chinese Historical Society Museum** (☎ 391-1188) at 650 Commercial St. It recounts the story of the city's Chinese community and is open Tuesday to Saturday from noon to 4 pm. A little further down, the **Pacific Heritage Museum** (☎ 399-1124), 608 Commercial St., is open Monday to Thursday from 10 am to 4 pm, Friday from 10 am to 5 pm. Both museums are free. Prior to the land reclamation that pushed the bayside much further out, Commercial St. led to a quay in Yerba Buena Cove with the "Long Wharf" that projected 2000 feet out into the shallow Bay.

Return to Kearny St., continue to California St. and turn right onto **St. Mary's Square**, the other large open

Emperor Norton:
San Francisco's First Tourist Attraction

Emperor Norton I was born Joshua Abraham Norton in 1819 and came to San Francisco as a young man, where he made a fortune off the city's boomtown economy. In 1852 he lost everything in a business gamble and never recovered. After eight years of increasing poverty he seems to have snapped, at least in one key respect: he declared himself the Emperor of the United States, and within a month added the title Protector of Mexico.

COURTESY OF THE BANCROFT LIBRARY

Norton spent the next 20 years of his life becoming an icon and widely loved mascot of San Francisco, living an oddly dignified life and causing no one any harm. He never appeared without his uniform with its bulky epaulets, a plumed hat, and a sword at his hip. He issued his own scrip in 50¢, $5, and $10 denominations and though it became mainly a collector's item, it was good-naturedly accepted by many shopkeepers. Among the many decrees he made as emperor, such as that to dissolve the republican form of government in the USA, was his famous injunction against the use of the word "Frisco":

> Whoever after due and proper warning shall be heard to utter the abominable word "Frisco", which has no linguistic or other warrant, shall be deemed guilty of a High Misdemeanor, and shall pay into the Imperial Treasury as penalty the sum of $25.

After his death in 1880, thousands attended his funeral. He now rests in Colma Cemetery under a prominent headstone unambiguously affirming his status in death, as in life, as "Emperor of the United States & Protector of Mexico". ■

space in Chinatown. Surrounded by high buildings, the square is home to a Benjamino Bufano **statue of Doctor Sun Yat-Sen**. When Chinatown was cleaned up in the late 19th century, the brothels, gambling dens, and bars from all over the area were concentrated here and then burned down in the aftermath of the 1906 earthquake. Like North Beach's Washington Square, this is a popular spot for early morning Tai Chi practitioners.

NORTH BEACH

North Beach links Chinatown and the Financial District to Fisherman's Wharf with Columbus Ave. as its spine, a clothesline angling across the symmetrical grid with the Transamerica Pyramid and The Cannery as its two poles.

North Beach started as the city's Italian quarter and their heritage lives on in the restaurants, bars, and lively nightlife. The Beats took over in the '50s and added cafes, jazz clubs, and the City Lights Bookstore to the mix. Today it's one of the liveliest parts of the city after dark and a great place for a cheap meal, a cold beer, or a strong cup of coffee.

TONY WHEELER

Looking towards downtown from North Beach

Getting There & Away

Muni bus Nos. 15 and 30 run from SoMa through downtown and Chinatown and then through North Beach on the way to Fisherman's Wharf. Bus No. 45 also goes through North Beach and then turns off to Pacific Heights while bus No. 41 goes from the Financial District through North Beach and on to Pacific Heights. Bus No. 39 shuttles back and forth between North Beach and Fisherman's Wharf with an excursion up Telegraph Hill to Coit Tower in the middle of its route.

A Walk along Columbus Ave.

Start from the Transamerica Pyramid and stroll up Columbus Ave. The green **Columbus Tower** of 1905 at the corner of Kearny St. was bought and restored by filmmaker Francis Ford Coppola in 1970.

The block from Pacific Ave. to Broadway can lay claim to being the literary heart of the city. A coffee at **Vesuvio Cafe**, under the banner announcing "we are itching to get away from Portland, Oregon," is sure to spark any

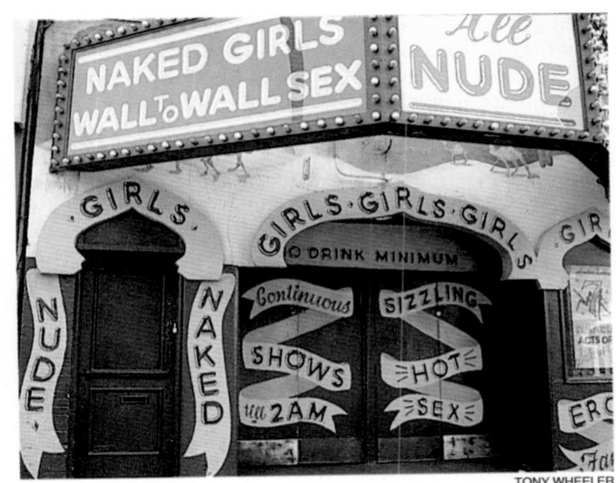

TONY WHEELER

TOM SMALLMAN

Patrons of the dwindling sex trade in North Beach can always absolve their sins at the Church of Sts. Peter and Paul.

literary hound into finding their way to the shelves of **City Lights Bookstore**, just across Jack Kerouac St. City Lights was founded in 1953 by poet Lawrence Ferlinghetti, who still owns it. It's always been a center for cutting edge books and poetry. On the other side of Columbus Ave. is **Specs'**, a great little bar with an eclectic collection of junk on the walls, and the adjacent **Tosca Cafe** is famous as a place for sighting the famous, but even more for its opera music jukebox.

At the junction of Columbus, Broadway, and Grant Sts. there's another historic San Francisco cultural site. The Condor Bistro is a very bland replacement for the old **Condor Club** where, a plaque solemnly announces, silicon-enhanced Carol Doda first went topless on June 19, 1964 and bottomless on September 3, 1969. Time moves on and the Doda boobs were put away in 1991. Sex is on the way out all over North Beach, and the odd remaining porn shop and strip show along Broadway looks distinctly out of place these days.

A right turn along Grant will lead to a wide choice of restaurants, bars, and cafes including the 1861 **Saloon** on the corner of Fresno St., one of the few North Beach buildings to survive the 1906 earthquake and fire. On the corner of Columbus and Vallejo the **Church of St. Francis of Assisi** was built in 1860 but rebuilt in 1913 after suffering heavy 1906 damage. Columbus Ave. trims a corner of Washington Square before leaving North Beach past the **Lyle Tuttle Tattoo Museum** (☎ 775-4991) at 841 Columbus Ave. (see Shopping).

Museum of North Beach

The museum (☎ 391-6210), 1435 Stockton St., in the Eureka Bank mezzanine, has photographs and memorabilia tracing the history of this colorful area in the late-18th and early-19th centuries, particularly around the time of the earthquake.

Washington Square

With a corner chopped off by Columbus Ave., Washington Square doesn't quite make it as a square but it is the best North Beach can drum up as a city park. An 1897 **statue of Benjamin Franklin** stands in the middle of the square. It was erected by teetotaling dentist Henry D. Cogswell, who made a fortune fitting miners with gold fillings, and the taps around the base originally dispensed mineral water. On the Columbus Ave. side of the square stands the **Volunteer Fireman's Memorial**, financed by none other than that dedicated fire engine-chaser Lillie Hitchcock Coit. For more on this eccentric lady see Coit Tower, below. Particularly in the morning, the square is a popular center for Tai Chi exercisers from nearby Chinatown.

Sts. Peter & Paul Church

The 1924 Sts. Peter & Paul Church (☎ 421-0809), 666 Filbert St., overlooks the square. It's the largest Catholic church in San Francisco and each October the Santa Maria del Lume (patron saint of fishermen) procession makes its way down Columbus Ave. to Fisherman's Wharf to bless the fishing fleet.

Ferlinghetti called it the Marzipan Church and its wedding cake design is clearly appropriate as this was where baseball star joltin' Joe DiMaggio and Marilyn Monroe had their wedding photos taken, though they weren't permitted to marry here because both had been divorced. In Cecil B. DeMille's 1923 film *The Ten Commandments,* the scene of the building of the Temple in Jerusalem is actually the construction of the church's foundations.

Telegraph Hill & Coit Tower

One of San Francisco's prime landmarks stands in Pioneer Park, atop Telegraph Hill. The hill was Alta Loma in Mexican San Francisco, then Goat Hill, and finally, in 1853, Telegraph Hill, when ships approaching the Golden Gate were contacted from here by a pioneering semaphore and optical telegraph station.

The 210-foot tower was built in 1934, financed by San Francisco eccentric Lillie Hitchcock Coit. Clearly a rebel against strait-laced Victorianism, Ms. Coit often dressed as a man to gamble in North Beach, wore short skirts to go ice skating, sneaked away on a men's camping trip, and harbored a life-long passion for a good fire. In 1863 the 15-year-old Lillie was adopted as the mascot of the Knickerbocker Hose Company No. 5 and it's said she "rarely missed a blaze." Contrary to what you may think, it's regularly repeated that the tower was *not* built to resemble a fire hose. After her husband's death in 1885, Lillie spent most of the rest of her life in Paris, but left a third of her fortune to build this monument.

Inside is a superb series of Rivera-style murals of San Franciscans at work. Painted by 25 local artists as part of a '30s WPA project, their sometimes leftist style caused some initial unease and the tower's opening was delayed for several months while the authorities and unions argued about the dangers of socialism. The tower itself had also been a controversial project.

TONY WHEELER

Coit Tower mural depicting San Franciscans at work

STUART WASSERMAN

Ever-present Coit Tower shows up in just about any panorama of the city.

Views of the City

Cable Car Views Somehow any view looks better from a cable car; try looking down Hyde towards Aquatic Park, down Washington to Chinatown and the Financial District, or down California from Nob Hill.

Coit Tower Yes, it's obvious, but the views over North Beach and across to the Financial District are superb, as are the tower's murals downstairs.

Lincoln Park Coastal Trail This interesting walk in Lincoln Park takes you from the ruins of the Sutro Baths to Lands End and there are some great views of the ocean and north to the Golden Gate.

Top of the Mark You've got do it - ride the elevator to the city's most famous view bar at the top of the Mark Hopkins Hotel on Nob Hill.

Twin Peaks A fantastic 360° view of the whole city.

Vista Point There are viewpoints at both ends of the Golden Gate Bridge but the northern one not only gives you the bridge but the San Francisco skyline as well.

Caldecott Tunnel Sweep through the tunnel from Walnut Creek into the East Bay and suddenly there's Oakland, the Bay, and San Francisco laid out before you; it's especially beautiful at night. ■

The tower (☎ 362-0808) is open daily from 10 am to 7:30 pm. The ride to the top, for superb views across the city and bay, costs $3, but the view is pretty special even from the bottom. Muni bus No. 39 swings past Fisherman's Wharf and Washington Square on its Coit Tower loop. Drivers also approach from Lombard St. but in summer there can be a long wait for a parking spot at the top. Pedestrians can climb steeply up Filbert St. from Washington Square to a stairway up to the top. On the other side the wooden **Filbert Steps** lead picturesquely down past the wooden cottages of Darrell Place and Napier Lane to Levi's Plaza and the Embarcadero. Go early in the morning and you might catch a glimpse of the family of wild red foxes that live in the underbrush. The Filbert Steps are paralleled by the Greenwich Steps.

RUSSIAN HILL

West of North Beach are the roller-coaster streets of Russian Hill, with some of the city's prime real estate as well as the famous Lombard St. switchback. It's said the hill takes its name from the burial site of early 19th-century Russian fur traders but the story is uncertain and no evidence of the mystery Russians has ever been found. Like Nob Hill, nobody lived up in these heights until the cable cars provided transportation.

Getting There & Away

The Powell-Mason and Powell-Hyde cable cars bracket Russian Hill with the latter going right by the top of Lombard's famous squiggly block. Muni bus Nos. 41, 45, and 30 also run past Russian Hill.

Lombard St.

For one block of Lombard St., between Hyde and Leavenworth, the city planners' single-minded intention to lay out the whole damn place as one straightforward grid was finally stymied by the city's uncooperative terrain. This Russian Hill stretch of street, the 1000 block, wiggles down the hillside to win the accolade as the world's "crookedest street," notching up 10 turns as it goes. It's not only a spectacular slalom but also a pretty one as the whole section is dense with flowers.

At one time, the crooked block was just as straight as any other, but with a 27% incline it was too steep for cars to manage. The steepest incline the cable cars have to tackle is 21%, so in 1922 the corners were added. That still didn't convert it into a tourist attraction. It was not until after WWII when local resident Peter Bercut personally imported a couple of thousand hydrangeas from France that the crookedest street became a postcard favorite.

San Francisco Art Institute

At 800 Chestnut St., just a block north of the Lombard wiggles, the Art Institute (☎ 771-7020) is renowned for its fine Diego Rivera Gallery with a wonderful example of the Mexican artist's famous murals from 1931. The institute was founded in 1871 and originally occupied the Nob Hill mansion built by Mark Hopkins for his wife

Steep Streets

Several of the steepest streets open to vehicles are on Russian and Nob Hills. The steepest street you can drive on? It's a 31.5% gradient tie between Filbert St. (between Leavenworth and Hyde) and 22nd St. (between Church and Vicksburg), in Noe Valley. In comparison, Mason (heading down Nob Hill by the Mark Hopkins Hotel) is 22.2% while Hyde (on the cable car plummet to Aquatic Park) is 21.3%. Lombard's crookedest stretch wimps out at just 18%. Is all this charging up and down hills tough on cars? Well, city taxis need a brake reline every 1500 to 2500 miles on average. ■

Mary. The mansion burned down in 1906 and the Mark Hopkins Hotel now stands on the site. The Institute's current collection of cloisters and courtyards dates from 1926 with a 1970 addition. There is a cafe, and fine views over the Bay from the terraces. The galleries are open Tuesday to Saturday, 10 am to 5 pm.

Parks, Buildings & Lookouts

Cable cars run precipitously up and down Mason St. and Hyde St. with superb Bay views. The top of Russian Hill is so steep that not all the roads manage to surmount it, making way for pocket-size patches of green like **Ina Coolbrith Park** and steep stairways like **Macondray Lane**, the Barbary Lane of Armistead Maupin's *Tales of the City*. Another lane of literary interest is Russell Place where, at No. 29, Jack Kerouac drafted *On the Road* and several other works while living with Neal and Carolyn Cassady in 1952.

At 1067 Green St., between Jones and Leavenworth, is the 1870 **Feusier Octagon House**. It's not open to the public, unlike the other surviving octagon house in Pacific Heights. It's one of an interesting little enclave of Victorian houses that make up a rare group of 1906 survivors in the 1000 block of Green St. The 1000 block of Vallejo St., just above Ina Coolbrith Park, is another small group of architectural interest.

NOB HILL

Nob Hill is just what its name suggests, a classy district perched atop one of the city's famous hills. It's been that way ever since the arrival of cable cars in the 1870s made the 338-foot summit accessible. Money poured in, mansions were thrown up, and the 1906 quake and fire brought the lot down. Eventually several of the burned-out mansions were replaced with hotels, which remain some of the most select, and expensive, establishments in the city. The Huntington, Mark Hopkins, Stanford Court, and the Fairmont are all perched atop Nob Hill. Although there's not much to see on Nob Hill, apart from the Grace Cathedral, it's worth a wander, a gawk at the elegant marble lobby of the Fairmont, and perhaps a drink in the Mark Hopkins rooftop bar, the Top of the Mark.

Getting There & Away

The California St. cable car runs up Nob Hill from the Financial District and Chinatown while the other two cable car lines skirt around the hill. Bus No. 1 goes along Clay and Sacramento, to and from the Embarcadero.

The Railroad Barons
Their names pop up all around the Bay Area and, in their prime, Nob Hill was their stomping ground. Mark Hopkins and Collis P. Huntington were the builders who, with financiers Charles Crocker and Leland Stanford, made fortunes from the Central Pacific Railroad, later renamed the Southern Pacific. They founded the railroad company in 1861 and built eastward, meeting the Union Pacific line on its way west in 1869. Stanford, Huntington, and Hopkins have given their names to Nob Hill Hotels, Crocker's name is applied to a bank, and Stanford went on to win election as the state's governor and to found Stanford University. Also known as the "Big Four" (there's a bar with that name in the Huntington Hotel) they were less kindly referred to as the "robber barons" as their methods of acquisition were far from scrupulous. ■

Pacific-Union Club

The sole residence surviving the 1906 earthquake and fire, the "Bonanza King" James C. Flood's brownstone mansion is now the private Pacific-Union Club (☎ 775-1234), 1000 California St. across Mason St. from the Fairmont Hotel. Built in 1885, the post-quake fire gutted the mansion but it was bought and rebuilt by the club. Don't expect to pay a visit if you're not in the millionaire class; that is, the male millionaire class. Since the club opened in 1911 women have only been allowed in twice and the last occasion was back in 1953.

Post-Quake Rebuilding

Several of Nob Hill's prominent hotels were built on former mansion sites. The **Mark Hopkins**, for example, was a 1925 replacement for the Mark Hopkins mansion although the granite retaining wall which surrounded the original flamboyant wooden mansion survives. The **Stanford Court Hotel** was built in 1911 on the site of Leland Stanford's home. The **Fairmont Hotel**, built by the daughter of silver magnate James Grantham Fair, was actually completed a few days before the Big One, was gutted by the conflagration, then rebuilt by architect Julia Morgan, and reopened a year to the day after the quake.

The open patch of **Huntington Park** has had a particularly colorful history. David Colton, Central Pacific Railroad's lawyer, built his mansion here but following his death his estate was sued by the railroad company for embezzlement. His widow retaliated with letters from Huntington to her husband detailing under-the-table deals with Washington politicians. The mansion was sold in 1880 and bought by none other than Collis P. Huntington in 1892! The quake destroyed it and Huntington's widow gave the site to the city in 1915. The park features a replica of the Tartarughe Fountain in Rome, but without the tortoises.

Grace Cathedral

After the big quake, hotels popped up on other mansion sites but Charles Crocker and his son William turned over their California St. sites to the Episcopalian church. It took from 1927 to 1964 to finally complete Grace Cathedral (☎ 776-6611), 1051 Taylor St. Although the construction is of reinforced concrete, it takes its inspiration from the Notre Dame in Paris. The bronze doors are casts of Ghiberti's Gates of Paradise in the Baptistry in Florence, Italy. Above the door the magnificent Rose Window was made in Chartres, France in 1964. Be sure to check out the Keith Haring Altarpiece, *The Life of Christ*, dedicated in 1995 by the AIDS Memorial Chapel Project.

Cable Car Museum

The 1906 disaster devastated the cable car system and the Cable Car Barn & Museum (☎ 474-1887), 1201 Mason St., dates from 1910. This is the powerplant that tows all the cable cars and the huge wheels over which the continuous cables whirr are a great sight. The museum's exhibits include Hallidie's original Clay St. cable car and at night the city's current collection comes here for a break. The museum is open in the summer, daily from 10 am to 6 pm and in winter until 5 pm. Entry is free.

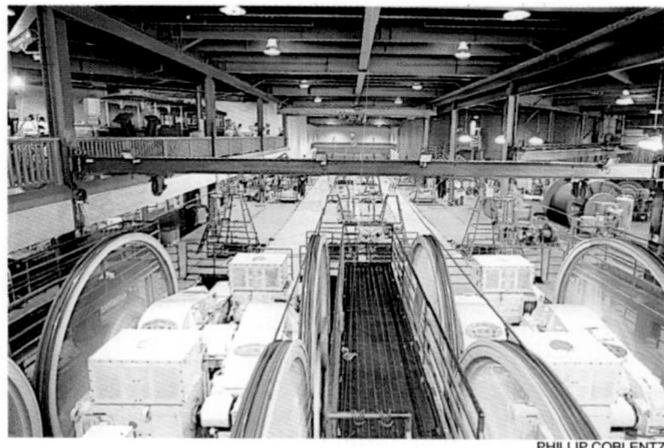

PHILLIP COBLENTZ

Inside the Cable Car Museum

Cable Cars

History The Transamerica Pyramid and the Golden Gate Bridge make fine city symbols but San Francisco has another much older icon, the beloved cable car. Cable cars were conceived by English mining engineer Andrew Hallidie as a replacement for the horse-driven trams which found the city's steep streets difficult and dangerous.

TONY WHEELER

From Hallidie's first experimental line on Clay St. in 1873, cable cars quickly caught on and by 1890 there were eight operators, 500 cable cars, and a route network of over 100 miles. By the turn of the century, the system was already past its heyday and shrinking in the face of new-fangled electric streetcars. The 1906 earthquake was a disaster for the cable car system , but the death knell sounded in January 1947 when the mayor announced the last lines would be replaced by bus services. He hadn't reckoned with Friedel Klussmann's "Citizens Committee to Save the Cable Cars," and a groundswell of public support which reprieved the Powell St. lines.

San Franciscans may have saved the system from politicians and accountants but saving it from old age became a new problem as derailments and runaways became increasingly frequent occurrences. In 1979, a six-month shutdown for a million dollars' worth of repairs was just a band-aid solution and in 1982 the system was finally closed for a $60 million complete overhaul. The rebuilt system, which reopened in 1984, consists of 40 cars on three lines covering a total of 12 miles. That may be a pale shadow of its heyday but the cable cars are an enormously popular tourist attraction and much loved by San Franciscans.

FISHERMAN'S WHARF

All serious guides to San Francisco are required by city ordinance to denounce Fisherman's Wharf as a tasteless, tacky tourist trap. Well it is, but there has to be a reason it remains so massively popular: it's the gateway for several top-class attractions (Alcatraz, the Maritime Museum, and the Historic Ships Pier) and all the accompanying kitsch may be unspeakably awful but it's certainly fun. The fishermen have almost all disappeared; now this tourist epicenter is packed with shopping centers, hokey museums, and countless accommodations.

Even before the fishermen arrived, this was a busy area. In the 1860s, ore from the Sierra Nevadas was smelted at a site where the Cannery now stands, and Beach St. really was the beach, before land reclamation

How it Works There are three key elements to the cable car system: the cable, the grip, and the brakes.

The Cable Cable cars do not have an engine. They're towed up and down the hills of San Francisco by continuous loops of cable driven by 510-horsepower electric motors housed in the Cable Car Museum. The cables move at a steady nine mph and can stretch three to 12 feet as cars grip and ungrip.

Cables on the busy Powell St. line only last 75 to 90 days before a new $20,000-plus cable must be installed. Cable replacement occurs in the middle of the night. The old cable is cut and the new cable, weighing over 30 tons on its drum, is temporarily spliced onto one end and pulled right through the system. The cables are inspected daily and if a broken wire triggers one of the 60 strand alarms the system is shut down and a temporary repair is made on the spot.

The Grip The process of grabbing hold (or "picking up") the cable to start off and letting go (or "dropping") the cable to stop is done by the gripman with the grip. Patented in 1877, the bottom grip weighs 327 lbs. and the metal dies in the grip's jaw clamp on to the cable when the gripman pulls back on the grip level. The soft metal dies wear very quickly and must be replaced every four days.

The Brakes Cable cars have four braking systems. First there is the cable itself; as long as the cable car is gripped onto the cable it cannot go faster than the cable is moving. Second are cast iron brake shoes on all eight wheels. Third are four pinewood block brakes which simply press down on the track; these only last two to four days and on steep downgrades you can actually smell woodsmoke. When all else fails, braking system four is a three-piece wedge which slides down into the cable car slot and jams everything up solid. It's used for emergencies only. ■

pushed the shoreline further out. When development forced the Italian fishing boats out of their Union St. moorings, where Levi's Plaza now stands, they moved round to Fisherman's Wharf, which for a time was known as Italy Harbor. San Francisco at that time boasted a diverse assortment of fishing vessels as each immigrant group used boats of their own traditional design, with the Chinese fishing from junks and the Italians fishing from Genovese feluccas.

Getting There & Away

The best way of getting to Fisherman's Wharf is by the Powell-Mason or Powell-Hyde cable car lines. You can also reach the Wharf by Muni bus No. 32 along the Embarcadero, No. 42 from SoMa through the Financial

District, or Nos. 15 and 30 from SoMa through downtown, Chinatown, and North Beach. Bus No. 39 runs a useful North Beach-Fisherman's Wharf shuttle with a Coit Tower excursion at the midpoint. Bus No. 28 goes from Fort Mason to the Golden Gate Bridge and then down to Golden Gate Park. If you come by car, remember that parking can be difficult and expensive.

Pier 39

If there's a single focus for the Fisherman's Wharf tourist crush, it's undoubtedly Pier 39. The pier, in its current incarnation, opened in 1978. Transforming a derelict working pier into a major shopping center and tourist attraction was no easy task but the numerous amusing "story of Pier 39" information plaques around the pier indicate that developer Warren Simmon's biggest battle was probably with the bureaucrats. Pier 39 has a host of restaurants, a huge collection of shops appealing to every conceivable touristic buying impulse, a pretty Venetian carousel for the kids, and the Center Stage for street entertainers.

The multi-media **San Francisco Experience** (☎ 388-6032) gives you the whole San Francisco story for $7, $5 for seniors, and $4 for students.

Sea Lions

Having put so much effort into attracting tourists to Pier 39 it's amusing that the pier's biggest attraction simply turned up, unplanned and uninvited. Around 1990, California sea lions began to haul out onto a section of the walkways at the marina beside Pier 39. Today the takeover has been complete, the boats have been cleared from K-dock, and hundreds of sea lions bask in the sun, woofing noisily and engaging in horseplay to the amusement of onlookers. The sea lion population varies during the year from a peak of around 600 in January and February down to virtually none in June and July, when they head south for the breeding season. Pier 39's sea lions are almost all male. They're big creatures; a fully grown male can be seven feet long and weigh over 800 pounds. By contrast a female may only reach six feet and 300 pounds. ■

TONY WHEELER

RON PICKUP

All sorts hang out at Fisherman's Wharf.

Shopping Centers

There is ample opportunity to empty your pockets at Fisherman's Wharf's enormously popular shopping centers, lined up to supply every conceivable tourist need. In 1964 **Ghirardelli Square** (pronounced gear-ah-deli) (☎ 775-5500), 900 North Point, was the first factory to be recycled into a shopping center, establishing a trend. Italian gold rush immigrant Domingo Ghirardelli arrived in San Francisco in 1849 and began making chocolate. His sons built a huge chocolate factory between 1900 and 1916, which was finally closed in the early '60s and redeveloped into a popular shopping center and tourist attraction.

The **Cannery** (☎ 771-3112), 2801 Leavenworth St., followed in 1967; in this case it was an old Del Monte fruit canning factory which metamorphosed into a shopping center. The Cannery also boasts the Museum of the City of San Francisco and the popular Cobb's Comedy Club. The **Anchorage** (☎ 775-6000), 2800 Leavenworth St., is a third, smaller shopping center.

Museum of the City of San Francisco

Established in 1991, the **Museum of the City of San Francisco** (☎ 928-0289) tells the story of the city with, hardly surprisingly, particular emphasis on the earthquakes of 1906 and 1989. The museum is on the 3rd floor of the Cannery, 2801 Leavenworth St., and it's open Wednesday to Sunday from 10 am to 4 pm; entry is free.

Hokey Museums

Just to prove Fisherman's Wharf really can be a tourist trap, Jefferson St. between Mason and Taylor features a collection of them – traps that is. You can savor the delights of the **Wax Museum** (☎ (800) 439-4305), where O.J. Simpson beckoned you in through 1994-95, the **Medieval Dungeon**, where you can thrill to repellent ancient tortures, or the **Ripley's Believe It or Not! Museum** (☎ 771-6188).

Pier 45

Get here early in the morning to discover that Fisherman's Wharf still does have fisherfolk, and thousands of tons of seafood are unloaded here each year. Later in the morning the sport fishing boats also make their way back to their moorings. The small **Fishermen's & Seamen's Chapel** was added to the pier in 1981.

U.S.S. Pampanito

At Pier 45 the *Pampanito* (☎ 929-0202) is a WWII, US Navy submarine which was built in 1943 and made six Pacific patrols during the last years of the war, sinking six Japanese ships. Tragically, among its victims were the *Kachidoki Maru*, and the *Rakuyo Maru* both of which carried British and Australian POWs.

The fascinating do-it-yourself audio tour of the 312-foot-long submarine conveys the incredibly cramped and claustrophobic conditions experienced by submariners and explains the operations and capabilities of this kind of sub. The *Pampanito* is open May to October daily from 9 am to 8 pm; November to April daily from 9 am to 6 pm. Entry is $5, $3 for seniors.

Hyde St. Historic Ships Pier

Moored along Hyde St. Pier, and part of the Maritime Museum, is a fine collection of historic ships with a Bay Area connection. The sidewheel steam ferry *Eureka* started life in 1890 as the railway ferry *Ukiah* and at the turn of the century was the largest ferry in the world. Refitted and renamed, the *Eureka* shuttled back and forth between the city and Sausalito from 1922 to 1941. She could carry over 2000 passengers and 100 cars but the Golden Gate and Bay Bridges sidelined her. Hyde St. Pier was used for the Bay ferries before the bridges ended their era.

In the latter half of the 19th century a huge fleet of magnificent sailing ships sailed around Cape Horn each year carrying Californian grain to Europe. The Scottish-built *Balclutha* of 1886 was a superb example of an iron hull square-rigger and after her retirement from the grain fleet she was conscripted for the Pacific Northwest timber trade, carrying lumber from Washington and Oregon to build the rapidly expanding cities of California. At one time, 900 sailing ships shuttled back and forth along this route. Retiring from this business and renamed *Star of Alaska*, she was then engaged in the Alaskan salmon fishing business. A final glory day came with a starring Hollywood appearance in the 1935 film *Mutiny on the Bounty*.

The smaller wooden *C. A. Thayer* of 1895 was built in California, and also worked the Pacific Northwest lumber trade and was later engaged in salmon and cod fishing off Alaska. The *Thayer* survived to be the last commercial sailing ship to operate from a West Coast port. Smaller ships along the pier include the 1914 *Eppleton Hall*, a British-built sidewheel tugboat, and the 1891 *Alma*, the last hay scow to operate on the Bay. These flat-bottomed sailing vessels once served as essential transport from the farms around the shallow waters of the Bay and the Maritime Museum tells their interesting story.

The Hyde St. Pier collection (☎ 556-3002) is open May to mid-September from 10 am to 6 pm; mid-September to April from 9:30 am to 5 pm. Entry is $2/1.

Aquatic Park

Hyde St. Pier and the long curve of Municipal Pier shelter the waters of Aquatic Park that boasts San Francisco's only real city beach. It's a popular place to laze on the sand or in the grounds of Victoria Park, and there are fine views of Golden Gate Bridge and the city skyline. Street entertainers add to the atmosphere, and even in the middle of winter hardy swimmers can be seen braving the frigid bay waters.

The **San Francisco National Maritime Museum** (☎ 556-8177) occupies a curiously ship-like 1939 building overlooking Aquatic Park at the waterfront end of Polk St. The museum's collection recounts the Bay Area's nautical history with a fine collection of ship models. The museum is open daily from 10 am to 5 pm, and entry is free.

THE MARINA

The term "yuppies" has gone out of favor since the big-spending '80s, but the Marina, with its pick-up bars, is

NIGEL FRENCH

The winds and scenery of the Marina make it a popular place for sailing.

still a district for swinging singles. Even the Safeway supermarket at 15 Marina Blvd. by Fort Mason has a reputation as a prime meeting place. Chestnut St. is the main cruising street while one block south is motel-lined Lombard St., a neat downscale divider between the upscale Marina and affluent Pacific Heights.

The Marina only popped up for the 1915 Panama-Pacific International Exposition, when the waterfront marshland was reclaimed to create the grounds for the exhibition commemorating San Francisco's phoenix-like post-earthquake rebirth. When the commemorations were over, the displays came down and the Marina district went up, along with the ritzy Golden Gate and St. Francis Yacht Clubs. Tragically, when the next Big One came along in 1989 the Marina was the most damaged area of San Francisco, proving once again that landfill is not an ideal foundation when you live in quake territory. Rebuilding was even quicker than after the 1906 tremblor and the Marina is as glossy as ever.

Getting There & Away

The Marina is just west of Fisherman's Wharf making for a pleasant bayside stroll. Useful Muni buses include No. 30 from downtown that heads through Chinatown, North Beach, and Fisherman's Wharf. No. 76 runs along Sutter St. through downtown, up Van Ness, and along Lombard. Bus No. 22 starts in Potrero Hill, runs through the Mission and up Fillmore past Japantown and Pacific Heights to the Marina. Bus No. 28 goes from Fort Mason, through the Marina and the Presidio to the Golden Gate Bridge and then south through the Presidio, Richmond, Golden Gate Park, and the Sunset districts.

Palace of Fine Arts

One of the few surviving structures from the 1915 Panama-Pacific Exposition, Bernard Maybeck's artificial classical ruin was so popular that it was spared from its intended demolition when the exhibition closed. Unfortunately, the stucco construction, intended to last the duration of the exhibition, eventually crumbled away to become a real ruin until, in the early '60s, it was resurrected in durable concrete. The exhibition featured everything from a Turkish mosque to a 432-foot high Tower of Jewels but the only other survivor at the site is the featureless shed which now houses the Exploratorium.

The Exploratorium

Behind Maybeck's ruin, the Exploratorium (☎ 561-0360) was established in 1969 as a museum of art, science, and human perception. Enormously popular with children, it has hundreds of exhibits with an emphasis on interactive discoveries of scientific principals. The exhibits

TOM SMALLMAN

The faux-ancient Palace of Fine Arts

are divided into 13 color-coded areas, with crowd-pleasers like a darkened tactile dome (reservations required) and the optical illusions of the distorted room.

The Exploratorium is open daily from 10 am to 5 pm, to 6 pm in summer and on Wednesdays until 9:30 pm. Entry is $9/5and free on the first Wednesday of the month.

Marina Green & the Wave Organ

Cyclists, in-line skaters, joggers, and kite flyers all enjoy the waterfront strip of Marina Green. Continue round the yachting marina to find the curious Wave Organ at the tip of the breakwater. Built as part of the Exploratorium, the theory is that incoming and outgoing tides will produce music in the organ's pipes. Well, so do flushing toilets.

Fort Mason

Adjoining the Aquatic Park, Fort Mason (☎ 979-3010) forms the border to the Marina. The site of a secondary Spanish fort, Fort Mason became a residential area before it was appropriated by the US Army during the US Civil War in 1861-65. It remained in military hands through WWII, when it was the transport hub for troops heading to the Pacific War. Most of the buildings were handed over for civilian use in the 1970s and now house a colorful mix of galleries, museums, theaters, and the city's finest vegetarian restaurant. The Golden Gate National Recreation Area (☎ 556-0560), responsible for much of the coastal park land north and south of the Golden Gate, has its headquarters and visitors center here, and Hostelling International's popular San Francisco International Hostel is also in Fort Mason.

Museums The **Mexican Museum** (☎ 441-0445), Bldg. D, has colorful exhibits on Mexican art and culture with particular reference to the Bay Area. It's open Wednesday to Sunday from noon to 5 pm. Entry is $3, free for children and free for everybody the first Wednesday of the month. There's also a small shop with excellent Mexican crafts.

The **Museo Italo-Americano** (☎ 673-2200), Bldg. C, has an equally vivid introduction to the activities of another important Bay Area community. It's open Wednesday to Sunday from noon to 5 pm, and admission is $2/1. The **San Francisco African-American Historical & Cultural Society** (☎ 441-0640), $3/2, and the **San Francisco Craft & Folk Art Museum** (☎ 775-0990), $1/50¢, are also headquartered at Fort Mason. See the entertainment chapter for information on the fort's performance centers.

PACIFIC HEIGHTS

This wealthy hilltop area has many of the city's finest old houses because Van Ness was where the fire was stopped after the 1906 quake. Known as Golden Gate Valley, it consisted of farms, market gardens, and nurseries before houses were built starting in the 1870s. Two parks, Alta Plaza and Lafayette, and the best houses, with the best views, are found along the east-west ridge. Divisadero, which climbs north-south over the ridge, was the "lookout path," the principal route between the Spanish settlements at the Presidio and Mission Dolores.

Inspecting the fine old Victorians of Pacific Heights is principally a wander-and-look operation; only a couple of houses are open to the public and for quite restricted hours. Union St. is the fashionable shopping and restaurant street; it was once known as Cow Hollow after a local dairy farm. Fillmore St., climbing uphill from Union St., and then dropping down to Japantown, is also packed with restaurants and shops.

Getting There & Away

The California St. cable car terminates at Van Ness Ave., close to Lafayette Park. Muni bus No. 1 runs from the bay (Embarcadero) to the ocean (Richmond district) taking California and Sacramento Sts. through Pacific Heights. Bus Nos. 41 and 45 take different routes from SoMa through Chinatown and North Beach and then continue along Union St.

Haas-Lilienthal House

This house (☎ 441-3004), 2007 Franklin St., was built in Queen Anne style between 1882 and '86 (for $18,500 plus $13,000 for the land), and is now the headquarters of the Foundation for San Francisco's Architectural Heritage. Built for wealthy merchant William Haas and inherited by his daughter Alice Lilienthal, it stayed with the Lilienthal family until her death in 1972. The house is externally impressive but inside it's surprisingly sparsely furnished considering the length of time the original owners were there and that it was handed over with contents intact. Worse, the one-hour tour is tediously slow. The house is open Wednesday from noon to 3:15 pm (last tour) and Sunday from 11 am to 4:15 pm. The tour costs $5/3.

Spreckels Mansion

Looking across Lafayette Park, this huge baroque mansion, at 2080 Washington St., stretches the entire block from Washington to Jackson, bordered by Octavia. It was built in 1912 by George Applegarth, who also created the Palace of the Legion of Honor, for mega-wealthy sugar magnate Adolph Spreckels. After years of decline the over-the-top home (it started life with 26 bathrooms) was bought in 1990 by romance novelist Danielle Steele. God knows what she's done inside but the peeling exterior still awaits the application of a large number of dollars.

Octagon House

The 1861 Octagon House (☎ 441-7512), 2645 Gough St. at Union, is one of the two survivors of the city's octagonal-shaped houses craze. It was proposed that the eight sides caught the sun from eight different angles, as this was supposed to be a sure-fire ticket to good health. The house is owned by the National Society of Colonial Dames and houses a collection of Colonial and Federal antiques. It's open the second and fourth Thursday and the second Sunday of each month from noon to 3 pm. Admission is a suggested donation of $3.

More Mansions

There are many other interesting houses which are not open to the public. The large reddish-pink **Whittier House** at 2090 Jackson St. was built for William Frank Whittier in 1896 by Edward R. Swain, who also designed McLaren Lodge in Golden Gate Park. This building was once open to the public but is now privately owned.

James Flood owned the only Nob Hill mansion to survive the 1906 quake and fire but there are also two **Flood Mansions** on Broadway in Pacific Heights. Flood's 1916 mansion at 2222 Broadway is now the **Convent of the Sacred Heart**, and the neighboring Grant and Hammond Mansions are also part of the convent. On the next block, at 2120 Broadway, the other Flood mansion was built in 1901 and despite appearances is made of wood. Just off Broadway, at 2550 Webster St., the dark and foreboding Georgian **Bourn House** was built in 1896. Far from being born with a mere silver spoon in his mouth, William Bourn started out owning one gold mine and became one of the wealthiest men in San Francisco; the Pacific Gas & Electric Company was just one of his many companies.

At 2727 Pierce St., on the steep ascent from Union St. to Alta Plaza Park, **Casebolt House** dates from the 1860s; one of the oldest houses in Pacific Heights, it's fashioned in an Italianate design and stands well back from the street. Visible from Alta Plaza Park, the 1894 **Gibbs House**, 2622 Jackson St., was built by Willis Polk. **Sherman House**, at 2160 Green St., is a handsome mansion built in 1876 and now an exclusive and expensive small hotel.

Churches

The **Church of St. Mary the Virgin** (☎ 921-3665), 2325 Union St., is a rustic Arts & Crafts-style creation of 1891 with a fountain still fed by one of the old farmland springs. The 1905 Hindu **Vedanta Temple** (☎ 922-2323), 2963 Webster St., is a curious conglomeration of architectural styles and is open only during the Friday night services. The **Holy Trinity Russian Orthodox Cathedral** (☎ 673-8565), 1520 Green St., is a 1909 baroque and Byzantine replacement for its Washington Square predecessor destroyed in 1906.

JAPANTOWN & THE FILLMORE

There have been Japanese in San Francisco since the 1860s and today only a tiny portion of them live in the compact Japantown area. Known as Nihonmachi in Japanese, the area only developed after the 1906 earthquake but the WWII internment of Japanese and Japanese-Americans was a major setback. Many former residents were unable to reclaim their homes after the war.

Japantown comes alive during the two-weekend Cherry Blossom Festival in April with music, dance, martial arts exhibits, a wide variety of demonstrations, a special program for children, a food bazaar, and a Japanese parade. A two-day Nihonmachi Street Fair takes place over the first weekend in August.

There are some areas of interest close to Japantown. Just north are several restaurant-packed blocks of Fillmore St. while St. Mary's Cathedral is a couple of blocks east. There are a number of restored Victorian row houses along Pine and Bush Sts., particularly the 1882 houses of Cottage Row, off the 2100 block of Bush.

Getting There & Away

From downtown, Muni bus No. 38 runs straight down Geary past the Japan Center. Bus Nos. 2, 3, and 4 run along Sutter (then eastbound on Post) just north of the center. Bus No. 22, on its long trek through the Mission to the Marina, also passes by the Japan Center on Fillmore.

Japan Center

The Japan Center opened in 1968 around Peace Plaza with its five-story Peace Pagoda. Unfortunately, the bare, windswept plaza has not been a success and there are plans to renovate and improve it. The three shopping centers which make up the center – the Tasamak Plaza, Kintetsu Restaurant Mall, and Kinokuniya Building – are packed with Japanese restaurants and shops including the excellent Kinokuniya Bookshop and the Maruma supermarket. The complex includes the eight-screen Kabuki Theater. More shops and restaurants can be found in Buchanan Mall, across Post St. from the center. The mall features fountains by sculptor Ruth Asawa, designed to look as if a stream flows through it.

Japantown can provide some real culture shock. After an hour or two wandering the shops and enjoying the food in the antiseptic Japan Center, it's a real surprise to emerge and find San Francisco's homeless problem is still there, right outside.

Kabuki Hot Spring

Japanese-style communal baths come to San Francisco at the Kabuki Hot Spring (☎ 922-6000), 1750 Geary Blvd. The baths are open weekdays from 10 am to 10 pm and weekends from 9 am to 10 pm. They're open for men Monday, Tuesday, Thursday, and Saturday and for women Wednesday, Friday, and Sunday. You can enjoy the baths, sauna, and steam room for $10.

Traditional Amma/Shiatsu massage is available weekdays from 2 to 9:30 pm and weekends from 10 am to 9:30 pm. Include a 25-minute massage with your bath and the cost goes up to $35. A 55-minute massage takes it to $55. In addition, there are private deep-tub baths and a session in these with a 25-minute massage is $40; with a 55-minute massage it's $65. Phone ☎ 922-6002 for massage appointments.

St. Mary's Cathedral

The 1971 St. Mary's Cathedral (☎ 567-2020), 1111 Gough St. at Geary Blvd., has a square floor plan rising to curving roofs which float over the nave. Some say that the building looks like a washing machine, thus the nickname St. Maytag. This is the city's third St. Mary's Cathedral. The original, in use from 1854 to 1891 still stands in Chinatown as Old St. Mary's. Its replacement, New St. Mary's, was on Van Ness Ave., but in 1960 it was completely destroyed by a fire.

HAIGHT-ASHBURY

Just east of Golden Gate Park the Haight-Ashbury area, locally known simply as "the Haight," is chiefly famed as the epicenter of San Francisco's brief fling as the city of love and home of flower power in 1966-67. As a San Francisco neighborhood, the Haight's earlier history was remarkably innocuous. In the 1860s it was mostly sand dunes rolling to the Pacific, but the construction of a tramway from the city center to Golden Gate Park in 1883 accelerated the change from rural to urban status. The Haight escaped the 1906 earthquake with minor damage, but shifting demographics turned the area's upward mobility around and many of the Haight's big Victorian houses were broken up into apartments. The decline continued in the '50s and the attractions of Victorian architecture and the adjacent Golden Gate Park combined with the biggest attraction of all, low rents, to draw the beatniks out of expensive North Beach. A younger counterculture generation made the Haight their own, and were soon dubbed the "hippies" for their emulation of the "hipsters" of the '50s.

Their famous decade, the '60s, proved to be a brief, if glowing, heyday. By late '67, drug overdoses and incidences of violence were increasing among the throngs of hippies, gawkers, media, and police. The Haight today is a colorful area and remarkably varied in its ethnic and economic composition, but contrary to the image of its tie-dyed stragglers, the Summer of Love is just a dream-like memory. Those long-lived Haight attributes – pretty Victorian houses and proximity to the park – are currently prompting yet another neighborhood transformation as the Haight is becoming increasingly gentrified.

The Haight is a compact zone, measuring eight blocks from Golden Gate Park to Buena Vista Park and most of the action is concentrated along Haight St. The Panhandle, the narrow strip of park which forms a "handle" to the Golden Gate Park's "pan," makes a natural northern border to the Haight, two blocks from Haight St. East of Haight-Ashbury, the **Lower Haight** is a colorful few blocks of grungy clubs and bars, and a few blocks south, tiny **Cole Valley** is a more upscale version with cafes, restaurants, and shops.

Getting There & Away

Muni bus Nos. 7 and 71 run from the Ferry Building to the Haight and No. 6 runs from the Transbay Terminal. No. 43 starts at the Marina, dips into the Presidio, and then heads south through the Haight and onwards.

The Summer of Love
When rock & roll combined with sex and, most importantly, drugs to light the fuse on the 1967 Summer of Love, the Haight was where it all took place. There was no single event that shaped the scene, but several forces seem to have been catalysts. In 1964, Ken Kesey took his acid-drenched voyage across the USA, chronicled by Tom Wolfe in *The Electric Kool-Aid Acid Test*, establishing Kesey and his Merry Pranksters as legends and LSD as the drug of choice. That same year, promotion-genius Bill Graham began his domination of Bay Area entertainment media as a business exec. who "dropped out" to produce theater with the San Francisco Mime Troupe, a politically radical performance group, staging their donation-only performances in the *commedia dell'arte* tradition. Other revolutionaries, like the anarchist Diggers, maintained that money, like church and state, was dead, and proved their point by providing meals ("free because it's yours") at their soon-famous Digger Feeds. By 1966 the area was attracting hundreds of new pilgrims daily; in January of that year Kesey's psychedelic Trips Festival – anticipating the Human Be-In, or Gathering of the Tribes, one year later – laid the path for the Summer of Love. ■

COURTESY OF THE BANCROFT LIBRARY

Flyer for an event sponsored by the Diggers

Haight St.

Let's be honest, there's not a lot to see around the Haight. You can take a glance at the street sign where Ashbury intersects Haight, but that's about the only icon of the Summer of Love which remains unchanged. The Haight-Ashbury Free Clinic (☎ 565-1908) at 529 Clayton St. is one of the few real reminders of the underlying spirit of that era. Any coffee bar, cafe, or head shop from the '60s has probably been recycled a dozen times since the flower power era, but that doesn't matter because the Haight is still a great place to wander. Start at the Golden Gate Park end, wander up Haight St., dive into a few of the strange shops, stop for a cheap meal and a cup of strong coffee – that's what the Haight is all about.

Parks & Victorian Houses

The eastern end of busy Haight-Ashbury is marked by **Buena Vista Park**, with great views from its steeply sloping site. This is another San Francisco park which is great to visit in the daytime and not so wise after dark. Buena Vista Ave. West runs up the west side of the park and features some fine old houses. The 1897 **Richard Spreckels Mansion** at No. 737 is the most impressive and most historically interesting, as it's where Jack London wrote *White Fang* and Ambrose Bierce spent the last years of his life. Don't confuse it with the other Spreckels Mansion in Pacific Heights; this one was built by Adolph Spreckels' nephew. Masonic Ave. and Piedmont and Delmar Sts., around the southwest side of the park, feature more interesting houses.

Northeast of the Haight, **Alamo Square** is notable for the row of "painted ladies," colorfully painted restored Victorian row houses, that make a postcard-popular view with the city skyline in the background. On your way up Steiner St. to this viewpoint the house at No. 601 is a fine example of the Queen Anne style from 1891.

Just south of Buena Vista Park is **Corona Heights Park**, with the Randall Museum (☎ 554-9600), 199 Museum Way, a kid's petting zoo with a variety of small wildlife and domestic animals.

THE CASTRO & NOE VALLEY

The compact Castro is the gay center of San Francisco, and is one of the city's best neighborhoods for strolling and watching the streetlife, stopping for a coffee, shopping, getting a body piercing, or having a leisurely lunch. The magnificent **Castro Theater** (see the Entertainment chapter) is the highlight of Castro St. and the center for the annual Gay & Lesbian Film Festival. **Harvey Milk Plaza**, at the Muni station at the intersection of Market and Castro, is dedicated to the unofficial "mayor of Castro," killed along with city Mayor Moscone in 1978.

Continue south along Castro or Noe Sts. and you'll come to **Noe Valley**, another of San Francisco's wonderful small neighborhoods. The mix of Victorian homes, upscale restaurants and coffeehouses, and eclectic shops gives it a villagey feel; 24th St. is the main drag.

Getting There & Away

The Muni F streetcar on Market St. terminates at Castro St. but the K, L, and M continue west. Muni bus No. 8

goes from the Ferry Building down Market St. to the Castro. Bus No. 37, on its winding route between Twin Peaks and the Haight-Ashbury, passes by the Castro. Bus No. 24 goes through Noe Valley and the Castro and up Divisadero to Alta Plaza Park in Pacific Heights. Muni's J Church line follows Church St. along Market from Embarcadero; for Noe Valley, get off at 24th St.

Names Project

The Castro's magnificent memorial to the swath AIDS has cut through the gay community is the AIDS Memorial Quilt. Each of the over 25,000 individually crafted, six-feet by three-feet panels commemorates an AIDS victim. The Names Project gallery (☎ 863-1966) at 2362 Market St. recounts the quilt's ongoing creation and its travels, most remarkably a display of panels in Washington, DC seen by over half a million people.

THE MISSION

The Mission district is – take your pick – one of the oldest parts of the city, a Spanish-speaking enclave, or a great place for a cheap meal. The Mission takes its name from the Mission Dolores, founded by the Spanish in 1776. It was Spanish then and is Spanish now, but in between it has hosted a moving parade of nationalities. German and Scandinavian settlers were followed by Irish and Italians and it was not until the 1960s that Mexican migration, along with Central and South American political refugees, reasserted the Latino atmosphere. The Mission Dolores is a prime attraction but the hundreds of colorful murals dotted around the district and the equally colorful street life are also worth seeing. Perhaps as a counterpoint to the district's Latin machismo, the Mission is a center for the city's lesbian community with a variety of feminist bookshops and the brightly painted Women's Building.

The heart of the mission stretches east-west, between Dolores and South Van Ness, and north-south, between 16th and 25th Sts. Valencia and Mission are the two main streets for shops and restaurants. The district manages relative immunity from San Francisco's fog so this is one of the warmest areas in the city.

Getting There & Away

BART will zip you out to the Mission in a matter of minutes, running along Mission St. with stops at 16th and 24th Sts. Visitors should take care around the BART stations at night. The J Church streetcar also runs to the Mission, passing down the west side of Mission Dolores Park. Useful Muni buses include No. 26, starting from 5th St. in SoMa and running down Valencia; No. 14, from the Ferry Building down Mission St.; and the circuitous No. 12 which starts at Alta Plaza Park in Pacific Heights, runs through the Financial District, and then loops back south on Folsom to the Mission.

Mission Dolores

The Mission San Francisco de Assisi acquired its familiar name, the Mission Dolores, from a nearby stream, the Arroyo de Nuestra Señora de los Dolores (Our Lady of the Sorrows). The stream may have disappeared long ago but the mission, with its four-foot-thick adobe walls, survives as the oldest building in San Francisco.

The mission was the sixth to be founded by Father Junipero Serra. Its site was consecrated on June 29, 1776 and a temporary structure was erected, so this oldest building in San Francisco can claim to be five days older than the USA. The permanent building was constructed in 1782 by Franciscan monks, with Native American labor. Today the mission building is overshadowed by the adjoining basilica, built in 1913.

The mission is entered via a small shop leading to the **cemetery** which is overlooked by a statue of Junipero Serra. It's said that more than 5000 Native Americans were buried here after measles epidemics devastated the Ohlone tribe in 1814 and 1826. The cemetery was once much larger and the international collection of gravestones are more recent, a surprising number of them marking Irish deaths from the gold rush era. Notable graves in the cemetery include Father Francisco Palou, who designed the mission and wrote Serra's biography; Don Luis Antonio Arguello, the first governor of Upper California under Mexican rule; Don Francisco de Haro, first alcalde (mayor) of San Francisco; and James Casey, Charles Cora, and James "Yankee" Sullivan, all 1856 victims of the Vigilance Committee, a lynch-first, ask-questions-later citizens organization. A small museum stands at one end of the mission and includes a tabernacle door brought from the Philippines, and the mission's baptismal register from 1776.

The mission **chapel** was built in 1782 and it's said the building's ceiling was originally painted with vegetable dyes by the local Indian tribes. Although it has been repainted, the original designs have been retained. The colorful altars and altar niche statues were brought from Mexico in the early 1800s. Four burial sites are marked

NIGEL FRENCH

CAROLINE LIOU

TONY WHEELER

TONY WHEELER

The murals of the Mission are a colorful depiction of history, diversity, politics, and fun.

TONY WHEELER

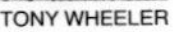
TONY WHEELER

SCOTT SUMMERS

within the mission building, those of pioneer businessman William Leidesdorff, of the Noe family, Lieutenant José Joaquin Moraga who led the Spanish expedition of 1776, and Richard Carroll, the first pastor of Mission Dolores after San Francisco became an archdiocese.

The sturdy mission survived the 1906 quake unscathed but the adjoining church, built to mark the mission's centenary in 1876, was severely damaged and its replacement dates from 1913. It was designated a **basilica** by the pope after his visit in 1952. The basilica's ornate *Churrigueresque* design is eye-catching and inside there are seven panels, one above the main door and three on the facades of each of the side balconies, depicting the Seven Sorrows of Mary. The choir windows picture St. Francis of Assisi, after whom the mission and the city of San Francisco are both named. The lower windows show the 21 Californian missions plus two more in honor of Father Junipero Serra and Father Francisco Palou.

The mission (☎ 621-8203) is at Dolores and 16th Sts. and is open daily from 9 am to 4 pm; entry is $1. Despite its historical significance the mission is a very low-key attraction with a mere dribble of visitors.

Levi Strauss Factory

The Mission's Levi Strauss factory was the second factory established by the San Francisco-based inventor of blue jeans and today it is their oldest and smallest factory, turning out just 7500 pairs per week. The factory is at 250 Valencia St. and a free 1¼-hour tour (☎ 565-9153, 565-9159 for bookings) takes place on Wednesdays at 10:30 am or 1 pm.

Mission Murals

The Mission is famed for the colorful murals depicting everything from San Francisco's labor history to Central American independence struggles, the women's movement, and depictions of local streetlife. Murals are scattered all over the place, so simply wandering the neighborhood at random is one of the best ways of coming across them. There's a nice batch at the intersection of Mission and 21st and another good collection at South Van Ness and 24th. Local guitar hero Carlos Santana overlooks the car park at South Van Ness and 21st. One of the most amazing examples of mural art is the wonderfully painted Women's Building at 3543 18th St. between Valencia and Guerrero where the paintings of heroic or oppressed women swirl dramatically from the sidewalk to the very top of the building. Narrow Balmy St., between Treat and Harrison off 24th, is lined from end to end with murals.

Other Mission Sites

Sloping up from Dolores St., between 18th and 20th, there are views of the Financial District from the high side of **Dolores Park**, where there is a statue of Miguel Hidalgo (1753–1811), a martyred Mexican priest and revolutionary hero. Like too many other parks in San Francisco, it's fine in the daytime but taken over by drug dealers after dark. Adjoining the park is **Mission High School**, built in the 1920s in the Mission Revival style and topped by a Churrigueresque tower mimicking the Mission Dolores basilica two blocks away.

The **Liberty Hill District**, bordered by Mission, Dolores, 20th and 23rd Sts., shelters some fine turn-of-the-century earthquake survivors in a variety of architectural styles. Mission St. is the main shopping street of the Mission but parallel Valencia St. is the home to many of the district's more recent feminist, political, and alternative organizations.

The **Mission Cultural Center** (☎ 821-1155), 2868 Mission St., is the area's Latino arts center.

Potrero Hill

Potrero Hill is an unsung little neighborhood in the eastern reaches of the Mission. It's usually the last place in the city to get fog and is fairly free of urban congestion. There's not much in the way of active sightseeing, but a good way to see the neighborhood is to drive down the "secret crookedest street in the world", and have a bite to eat at one of the many restaurants on 18th St.

The **McKinley Square** park and playground, at 20th and Vermont Sts., sits at the top of the hill and is a great place for a picnic. For those not prone to vertigo, the swingsets at the ledge of the park provide quite a thrill as they swoop you out into space over the Mission. Continue down one-way Vermont St. towards 21st St. on what locals will tell you is the *real* crookedest street in the world. It's less traveled and longer than Lombard St., but not gingerbreaded out like its touristy counterpart.

The **Anchor Brewing Company** (☎ 863-8350), 1705 Mariposa St., is where the city's famous Anchor Steam Beer is brewed. There are small group tours daily at 2 pm; reserve well in advance.

THE PRESIDIO

The northwest corner of the San Francisco peninsula has for many years been occupied as a rather low-key army base; as a result it has not been developed and most of it remains green and park-like. Highways 1 and 101 meet in the middle of the Presidio and become the Golden Gate Bridge Freeway but despite the steady flow of traffic along these arteries the Presidio has remained a refreshingly relaxed escape from the city.

The Presidio has had a long military history. In the Spanish era it was established in 1776 as the site of the first fort, or presidio, and was linked with the religious center of Mission Dolores, three miles to the south, by the Divisadero; the modern street follows that old route. Under American rule, Fort Point was built at the start of the 1861-65 Civil War to guard the entrance to the Bay. The Presidio's military role ends in 1996 with the completion of a three-year changeover to a National Park.

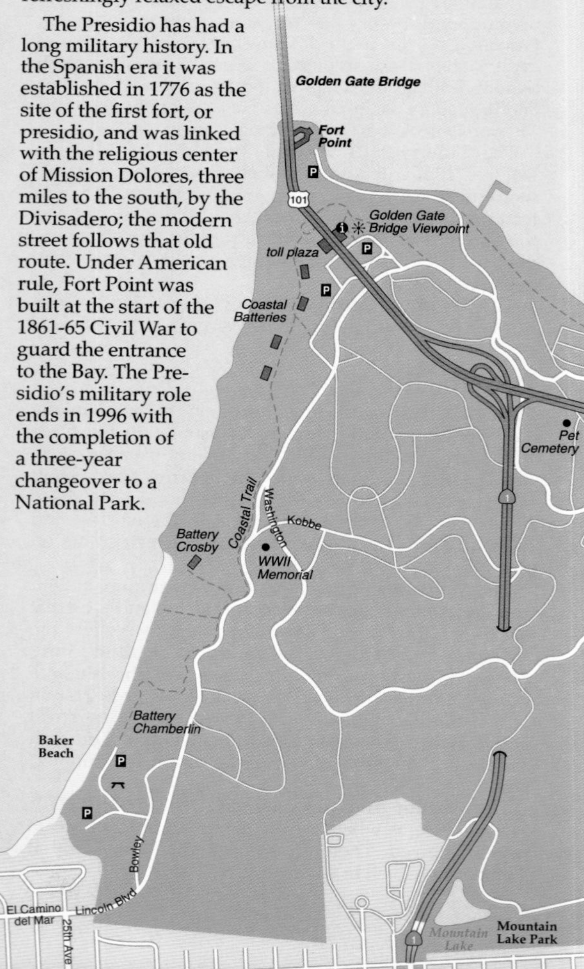

Getting There & Away

Muni bus No. 28 goes from Fort Mason through the Presidio to Fort Point and then south through Golden Gate Park. Golden Gate Transit buses heading to Marin County all stop at the bridge toll plaza.

Fort Point

Some of the most spectacular views of the Golden Gate Bridge and the bay are from this lookout. The small Spanish fort that originally occupied the site was replaced by the US Army with a much larger triple-tiered fortress between 1853 and 1861. Though it had 126 cannons, it never saw battle or cannon fire and was abandoned in 1900. The bridge is built right over it, and it houses displays relating to the Civil War. It's open Wednesday to Sunday from 10 am to 5 pm and entry is free. There's another military gunpoint at Battery Chamberlin on the bluffs above Baker Beach.

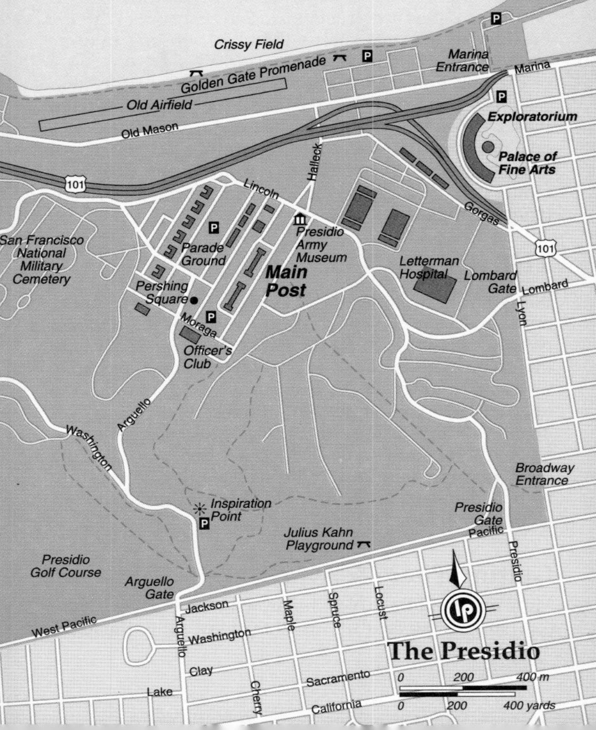

Presidio Army Museum

Housed in a Civil War-era hospital building, the Presidio Museum (☎ 556-0865), at Funston Ave. and Lincoln Blvd., documents the history of California and the West Coast with a military emphasis. The Presidio sheltered many residents left homeless by the 1906 earthquake and there are exhibits on the disaster and examples of the temporary cabins used as shelters. The museum is open Wednesday to Sunday from 10 am to 4 pm and entry is free.

Other Sites

The relatively quiet and winding roads of the Presidio are ideal for exploring by bicycle. Along the ocean side of the peninsula is **Baker Beach**, the most picturesque of the city's beaches with craggy rock formations backed up against cliffs. Due to the cold water and currents, it's not much of a swimming beach. The **Presidio Officers' Club** (☎ 921-1612), 50 Moraga Ave., houses fragments of the old Spanish fort and, along with Mission Dolores, is one of the oldest constructions in San Francisco. With the Presidio's new park status the club building may be opened to the public.

The **San Francisco National Military Cemetery** was established in 1884 and is the burial site for soldiers from the Civil War to the present. The **Presidio Pet Cemetery**, on Crissy Field Ave., is a strange and forgotten patch of ground holding the remains of many army dogs and family pets, their graves marked with sentimental hand-painted tombstones.

THE RICHMOND

Bordered by the green park land of the Presidio to the north and Golden Gate Park to the south, the uniform rectangles of the Richmond district stretch all the way to the ocean. The restaurants and bookshops along busy Clement St. make up the heart of the area, and also the heart of New Chinatown. In addition to excellent Chinese restaurants, there's an international smorgasbord of other ethnic eateries. The Richmond district has a couple of interesting religious buildings, while the recently reopened Palace of the Legion of Honor and the Cliff House are in Lincoln Park.

Getting There & Away

Muni bus No. 1 links old Chinatown with the new, while bus Nos. 31 and 38 also run all the way out to the Richmond from downtown. Bus Nos. 28 and 29 both wander through the Presidio and cut across the Richmond district and Golden Gate Park.

Lincoln Park Hiking Tour

Golden Gate park-keeper John McLaren took time out from his favorite park to establish Lincoln Park. There's a fine walking path along this surprisingly rugged stretch of coast from the Cliff House to Lands End from where there are terrific views across the Golden Gate; it only takes about an hour roundtrip and is worth it – fog or no fog. The walk starts by the remains of the gigantic Sutro Baths and pass the U.S.S. *San Francisco* memorial, looking out from Point Lobos. The ship was sunk during the WWII battle of Guadalcanal in the Solomon Islands and its bridge is preserved on the clifftop.

Cliff House & Sutro Baths

Fires and earthquakes have resulted in multiple incarnations for a number of San Francisco buildings but none have come back as often as the Cliff House (☎ 386-3330), originally built in 1863 as an escape from the crowds and the hectic pace of the city. The most impressive of the myriad of Cliff Houses was the elegant eight-story gingerbread resort built by Adolph Sutro in 1896 containing art galleries, dining rooms, and an observation deck. It survived the 1906 earthquake but was destroyed

COURTESY OF THE BANCROFT LIBRARY

The 1896 Cliff House stood for a mere 11 years.

by fire the following year. The 1909 replacement was nowhere near as grand but it's still a popular restaurant with great views and unexciting food, although sunset over the Pacific can be worth the price of a drink. Seal Rocks, just offshore from Cliff House, is washed by crashing waves but is no longer as densely populated by seals since they've discovered the greater comforts of Fisherman's Wharf.

On the deck below the restaurant is a giant **Camera Obscura**, a Victorian invention that projects the view outside onto a parabolic screen. It's open daily from 10 or 11 am to sunset and entry is $1/50¢. Underneath the restaurant is the **Musée Mécanique** (☎ 386-1170) which traces the history of arcade games from some wonderfully whimsical early versions to the latest computerized devices. It's open daily from 10 or 11 am to 7 or 8 pm and entry is free. There's also the Golden Gate National Recreation Area Visitors Center (☎ 556-0560) on the deck, dispensing information about all the GGNRA coastal parks.

In the cove just north of the Cliff House are the remains of the Sutro Baths. At the same time that he built the Cliff House in 1886, the wealthy Sutro built a magnificent indoor swimming pool complex which could accommodate 25,000 visitors a day, but despite initial awe the pools never made money. An ice-skating rink was added in 1937 and the whole complex converted to ice skating in 1952 but, on the point of bankruptcy, it mysteriously burned down in 1966. Period prints show what an amazing creation the six-pool (some saltwater, some freshwater), three-acre palace must have been. Across the street tourists are welcome to stroll around the grounds of the Adolph Sutro Estate, now known as **Sutro Heights Park**. The mansion is gone but some of the walls and gardens remain and there are wonderful views.

ERIC KETTUNEN

The ruins of the once glorious Sutro Baths

Palace of the Legion of Honor

Sugar magnate Adolph Spreckels' name pops up regularly around San Francisco and this magnificent art museum was the creation of his wife, Alma Spreckels. The French pavilion for the 1915 Panama-Pacific Exposition at the Marina was a replica of the Palais de la Légion d'Honneur in Paris and was stocked with French art. The exposition buildings were temporary structures – the Palace of Fine Arts is the sole survivor – but Mrs. Spreckels decided to construct a permanent replica, built by architect George Applegarth who also created the Spreckels mansion in Pacific Heights.

The museum opened in 1924 and has a world-class collection of medieval to 20th-century European art including many works by the impressionists and a huge Rodin collection. The 1989 earthquake caused severe damage to the building and it took over five years to complete the repairs and seismic strengthening. Reopened in late 1995 with a number of new galleries, the museum (☎ 863-3330) is open Tuesday to Sunday from 10 am to 5 pm and the first Saturday of each month to 8:45 pm. Entry is $6; children are free, and on the second Wednesday of each month it's free to all. The entrance to the museum is from 34th Ave., which becomes Legion of Honor Drive inside Lincoln Park.

The Holy Virgin Cathedral

The golden onion domes of the Holy Virgin Cathedral (☎ 221-3255), 6210 Geary Blvd., look very out of place in the suburbs but it's an appropriate focus for the city's surprisingly active Russian communities. It's a reminder that California's Russian links go right back to the Mexican era; in fact, the Mexican authorities were just as worried about incursions by Russian fur traders as American frontiersmen. The cathedral is also known as St. Mary-the-Virgin-in-Exile and is open daily from 8 am to 6 pm. The Sunday services are held at 9:45 am.

RON PICKUP

Temple Emanu-El

With a dome modeled after the 6th-century church of Sancta Sophia in Istanbul, the 1925 Jewish Temple Emanu-El (☎ 751-2535), Lake St. and Arguello Blvd., manages to blend Mission revival with elements of Byzantine design. Designed by Arthur Brown, who was also responsible for the fine City Hall at the Civic Center, the temple was also inspired by the city's Russian community. It's open Monday to Thursday from 1 to 3 pm and for services on Friday (5:30 pm) and Saturday (10:30 am).

St. Ignatius Church

The twin towers of the 1914 St. Ignatius Church loom over the University of San Francisco, just off the northeast corner of Golden Gate Park. They're a landmark for much of the Western Addition. The university began as the St. Ignatius College in 1855.

GOLDEN GATE PARK

San Francisco's biggest park stretches almost halfway across the six-mile-wide peninsula. In 1866 Mayor Frank McCoppin led the push to create the park, at a time when San Francisco's meteoric gold-fueled growth had left little time to think about such civic niceties. An 1870 competition to design the park was won by 24-year-old William Hammond Hall, who devised a way to reclaim the windswept sand dunes. In 1871 he commenced the task of turning 1017 acres of dunes into the largest man-made park in the world. Battles with land speculators forced him to resign five years later, but by the 1880s the park had become the city's most popular attraction. Hall was recalled in 1886 but a year later handed over the park's management to John McLaren, who administered the park for the next 56 years. As astute at managing politicians as he was at growing plants, the indestructible Scottish-born gardener was 97 years old when he died, still in charge of his beloved park.

Apart from gardens, lakes, sporting facilities, and drives the park also has a host of museums and other indoor attractions. They can be a useful escape on days when the fog rolls in and the temperature plummets. Initial inspiration for Golden Gate Park came from Frederick Law Olmsted, designer of New York's Central Park, but he quickly decided that reclaiming the dunes was an impossible task, and was suitably astonished when Hall managed the feat.

Park information (☎ 666-7200) is available from McLaren Lodge at the entrance to the park. Built in 1896 this was park administrator John McLaren's home. The lodge, now the offices of the Friends of Recreation & Parks (☎ 750-5105), is open weekdays from 9 am to 5 pm. They organize free walking tours of the park.

The Academy of Science, M.H. de Young Museum, Asian Art Museum, and Japanese Tea Garden cluster around the Music Concourse, where the Midwinter Fair of 1894 was held, towards the eastern end of the park. A $10 Culture Pass gives admission to the five park attractions which charge entry fees, giving a $5.50 savings. The pass can be used over a number of days.

Getting There & Away

From Union Square to the museum area of the park take a No. 38 bus and change to a southbound No. 44 at 6th Ave. From Market St. a No. 5, 7, 21, or 71 will get you to the eastern or southern park edge. Or take the N streetcar to 9th Ave. and then the northbound No. 44. From Fisherman's Wharf take a southbound No. 42, 47, or 49 to McAllister St. and change to a westbound No. 5 Fulton. No. 28 runs from Fort Mason through the Presidio and then south right through the park.

Bicycles can be rented just outside the park at the Start to Finish Biking Shop (see the Getting Around chapter). Horses can be rented at Golden Gate Park Stables (☎ 668-7360) near the Polo Fields off John F. Kennedy Drive; rates are $20 per hour and reservations are required.

A Park Circuit

From McLaren Lodge at the eastern entrance to the park, a six-mile circuit can be made following John F. Kennedy Drive westbound and Martin Luther King, Jr. Drive back to the starting point. The Conservatory of Flowers is the first site passed. The entrance to the Music Concourse with its surrounding museums is further along on the left. The Golden Gate Park Band performs regularly every Sunday during summer at 1 pm in the Spreckels Temple of Music at the west end of the Music Concourse.

The drive passes the 1911 Pioneer Log Cabin and the boat rental house on Stow Lake. The Huntington Falls on the east side of Strawberry Hill, the island in the lake, was one of the few features of the park damaged by the 1906 earthquake and it was not repaired until the late 1980s. A pretty Chinese pavilion stands at the foot of the falls. Reflected in the waters of Lloyd Lake, continuing west, are the Portals of the Past, the entrance portico to a Nob Hill mansion destroyed in the 1906 earthquake. It's the city's only memorial to the Big One.

Golden Gate Park Stadium is a combined polo field, football field, and trotting track to the south of the drive. The great hippie-fest of 1967, the 14,000 strong "Gathering of the Clans," took place here. Spreckels Lake is just to the north of the drive. The bison paddock is a park surprise; the original herd was brought here in 1894 but a replacement herd was relocated from Wyoming in 1984 after a tuberculosis epidemic. The John F. Kennedy Drive winds on past the golf course to end at the 1902 Dutch Windmill, which once pumped water to the Strawberry Hill reservoir atop the Stow Lake island. The Beach Chalet on Great Highway was built in 1925 and its interior painted with murals during the Depression.

Return along Martin Luther King, Jr. Drive, starting with the 1905 Murphy Windmill, also built for the Strawberry Hill reservoir. The drive goes around the south side of Stow Lake and the north side of Strybing Arboretum before ending near the Children's Playground with its 1912 carousel. Built in 1888 the playground was the first ever in an American park.

Conservatory of Flowers

KITTI HOMME

The oldest building in the park was brought from Ireland for millionaire James Lick's San Jose property and was modeled on a greenhouse in London's Kew Gardens. When Lick died only a year later the greenhouse was still in its shipping crates and it was bought and assembled in Golden Gate Park in 1878. A fire caused severe damage in 1883 and the dome was rebuilt to a different design. The conservatory (☎ 666-7200) houses a steamy collection of tropical flora. It's open daily from 9 am to 5 pm and entry is $2.50.

California Academy of Sciences

This large natural history museum houses a variety of exhibits and many of them are real child pleasers, like the interactive tidepool. It's part of the **Steinhart Aquarium** which features a 180-foot-diameter fish roundabout and some very strange fish in the smaller tanks. The aquarium's seals and dolphins are fed Thursday to Tuesday, every two hours from 10:30 am; Wednesday, from 12:30 pm. The Life through Time exhibit traces the development of life on earth and has some superb dinosaur models. Wild California, with displays of Californian wildlife, is of special interest and the trippy shows at the

TONY WHEELER

Bronze Buddha in the Japanese Tea Garden

Morrison Planetarium are worth catching but the most earth-shaking exhibit is undoubtedly the earthquake platform where you watch an earthquake video while the ground rolls beneath your feet, simulating increasingly larger tremblors building up to the "Big One" of 1906.

The Academy (☎ 750-7145) has a shop and a cafe. It's open daily from 10 am to 5 pm (9 am to 6 pm from July 4 to Labor Day) and entry is $7/4.

M.H. de Young Memorial Museum

The museum building began as the Fine Arts Museum at the huge Midwinter Fair of 1894, a predecessor of modern World Fairs. The six-month-long fair attracted millions of visitors and was dominated by an Eiffel-like Electricity Tower but today the museum is one of the few surviving reminders. The museum has a fine collection of American art, much of it from the collection of Mr. & Mrs. John D. Rockefeller III. There are other exhibits of art from Africa, Oceania, and the Americas as well as an important textile collection.

The museum (☎ 863-3330) is open Tuesday to Sunday from 10 am to 5 pm and entry is $5/2. On the first Wednesday of each month the museum stays open until 8:45 pm and entry is free. Entry is also free on the first Saturday of each month from 10 am to noon.

Asian Art Museum

Adjacent to the M.H. de Young Museum, the Asian Art Museum (☎ 668-8921) houses the Avery Brundage Collection and other superb art from the Middle East, the Indian subcontinent, Southeast Asia, Tibet, China, Korea, and Japan. The collection is so extensive that less than 20% of it can be displayed at one time. Opening hours are the same as the M.H. de Young and entry is combined with that museum.

Japanese Tea Garden

Like the M.H. de Young Museum the popular Japanese gardens (☎ 666-7200) were originally built for the 1894 Midwinter Fair. The gardens feature a pagoda, gates, bridges, a variety of statues, and a nice little tea house where you can enjoy green tea and fortune cookies for $2. It's claimed fortune cookies were actually invented here, back in 1909.

The gardens have had an interesting and at times rather sad history. Makoto Hagiwara, who constructed the garden for the fair, lived in the garden until 1925, during which time he extended it from one to five acres. After his death the garden remained in the Hagiwara family's care until 1942, when anti-Japanese prejudice resulted in their eviction from the garden, the demolition of a number of structures, and even a name change to the "Oriental Tea Garden." Things gradually improved after the war; the original name was reinstated, the large 1790 bronze Buddha was installed, and in the early '50s a dry stone Zen Garden was added.

The gardens are open daily in summer from 9 am to 6:30 pm and in winter from 8:30 am to 6 pm. Entry is $2/1.

Park Gardens

There are a host of smaller parks and gardens within Golden Gate Park, and the **Strybing Arboretum & Botanical Gardens** (☎ 661-1316) in turn encompasses a number of smaller gardens within its 70 acres. They include a Garden of Fragrance with special appeal to the blind, the California Collection of Native Plants, and the Japanese Moon-Viewing Garden. Free tours of the Arboretum take place every day.

Behind the Academy of Science the 1928 Shakespeare Garden has 150-odd plants, all of which are featured in Shakespeare's writings. The Redwood Memorial Grove to the dead of the 1898 Spanish-American War and WWI also includes the WWI Doughboy memorial. There is also a Dahlia Dell, a Fuchsia Garden, a Rhododendron Dell, a Rose Garden, and beside the Dutch Windmill, the Queen Wilhelmina Tulip Garden.

Sporting Facilities

The park is packed with sporting facilities including 7½ miles of bicycle trails, many miles of jogging trails, and 12 miles of horse riding trails. Some of the park roads are closed to vehicles on Sundays to allow more space for cyclists, skateboarders, in-line skaters, joggers, and other forms of human-powered transport.

The park has an archery range, baseball and softball diamonds, fly-casting pools, a cramped nine-hole golf course, lawn bowling greens, horseshoe pitching and petanque courts, four soccer fields, and 21 tennis courts. Rowboats, pedal boats, and electric boats can be rented (☎ 752-0347) on Stow Lake for around $10 to $13 an hour. Model sailboats and power boats can be unleashed on Spreckels Lake.

THE SUNSET & TWIN PEAKS

South of Golden Gate Park, the city's hilly terrain makes two final skyward lunges at Twin Peaks and Mt. Sutro, then rolls westward in block after uniform block to the ocean. Originally known as El Pecho de la Chola, "The Breasts of the Indian Girl," the summit of the appropriately named 900-foot Twin Peaks is a superb viewpoint over the whole Bay Area, especially at night. Just northwest of Twin Peaks is Mt. Sutro (981 feet), topped by the triple-pronged antennae which broadcasts most of the city's TV and radio.

The area south of the park down to Sloat Blvd. and from about 16th Ave. to the ocean is known as the Sunset district, a mostly residential area filled with pastel-colored stucco homes built between the 1930s and 1950s. The Inner Sunset, centered around 9th Ave. at Irving and Judah Sts., has the most to offer, with a variety of ethnic restaurants and fun cafes only a block or two from Golden Gate Park.

Ocean Beach bounds the district to the west, and the San Francisco Zoo, Lake Merced, and Fort Funston all lie to the south.

Getting There & Away

The L and N streetcar lines will take you through the Sunset to the ocean and the L stops right by the zoo. Muni bus No. 71 starts from the Ferry Building, passes through the Haight-Ashbury and along Golden Gate Park and ends at the ocean.

Ocean Beach

Ocean Beach stretches for miles along the coast, from the Cliff House to the cliffs of Fort Funston. On sunny days you'll find a classic California beach scene, packed with sunbathers, surfers, and picnickers. Unfortunately, sunny days are few and far between. From June to September Ocean Beach is often covered by thick, cold fog or equally demoralizing coastal clouds and as a result tends to be deserted except for fisherfolk and wetsuit-clad surfers.

San Francisco Zoological Gardens

The zoo (☎ 753-7061), Sloat Blvd. and 45th Ave., is sandwiched between Lake Merced and the sea. Though not one of the country's best, there are some fine attractions, like the Primate Discovery Center and Gorilla World, one of the largest gorilla enclosures in the world. It's open daily from 10 am to 5 pm. Entry is $7/3, and free on the first Wednesday of the month.

Fort Funston

A mile south of the zoo, Fort Funston is a beautiful windswept area of cliffs, trails, and beach and a great place to spend an afternoon hang-gliding or, more likely, watching the hang-gliders float above the cliffs. To get there, just stay on Great Hwy past Lake Merced.

RON PICKUP

Ocean Beach: sunset in the Sunset

THE BAY

San Francisco is a contender for any "city by the bay" beauty contest but it's a curiously shy bay. The San Francisco Bay is not like Sydney Harbor, a living, breathing part of the city or even Hong Kong Harbor, a working part of a hard-working city. The San Francisco Bay always seems to be around the corner, glimpsed in the distance, seen from afar, spanned by bridges, and dotted with sails and fast-moving ferries.

The Bay is the largest on the California coast, stretching about 60 miles in length and up to 12 miles in width. It's fed by the Sacramento and San Joaquin Rivers and enters the sea through the Golden Gate. It is, however, very shallow, averaging only six to 10 feet in depth at low tide! In the pre-bridge ferry days the pier at Berkeley had to be built three miles out into the Bay in order to reach the 13-foot-deep water necessary for ferries to dock. There's a surprising amount of reclaimed land around the Bay, a practice that started with the 1849 Gold Rush when arriving ships were abandoned and their wreckage was added to landfills that extended the city shoreline. Its shallow waters means it's very easy to change Bay into land but since 1969 the Bay Conservation & Development Commission has put the brakes on further landfills.

Golden Gate Bridge

NIGEL FRENCH

Commenced in January 1933 and opened in May 1937, the beautiful Golden Gate Bridge (☎ 921-5858) links San Francisco with Marin County and, despite competition from modern constructions like the Transamerica Pyramid, remains the symbol of the city. The bridge is nearly two miles in length with a main span of 4200 feet. At the time of its completion, it was the longest suspension bridge in the world and the 746-foot suspension towers were higher than any construction west of New York City. A Depression-era project, the bridge tested engineering limits at the time with the tricky harbor currents causing special difficulties. Joseph B. Strauss, the bridge's builder, was a specialist in steel bridge design who built more than 400 all over the world. The bridge's name comes from the Golden Gate entrance to the harbor, but could just as easily have come from the "international

Death at the Golden Gate

Eleven men died during construction of the Golden Gate Bridge and it has continued to chalk up a steadily rising death list ever since: this is San Francisco's favorite suicide site. It's 220 feet down from the roadway to the water and if the impact doesn't kill you immediately you're likely to be so badly injured that drowning soon follows. Of course there have been survivors including an 18-year-old woman who jumped twice in 1988; she survived the first time but died on her second attempt two months later. At least one jumper wasn't a suicide: a German stunt man made the jump in 1980 intending to survive. He didn't.

Suicide victim number 1000 probably made the leap some time in 1995, but the count went quiet for a time as it approached that number, for fear there would be a rush to be the 1000th. Popular mythology relates that bridge suicides jump facing the city so San Francisco is their final sight, but as the pedestrian walkway is on the San Francisco-facing side, the explanation is likely much more mundane. ■

orange" paint scheme. Painting the bridge is a never-ending job and a team of 25 painters add another 1000 golden gallons every week.

A prime starting point for a bridge inspection is the Fort Point Lookout (☎ 556-1693), on Marine Drive at the southern end of the bridge. The lookout offers excellent views and has a gift center, a statue of Strauss, and a section of the three-foot-diameter suspension cable. Muni bus No. 29 runs to the lookout and to the Toll Plaza and No. 28 just to the Toll Plaza. Any Golden Gate Transit bus bound for Marin County stops at the Toll Plaza. There are even better views from the lookout at Vista Point, on the north side of the crossing since from there San Francisco forms part of the backdrop.

Unlike the Bay Bridge, it is possible to walk or cycle across the Golden Gate Bridge. From the Fort Point Lookout a pathway leads up to the toll plaza and then it's a couple of miles across to the other side. By bicycle simply follow the 49-Mile Drive signs along Lincoln Blvd. through the Presidio to the toll plaza. Normally there's a $3 toll for southbound (Marin to San Francisco) cars. During the morning and evening rush hours car pools (four occupants in the car) cross free. It's estimated that over 100,000 cars cross the bridge every day.

The Bay Bridge

The Bay Bridge, connecting San Francisco and Oakland, is five times as long as the Golden Gate Bridge, carries far more traffic and predates it by six months but it's never going to have the same iconic fame.

The Bay Bridge was built between April 1933 and November 1936 and actually consists of three separate parts: a double suspension bridge leads from San Francisco to the mid-Bay island of Yerba Buena; a tunnel then cuts straight through the rocky island; and a series of double-decked lattice work spans connect Yerba Buena Island to the Oakland side. The bridge is just over six miles long but the 1989 earthquake revealed that it was not 100% earthquake proof when a 50-foot top deck piece of the Yerba Buena-Oakland section slumped on to the lower deck, killing a motorist. Like the Golden Gate Bridge the San Francisco-Yerba Buena section is pinned on to solid rock but the Oakland side is based on bay bottom clay, not the best foundation when a tremblor comes along.

The best views are from the top deck (westbound to San Francisco) but the Bay Bridge does not offer wide open views like the Golden Gate. There's a $1 toll westbound. During the morning and evening rush hours a car with three occupants counts as a car pool and not only crosses free but also avoids the toll booth lines.

Treasure Island

The rock cut out from the Yerba Buena tunnel formed the basis of adjacent Treasure Island, halfway from San Francisco to Oakland. Named after the Robert Louis Stevenson novel, the island was the site of the International Golden Gate Exposition in 1939-40, celebrating the completion of the two bridges. The **Treasure Island Museum** (☎ 395-5067) in the Administration Building has relics of the exhibit, displays about the construction of the bridge and on the Pacific-crossing China Clipper flying boats.

The museum is at 410 Palm Ave., just inside the naval base, and is open weekdays from 10 am to 3:30 pm and on weekends from 10 am to 4:30 pm. Entry is $3. The naval base on Treasure Island is marked for closure which may leave the museum's survival in question.

Alcatraz

For 30 years from 1933 to 1963 the rocky island in the middle of San Francisco Bay was the most famous prison in the USA. The 12-acre island was named by Lieutenant Juan Manuel de Ayala, commander of the *San Carlos*, the first European vessel to enter the Bay, as Isla de Alcatraces (Isle of the Pelicans) and was uninhabited until a military fortification was begun in 1853 and a lighthouse was built in 1854. The current lighthouse dates

TONY WHEELER

Prisoners at Alcatraz enjoyed a breathtaking view of the Bay.

from 1909. During the Civil War the fort was used as a military prison.

Alcatraz became the prison of choice for serious offenders for a simple reason – "the Rock" was escape-proof. It's only 1½ miles from the island to the mainland but they're 1½ very cold miles and swept by the Bay's often ferocious currents, not to mention the occasional shark. There were no escapees known to reach land alive, though one escape was made famous by the Clint Eastwood movie *Escape from Alcatraz,* which tells the story of the Anglin brothers and Frank Morris who, indeed, floated away in a self-made raft, and were never seen again. Remarkably, Alcatraz was never packed to capacity; there were 450 cells but the population averaged 264 and only 1576 convicts were imprisoned there during the island's entire penal history.

After its closure, the island was more or less forgotten for six years and then taken over by Native Americans who conducted a protest sit-in from 1969 to 1971. Although the island has been a major tourist attraction since 1973, only basic repairs have been made to the prison buildings and discussion continues about the island's long-term future.

The tour points out the cells occupied by famous residents like Al Capone, "Machine Gun" Kelly, and Robert Stroud, the "birdman of Alcatraz." Stroud, who despite the movies was a thoroughly difficult person, spent most of his 17 years on the Rock in the unpleasant D-block solitary cells and was really the "birdman of Leavenworth," as he wasn't allowed to keep birds after he was transferred to the Rock in 1942.

Red & White Ferries (☎ 546-2896 for information,

546-2700 for tickets) run to the island from Pier 41 and it's wise to phone ahead and book or pick up tickets well in advance. There's an extra $2 charge for phone orders. The boats can be sold out days ahead during the summer. The pier booking office is open 8 am to 5 pm.

Departures to the island are 9:30 am to 2:45 pm on weekdays and until 2:15 pm on weekends. The roundtrip fare is $5.75/3.25 or for $9/4.50 an excellent audio tour is included. It features guards and inmates talking about their Alcatraz experiences and is well worth the cost. Tickets can also be booked through Ticketron (☎ 392-7469). The park ranger station (☎ 705-1042) has information on the island and its history.

Angel Island

Angel Island State Park (☎ 435-1915), the 750-acre island north of Alcatraz, is a popular place for walking, biking, picnics, and camping. There are 12 miles of roads and trails including a hike to the summit of 781-foot Mt. Livermore and a five-mile perimeter trail that offers a 360° panorama of the Bay. In Ayala Cove, the sheltered harbor on the Tiburon side of the island, a small beach backs up to grassy picnic lawns fringed by forest. A number of historical buildings are also found on the island: Camp Reynolds, on the western side, dates to the Civil War and Fort McDowell, and on the eastern side, to the Spanish-American War. The Immigration Station operated from 1910 to 1940 but this "Ellis Island of the West" was an even less welcoming place than its New York counterpart. During WWII it housed prisoners of war. These sites are open weekends and holidays from 11 am to 3:30 pm.

You can make camping reservations ($9 in summer, $7 off-season) through Destinet (☎ (800) 444-7275). Angel Island is accessible by the Red & White Fleet ferry from Fisherman's Wharf or by the Tiburon-Angel Island Ferry (☎ 435-2131) on the Tiburon peninsula. Bicycles are available to rent in Ayala Cove.

ACTIVITIES

San Franciscans are an energetic lot and there are plenty of opportunities to burn calories even within the city limits.

Bicycling

Those precipitous streets should shout that this is no bicycle riders' city. But even if you're not suicidally inspired (or a bike messenger), Golden Gate Park and the Presidio have great cycling potential, and the mountain bike *was* invented in Marin County. You can bike across the Golden Gate Bridge to the Headlands or transport your bike up to Mt. Tam, the Bay Area's supreme mountain biking challenge. Or, take your bike on the ferry to Tiburon and Angel Island.

For more about Bay Area biking get *Bay Area Bike Rides* by Ray Hosler (Chronicle Books, San Francisco, 1994) or *Cycling the San Francisco Bay Area: 30 Rides to Historic Sites & Scenic Places* by Carol O'Hare (Bicycle Books, Mill Valley, 1993). For the clearest evidence that this is a bicycling city, join Critical Mass on the last Friday of the month. See the Getting Around chapter for more on this inspired piece of urban guerrilla warfare.

Golf

There are three public golf courses in San Francisco; most have twilight fees if you're economizing. Harding Park (☎ 664-4690) at Harding and Skyline Blvds. near Lake Merced is a beautiful 18-hole course near the ocean and charges $26 on weekdays and $31 on weekends. Also on the site is the Jack Fleming nine-hole course which charges $13.

For spectacular views, the hilly, 18-hole Lincoln Park course (☎ 750-4653), 34th Ave. and Clement St., wraps around the California Palace of the Legion of Honor and runs along the coast west of the Golden Gate Bridge. Greens fees are $23 on weekdays and $27 on weekends and there's a par of 68.

Golden Gate Park has a challenging nine-hole, par 27 course (☎ 751-8987) near the beach at the Fulton St. and 47th Ave. entrance and charges $10 on weekdays and $13 on weekends.

Exciting news for golfers: in the summer of 1995, the Presidio Golf Course (☎ 561-4653) near the Presidio's Arguello Gate, opened to the public for the first time after a century of exclusive use by US military peronnel. Now operated by the National Park Service, this gorgeous course runs along the Bay and is considered one of the country's best. Greens fees are $35 on weekdays and $45 on weekends ($25 and $35 after 1 pm). Book far in advance.

There are two 18-hole championship courses in the East Bay with more reasonable greens fees ($14 weekdays, $18 weekends). These are the City of Alameda-Chuck Corica Golf Complex (☎ (510) 522-4321), at Island Drive and Clubhouse Memorial Drive, and Tilden Park Golf Course (☎ (510) 848-7373), in the Berkeley Hills off Grizzly Peak Drive.

Running & Skating

In San Francisco, Marina Green has a 2½-mile jogging track and fitness course and there are many running paths through Golden Gate Park. There are a couple of routes all the way from the Panhandle to the ocean, covering about three miles, and on Sundays motor vehicles are banned from most of the park. The Presidio is another great park running area with plenty of routes from the Marina right past the Golden Gate Bridge to Baker Beach.

The Bay to Breakers race (☎ 808-5000, ext 2222) in May is as much a festival as a run with tens of thousands of often wildly costumed participants making their way from the Embarcadero across the city to the ocean. In the grueling Dipsea (☎ 331-3550) in Marin County, runners take any route they choose over Mt. Tam from Mill Valley to Stinson Beach.

In-line skating is very popular in Golden Gate Park; you can rent skates at Skates on Haight (☎ 752-8376), 1818 Haight St., and cruise directly into the park.

Sailing & Windsurfing

Any view over the bay, dotted with sails, shows this is prime sailing country. It's not, however, the easiest stretch of water to sail on and much of the year the wind can be as chilly as the water. It's also extremely important to pay attention to the tides. If you go out in a small boat at ebb tide, you might just find yourself waving goodbye to San Francisco as you're sucked out to sea. The bay is at its best during the west winds of April to August.

A good place for sailing lessons is the Berkeley Marina with the Cal Sailing Club (☎ (510) 287-5905) or the Olympic Circle Sailing School (☎ (510) 843-4200), but Sausalito's Richardson Bay is a much more scenic option. Cass's Marina (☎ 332-6789), 1702 Bridgeway, is one of many places that offer lessons and rentals. In the city, Spinnaker Sailing (☎ 543-7333), Pier 40, offers lessons and charters boats.

The Bay has great windsurfing but can be difficult for beginners. The San Francisco School of Windsurfing (☎ 753-3235) offers lessons on Lake Merced and at Candlestick Park. Before venturing out on the Bay make sure you're up to it and seek local advice on winds and currents. Once you know what you're doing, Crissy Field in the Presidio, and Candlestick Park and Coyote Point south of the airport, are all good places to get out on the Bay, but none of them are kind to beginners. For begin-

TOM SMALLMAN

Golden Gate Park's JFK Drive is popular with skaters and cyclists on Sundays, when it is closed to traffic.

ners and intermediates, Larkspur Landing in Marin is a favorite spot, while in the East Bay, the Berkeley Marina is a popular launching place. Crown Beach, Alameda, on the bayside of downtown Oakland, is probably the easiest place to get on to the Bay and the prevailing westerlies blow you back on to shore, rather than out into trouble.

Swimming & Surfing

None of those sunny surf city and "California girl" visions apply to San Francisco. The waters around the Bay Area, bayside or oceanside, are cold and current-plagued. Swimming is often unsafe and never very pleasant. Walking, jogging, and sunbathing (nude at some spots) are the popular waterside activities.

There's a tiny patch of beach at Aquatic Park, just west of Fisherman's Wharf, and you even see the occasional hardy swimmer in the chilly waters. Baker Beach, the ocean beach immediately south of the Golden Gate Bridge, is strictly for spectators, walkers, and surf fishing. Nude sunbathers lay out at the northern (Presidio) end. There are great views from China Beach, at the southern end of Baker Beach, and more nudity at Land's End. Past Point Lobos is Ocean Beach, starting at Geary Blvd., north of Golden Gate Park, and heading south for four miles with surfers at the northern end and hang gliders at the south.

Ocean Beach is one of the most challenging and exhausting places to surf in California, especially in winter when the powerful, cold swells can reach 12 feet or more. There are no lifeguards and you should never surf alone or without at least a three-mm full-length wetsuit. For a recorded message of the latest surfing conditions at Ocean Beach call Wise Surfing at ☎ 665-9473.

Tennis

There are free public tennis courts all over San Francisco. The courts at Mission Dolores Park are popular; for others, call San Francisco Recreation & Park Department (☎ 753-7001). The 21 courts in Golden Gate Park charge a fee.

Walking Tours

San Francisco lays out a rich feast for those keen on doing their sightseeing on foot. The visitor information center caters to walkers with an excellent line of walking-tour leaflets to Chinatown, Fisherman's Wharf, North Beach, Pacific Heights, and Union Square.

If you'd rather have a local expert providing the guidance, there are plenty of those and their walks are as varied as the city. Chinatown is a walker's favorite, of course, and you can tag along on a Chinese Heritage Walk (Saturday afternoon, $15) or a Chinese Culinary Walk & Luncheon (Friday morning, $30) from the Chinese Culture Center (☎ 986-1822). Or, take a 2½- to 3½-hour Chinatown Adventure Tour with the Wok Wiz (☎ 355-9657) for $25 or $35 with lunch.

The Mission is great for walking, and especially for seeking out the district's many superb murals on a Mission District Mural Walk (☎ 285-2287). The Saturday afternoon walk lasts two hours and costs just $4 for adults. Want the inside line on San Francisco's gay mecca, the Castro? Then try Cruisin' the Castro (☎ 550-8110, preferably 5 to 8 pm) with local resident Trevor Hailey; her Tuesday to Saturday morning, 3½-hour walk costs $30 including brunch. Keen to relive the Summer of Love? Join a Flower Power Haight-Ashury Walking Tour (☎ 221-8442) to find the site of the Human Be-In, the Drugstore Cafe, and the Grateful Dead's house. The two-hour walk takes place Tuesday and Saturday mornings and costs $15.

Helen's Walk Tours (☎ (510) 524-4544) offer a variety of walks from two hours for $20 to a 3½-hour grand tour for $40. San Francisco Strolls (☎ 282-7924) also offer lots of possibilities including a Brothel Stroll and a Barbary

Coast Stroll; these 2½-hour perambulations cost $20. A two-hour Javawalk (☎ 673-9255) costs $15. That's just a small taste of walking possibilities. There are architectural walks around Pacific Heights (☎ 441-3004) and explorations of North Beach (☎ 648-8159). The Friends of the San Francisco Public Library (☎ 557-4266) offer an eclectic variety of free (donations accepted) walking tours led by savvy local historians. Some of their offerings are the Art Deco Marina tour, Victorian San Francisco, Cityscapes & Roof Gardens, and Coit Tower Murals.

Whale Watching

Mid-October through December is the peak season for whale watching in the Bay Area, as gray whales make their annual migration south from the Bering Sea to Baja California. It's the longest annual mammal migration in the world, and as the whales tend to cruise along the coastline, they're easy to spot from land. Point Reyes, to the north, is a prime whale-watching spot. The whales pass by on their way home in March, but are further from shore on the northward leg of the journey. Bay & Delta Charters (☎ 332-6811) runs all-day, naturalist-led whale-watching expeditions on weekends during both migration seasons. They depart from Sausalito for the Farallon Islands, 28 miles outside the Golden Gate. It's $59 per person (15% discount for three or more) and reservations are required.

Places to Stay

Deciding where you're going to stay in San Francisco is a two-part process: Where do you want to stay and what do you want to stay in? The decisions are interrelated; if you want a cheap motel or a romantic little B&B you're not going to end up in the Financial District, for example. Apart from the solitary RV park and the numerous backpacker hostels the categories that follow are divided up by area. Some are then subdivided; the Union Square area is subdivided by hotel price range for example. But first a brief description of accommodations possibilities:

Camping There's nowhere to camp in San Francisco proper; you have to head to Marin County, north of the Golden Gate, or down the coast towards Half Moon Bay, to find the nearest campsites. There is, however, an RV Park in SoMa, close to downtown.

Hostels A bed in a backpacker hostel typically costs $12 to $15 and may be in a dormitory (typically with four to eight beds) or a double room. The general standard of accommodations will usually be much better than cheap hotels.

Hotels There are cheap hotels in San Francisco but the cheapest places are no fun at all; if you're really economizing, you'll find the hostels are a much better bet. That said, there are some safe, comfortable hotels at $40 to $80 for a double room. Middle-range hotels run $80 to $200, and once you get over $200 a night, you're in the "top end" at the deluxe establishments with international reputations and very high standards.

Motels A city motel room typically costs $50 to $80. There are some convenient ones in SoMa, just a short stroll from Union Square. The big advantage is free parking – overnight parking in city garages can end up costing nearly as much as a room!

B&Bs San Francisco has lots of very comfortable and very romantic B&Bs with prices for two typically ranging from $80 to $150. Bed & Breakfast Reservations (☎ 696-1690, (800) 872-4500), P.O. Box 282910, San Francisco, CA 94128-2910, can make free bookings at B&Bs throughout California.

RV PARK

The *San Francisco RV Park* (☎ 986-8730, (800) 548-2425), 250 King St., is between 3rd and 4th Sts., three blocks south of I-80 and right by the CalTrain Station. There are 200 full hookup spaces to park your RV for $34 a night. The park has picnic tables and barbecues, showers, restrooms, and a convenience store.

HOSTELS

San Francisco has a surprising number of backpacker hostels. They're predominantly used by overseas visitors; some of the hostels actively discourage local users. Hostels usually offer kitchen and laundry facilities, a meeting room, a TV lounge, and other useful conveniences. Their noticeboards are inevitably great sources of local information and travel hints.

Hostelling International (HI) are the long-term survivors of the hostel business. You usually don't have to be an HI/AYH member to use their hostels although membership ($25 a year in the USA) does give you a discount and other advantages. Their main hostel in San Francisco is the largest and best-equipped hostel in the city and has a site five-star hotels would kill for. The *Hostel at Union Square* (☎ 788-5604) is at 312 Mason St., a stone's throw from **Union Square**, and has 230 beds divided between dorms and double rooms. The cost is $15 in the July-September peak season and usually $14 the rest of the year with HI/AYH membership (an extra $3 without). It's very well-equipped with a kitchen, lounges, a TV room, and laundry facilities and organizes lots of sightseeing and entertainment activities. To get there, take a No. 38 Geary bus from the Transbay or Greyhound Terminals. If you arrive by Amtrak take the free shuttle to the Ferry Building and a No. 5 or 21 bus up Market St.

Their second hostel, the *San Francisco International Hostel* (☎ 771-7277) trades downtown convenience for a pleasantly quiet setting in Building 240 at **Fort Mason** near Fisherman's Wharf. To get there take Muni bus No. 42 from the Transbay Terminal to the stop at Bay and Van Ness. Bus Nos. 30 and 47 also stop there. Nightly cost is $15 and $6.50 for kids; there's a 1 am curfew.

The other hostels are mainly downtown and all privately run although they operate in much the same fashion as the two HI/AYH hostels. There are other hostels apart from the following ones listed but these are the best in the city at press time.

Globetrotters Inn (☎ 346-5786), 225 Ellis St. at Mason in

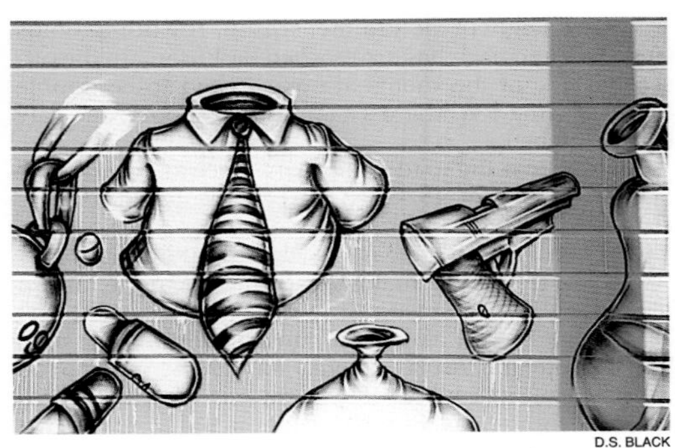

D.S. BLACK

"Grafitti art is one of the last forms of free expression." – artist "Twist"

the Union Square/**Tenderloin** area, is just around the corner from the HI hostel. Accommodations in this smaller hostel are either in dorms for four or in double rooms and cost $12 per night or $75 a week. In the fuzzy zone where **Chinatown** fades into the Financial District, the *Pacific Tradewinds Guest House* (☎ 433-7970), 680 Sacramento St., is the smallest of the city hostels with room for just 28 people, all in dorms. This friendly 4th-floor hostel has a kitchen and guest room and offers free tea or coffee all day. Rates are $14 or seven nights for the price of six (if paid in advance).

Move over towards **North Beach** and the medium-size *Green Tortoise Hostel* (☎ 834-1000) is at 494 Broadway. Run by the same people who run those funky buses, the hostel has beds in dorms for two to six at $14 or some single rooms at $20 and double rooms at $32. There's a free breakfast and kitchen and laundry facilities.

Near the **Civic Center** the *Grand Central Hostel* (☎ 703-9988), 1412 Market St., is one of the city's largest hostels with beds ($12) for over 200, or singles/doubles at $20/30 and the location is quite convenient.

There are three hostels in **SoMa**, two small and one large, great for nightclubbers yet generally pretty quiet. The big one is the *Globe Hostel* (☎ 431-0540), at 10 Hallam Place; the hostel is actually right on Folsom between 7th and 8th but the entrance is on this small side street. Well-run and gregarious, it's set in a surprisingly quiet location. It's for "international travelers" only, which doesn't necessarily exclude Americans; US citizens must, however, show a passport or other proof of international travel intentions. There's room for about 150 people at $12 a bed but the cost increases to as much as

$15 at the height of the summer season. The dorm rooms sleep five and each has an attached bathroom. In the off-season, five of the rooms are rearranged to be double rooms costing $36. There's a laundry, TV room, and cafe but no kitchen.

Right across the road is the *San Francisco International Student Center* (☎ 487-1463), 1188 Folsom St. There's room for around 50 people in dorms for three to five. Nightly cost is $12, increasing a bit at the summer peak. There are tea/coffee-making facilities, a fridge, and a microwave. The *European Guest House* (☎ 861-6634) is at 761 Minna St., an alley that runs parallel to Mission, between 8th and 9th Sts. There's room here for about 70 people, some in double rooms, others in dorms for three or four. Nightly cost in the summer is $14 and there's a TV room, kitchen, and laundry facilities.

HOTELS, MOTELS, & B&BS

Union Square

Cheaper overnight parking downtown can be found at the parking garage at 123 O'Farrell St. (☎ 986-4800) (6 pm to 8 am for $5) or by the day at the garage at 5th and Mission (☎ 982-8522), that charges $12 for 24 hours.

Bottom End The area to the west of Union Square has San Francisco's greatest density of hotels and among the five-star luxury and middle-range hotels are some real bargains.

The *Dakota Hotel* (☎ 931-7475), 606 Post St., is a small 42-room hotel from the 1920s. There's a TV, microwave, and refrigerator in every room and local phone calls are free but the rooms are sometimes a little threadbare. At $50 to $60 a night and just two blocks from Union Square, it's hard to complain.

Just south of Post St., the *Adelaide Inn* (☎ 441-2261), 5 Isadora Duncan Court, off Taylor, also aims to appeal to foreign visitors with singles from $35 to $40 and doubles from $45 to $50, depending on the room size and demand. All rooms share bathrooms but there's a continental breakfast included.

The name may conjure up visions of '70s sitcoms but *Brady Acres* (☎ 929-8033, (800) 627-2396), at 649 Jones St., just off Geary, is a friendly little 25-room establishment with singles at $50 to $55 and doubles at $60 to $65. They also have seven nights for the price of six specials. It's a great value as each room has its own bathroom, a mini-kitchen, and local telephone calls are free, and there are laundry facilities. Phone ahead as the office is open limited hours.

The 46-room Victorian-style *Pensione International* (☎ 775-3344), at 875 Post St. between Hyde and Leavenworth, has rooms from $30 to $50 with shared bathroom and $40 to $75 with private bathroom, all including a continental breakfast. A block north at 620 Sutter St., the *Sheehan Hotel* (☎ 775-6500, (800) 848-1529) has 64 rooms. Including continental breakfast, a room costs $40 to $60 or $50 to $80 with a private bathroom. Larger rooms are $75 to $100. The building used to be a YMCA and as a result has good fitness facilities and an indoor swimming pool, unique among the city's lower-priced hotels.

Further down Sutter St., the *Beresford Manor* (☎ 673-3330, (800) 533-6533), 860 Sutter, is the most affordable of the three Beresford properties in the area, and specializes in long-term accommodations for foreign students. Rates by the night are $50/60 with a shared bath and $60/70 with a private bath. By the week, you pay $200/280 with a shared bath and $300/380 with a private bath.

The *Grant Hotel* (☎ 421-7540, (800) 522-0979), 753 Bush St., is on the way up Nob Hill and equidistant between Union Square and Chinatown. It's another basic low-priced hotel offering clean, simple accommodations at $45 for singles and $49 to $57 for doubles and twins, all with attached bathrooms. Almost next door, the *Golden Gate Hotel* (☎ 392-3702), 775 Bush St., has rooms at $59 or $89 with attached bathroom. The very much no-frills *Amsterdam Hotel* (☎ 673-3277, (800) 637-3444), 749 Taylor St., is between Bush and Sutter, on the way up Nob Hill. It's in the same category and popular with international visitors with rooms at $50/60 or with attached bathroom at $65/75.

Finally, further along at 1040 Bush St., between Jones and Leavenworth, the *Mary Elizabeth Inn* (☎ 673-6768) is a women-only establishment run by the United Methodist Church. There are 86 rooms with shared bathrooms for $45 a day including two meals, and a weekly rate of $147.

The *Hyde Plaza Hotel* (☎ 885-2987), 835 Hyde St. near Sutter, is west of Union Square, a region where Nob Hill starts to descend into the Tenderloin and sometimes referred to as the "tender nob." The less-than-wonderful location is balanced by basic but clean standards and the very reasonable prices; doubles without bath can be $35 or even less. At 520 Jones St., near O'Farrell, the *Pacific Bay Inn* (☎ 673-0234, (800) 343-0880) has had a recent renovation and has rooms with attached bathroom at $50.

A block south of Union Square the *Herbert Hotel* (☎ 362-1600), 161 Powell St., is about as cheap as they come with rooms at around $35 to $40 (less without private bathroom) although most are let out for longer periods. The big Parc 55 Hotel more or less encircles the *Olympic Hotel* (☎ 982-5010), 140 Mason St. near Hallidie Plaza. Popular with the internationally impecunious, the rooms are spartan but in reasonable condition and cost from $30 without bath and $45 with bath. There are other very cheap hotels in the Tenderloin but this is not an area where visitors are likely to feel comfortable, no matter how tight their budget.

Middle Post St. runs across the north side of Union Square while Geary St. runs across the south side, and there are many excellent middle-range hotels in the blocks to the west of the square. Starting along Geary St., just one block brings you to the older *Raphael Hotel* (☎ 986-2000, (800) 821-5343), at 386 Geary St., which claims to be San Francisco's "elegant little hotel," with 152 rooms. Some of the standard sized rooms at $99/109 are perhaps a little on the cramped side of standard; larger rooms are $109/119 and $124/134. Equally convenient at 440 Geary St., the *Diva Hotel* (☎ 885-0200, (800) 553-1900) is cleanly modern in the glass, chrome, and black enamel style. There are 108 rooms (each with a VCR) from $115 to $150 including continental breakfast delivered to your room.

Just a few steps from Union Square along Post St., *The Inn at Union Square* (☎ 397-3510, (800) 288-4346), at 440 Post St., has 30 elegantly old-fashioned rooms and suites from $130 to $190. The inn is a nonsmoking hotel and rates include a continental breakfast served on each floor, and afternoon tea and wine. In the next block, the *Savoy Hotel* (☎ 441-2700), 580 Geary St., is an excellent value for $100 to $140, with a homey style and afternoon tea and sherry; a continental breakfast is included in the price.

The *Beresford Arms Hotel* (☎ 673-2600, (800) 533-6533), 701 Post St., is a well-kept older hotel with some very spacious rooms, some of them with kitchens. You can breakfast on coffee and doughnuts or pastries in the lobby in the morning and there's wine in the afternoon. It's a great value with 90 rooms from $90/100. One block north at 635 Sutter St. is its sister establishment, the *Beresford Hotel* (☎ 673 9900, (800) 533-6533) with 114 rooms from $90/100.

Continue three blocks further west to the Art Deco *York Hotel* (☎ 885-6800), at 940 Sutter St. There are 96 rooms from $95 to $110 in this rather elegant hotel which was used for the stairway scenes in Hitchcock's *Vertigo*. Backtrack towards the center and the *Cartwright Hotel* (☎ 421-2865, (800) 227-3844), 524 Sutter St., is a good value at $110 with excellent service and a convenient location only a block from Union Square.

The *White Swan Inn* (☎ 775-1755), 845 Bush St., is half hotel, half B&B. There are just 26 spacious and well-equipped rooms at $145 to $165 and a nice combination of hotel service and B&B atmosphere. The breakfast room opens out onto a small garden. The nearby *Petite Auberge* (☎ 928-6000), 863 Bush St., is under the same management and offers similar facilities and an even more overly romantic look.

Only a few steps from the entrance to Chinatown and an easy stroll from Union Square the *Triton Hotel* (☎ 394-0500, (800) 433-6611), 342 Grant Ave., is notable for its 140 exotically designed guestrooms. The hotel lobby, is a hint of what is to come and Deadheads might even care to try the Jerry Garcia suite. Complimentary morning coffee and evening wine is served in the lobby and the popular Cafe de la Presse and Aioli restaurant are part of the hotel. Rooms range from $105 to $175.

Top End The *Westin St. Francis Hotel* (☎ 397-7000, (800) 228-3000), 335 Powell St. on Union Square, is one of the city's most famous hotels. Occupying the entire west side of Union Square, it was built just before the 1906 earthquake and burned out by the post-quake fire. The St. Francis was completely rebuilt and more recently a tower was erected behind the original hotel, bringing the room count up to 1300. A standard room rates $170 to $265/295 for a deluxe single/double. Prices skyrocket for their range of suites.

The *Grand Hyatt on Union Square* (☎ 398-1234, (800) 233-1234) is on the north side of the square at 345 Stockton St. There are 693 rooms at $215 to $250 for singles and $240 to $275 for doubles. Right across the road, the *Campton Place Kempinski Hotel* (☎ 781-5555), 340 Stockton St., is a small and serene hotel which makes a special effort to appeal to businesswomen. There are 117 rooms from $195 to $330 and an attached well-regarded restaurant.

The *Sir Francis Drake Hotel* (☎ 392-7755, (800) 227-5480), 450 Powell St. at Sutter, is an opulently decorated luxury hotel with beefeater-costumed doormen to add even more pomp and circumstance. The lowest rates are $129 to $189 for rooms and $350 to $650 for suites. The *Clift Hotel* (☎ 775-4700, (800) 437-4824), 495 Geary St. at Taylor, is another favorite with the rich and famous, and is known for its stand-out service. Room rates start at $225; suites range from $375 to $675.

There are a number of upper-bracket hotels around the theater district, just southwest of the square. The *Hotel Nikko* (☎ 394-1111), 222 Mason St. at O'Farrell, has singles at $185 to $245 and doubles at $215 to $275. The name reflects this very modern establishment's Japanese flavor and this is one of the limited number of San Francisco hotels with an indoor swimming pool. A block west of Union Square at 500 Post St., the *Pan Pacific Hotel* (☎ 771-8600, (800) 327-8585) has 330 stylish rooms starting from $205/225 for superior (that's the basic level!) rooms, moving up through $225/275 (deluxe) and $305/325 (luxury) before you start talking about suites.

Civic Center & Tenderloin

The *Inn at the Opera* (☎ 863-8400, (800) 325-2708), 333 Fulton St. at Franklin, is right behind the Opera House and Symphony Hall and used to be the place where visiting opera singers stayed. Now it's a small boutique hotel with 48 rooms from $125 to $200 including a continental breakfast.

The *Central YMCA Hotel* (☎ 885-0460), 220 Golden Gate Ave. at Leavenworth, is not the best address in town, on the Tenderloin side of the Civic Center, but it offers simple, clean rooms with shared bathroom facilities for $28/38 for men and women. The Y's fitness facilities are available for residents and coffee and muffins are provided in the morning; students with ISIC get a discount.

At 601 Eddy St. and Larkin, the *Phoenix Motel* (☎ 776-1380) is not the place to consider a stroll around at night, but this recycled motel is a wonderful fantasy. Close your eyes and you can really imagine that the hotel is just off Miami or Waikiki Beach. The presence of the popular Caribbean restaurant Miss Pearl's Jam House only adds to the mood. The lobby has a great collection of movies featuring San Francisco and a second collection of "rock band on the road" movies, reflecting that the Phoenix has become a favorite resting place for visiting bands. Free parking and a continental breakfast make the rooms at $89 to $99 a great value. There's also a *Day's Inn* (☎ 441-8220) at 895 Geary St. at Larkin, with rooms at $75 to $95. This motel's free parking and proximity to downtown make it a good value.

SoMa

South of Market has a variet of accommodation options, from a trio of youth hostels (see Hostels) to a pair of top-notch luxury hotels. There are also middle range hotels and a small enclave of motels along 17th St which are a great value if you want a reasonable hotel close to downtown that offers free parking. Shuttle bus services are often provided by these motels to Union Square.

Bottom End In the small 7th St. motel enclave the *Hotel Britton* (☎ 621-7001), 112 7th St., has 79 rooms at $49 to $62 for singles and $54 to $67 for doubles.

Mosser's Victorian Hotel (☎ 986-4400, (800) 227-3804), 54 4th St. off Market St., is just across the street from the big Marriott Hotel and has simple rooms from $60 for singles.

There are also a number of good values along Market St. towards the Civic Center. The *Aida Hotel* (☎ 863-4141, (800) 863-2432) is at 1087 Market St. between 6th and 7th. It's neat and tidy and an excellent value with 174 rooms at $30/35 for singles/doubles with attached bathroom. There are some very spacious rooms for $45 and a continental breakfast is included. The *Pensione San Francisco* (☎ 864-1271), 1668 Market St., is a pleasant little place with rooms with shared bath at $42 to $45 for singles and $52 to $55 for doubles, all including continental breakfast.

Middle The *Best Western Americania* (☎ 626-0200, (800) 444-5816), 121 7th St., has 143 standard motel-style rooms from $70 to $120. There's a pool, sauna, and restaurant. Across the road is the *Best Western Carriage Inn* (☎ 552-8600, (800) 444-5817), 140 7th St., a smaller motel with 48 rooms varying in price throughout the year from $80 to $110, including a continental breakfast. Again, there's a pool.

The *Griffon Hotel* (☎ 495-2100, (800) 321-2201) has a great location at 155 Steuart St. at the waterfront, close to the Embarcadero Center and the Ferry Building. The 59 rooms are modern, well-designed and comfortable and cost from $145 to $175 and include a light breakfast. Downstairs there's the popular Rôti Restaurant and there's an adjoining fitness center.

The adjacent *Harbor Court Hotel* (☎ 882-1300, (800) 346-0555), 165 Steuart St., is a larger establishment with 130 rooms at $155 to $170. Rooms looking out over the harbor offer some of the best views in the city. There's a pool and health club facilities available to guests at the adjacent YMCA. Harry Denton's Restaurant is part of the hotel.

Top End One of San Francisco's most famous and elegant hotels, the *Sheraton Palace Hotel* (☎ 392-8600, (800) 325-3535), 2 New Montgomery St. at Market, was the ultimate in luxury when it opened in 1875. It was rebuilt after the post-earthquake fire destroyed it in 1906 and has recently undergone a major renovation. The central Garden Court is worth seeing even if you don't stay here. There are 550 rooms from $235/255 to $295/315 plus a range of suites. The hotel has a pool and health club.

TONY WHEELER

Often referred to as the "giant jukebox of the city", the Marriott towers over SoMa.

The *San Francisco Marriott* (☎ 896-1600), at 55 4th St., looks across Yerba Buena Gardens. It isn't old and no one has ever called it elegant – in fact, most liken it to a jukebox. One thing for sure: missable it is not! Whatever the virtues of its architecture, the Marriott is big and brash with 1500 rooms at $150 on weekdays and $215 to $240 on weekends.

Financial District

Bottom End A cheap night in the Financial District is a pretty remote possibility. Apart from a popular backpacker hostel (see the Hostels section), however, there is a fairly spartan but very economically priced and quite respectable hotel right across from the Bank of America. The *Temple Hotel* (☎ 781-2565), 469 Pine St. between Montgomery and Kearny, has 88 rooms at $30/35 for singles/doubles without attached bathroom and $40/45 with bathroom. There are discounts for stays of three days or more.

Top End The *Mandarin Oriental San Francisco* (☎ 885-0999, (800) 622-0404), 222 Sansome St., has 158 rooms from the 38th to 48th floors of the third-highest building in the city. The views are obviously spectacular (even from the bathtubs) and the rooms have every luxury and cost $275 to $395; weekend rates from $170 to $300 are sometimes available.

The *Hyatt Regency* (☎ 788-1234, (800) 233-1234), 5 Embarcadero Center, is probably San Francisco's most architecturally memorable hotel: with its backward leaning 20-story atrium, it gave Mel Brooks vertigo in his film *High Anxiety*. If you can stand the heights, the 800 rooms are $195 to $215 for singles and $220 to $245 for doubles. There are also business rooms with a fax and other amenities for an extra $15, or you can get a second room for children at a 50% discount. There's a second, less exotic, Financial District Hyatt, the *Park Hyatt* (☎ 392-1234, (800) 233-1234), at 333 Battery St. This very business-like hotel has 360 rooms at $245 to $270 during the week and $170 on weekends.

Chinatown

Bottom End The *YMCA Chinatown* (☎ 982-4412), 855 Sacramento St., just steps away from busy Grant Ave., only takes men, requires reservations well in advance, and the office is only open from 6:30 am to 4:30 pm. If you can surmount those hurdles, rooms are $28/38 with the seventh night free. The female alternative is the *Gum Moon Women's Residence* (☎ 421-8827), 940 Washington St. at Stockton. Similar obstacles must be dealt with and rooms are $20 to $25.

The *Grant Plaza* (☎ 434-3883, (800) 472-6899), 465 Grant Ave. at Pine, has a real Chinatown feel, just a block from the Chinatown gateway and the California St. cable car. It's neat and tidy, the rooms have attached bathrooms, and singles are $39 to $42 and doubles and twins are $47 to $73.

The *Astoria Hotel* (☎ 434-8889), 510 Bush St. at Grant, is right by the Chinatown gates but only a couple of blocks from Union Square. It's a very simple, very Chinese hotel with basic rooms for less than $40 with shared bathroom, and around $60 with a private bathroom. The *Obrero Hotel* (☎ 989-3960), 1208 Stockton St., between Pacific and Broadway, on the border between Chinatown and North Beach, has just 12 rooms with shared bathrooms and rock-bottom prices of $40 to $50.

Middle The *Holiday Inn Financial District* (☎ 433-6600), 750 Kearny St., is also known as the Chinatown Holiday Inn since it's linked with Portsmouth Square by a pedestrian bridge. It's one of the city's least favorite architectural creations and has 566 rooms at $120 to $170, although there are regular special deals available. There's also a swimming pool.

North Beach

There's not much right in North Beach although Fisherman's Wharf and Chinatown are both nearby. The *Washington Square Inn* (☎ 981-4220, (800) 388-0220), 1660 Stockton St., right on the square, has 15 rooms. A handful of them have shared bathrooms and cost $85 to $95; with a private bathroom they're $95 to $165, or $180 if you opt for a park view. Parking in this area can be difficult.

There's also a newly refurbished, absolutely grand small hotel in the heart of North Beach, *Hotel Bohème* (☎ 433-9111), 444 Columbus Ave. The decor is heavy into that gangster-era/Naked Lunch/Beat Generation chic – very American, very stylized, and, at $95 to $115, a hell of a lot cheaper than most of the hotels in the area.

Nob Hill

Middle The *Nob Hill Lambourne* (☎ 433-2287, (800) 275-8466), 725 Pine St., is an interesting smaller establishment best described as a boutique business hotel. The rooms each have a computer, fax, and voice mail facilities, and cost from $125 for standard rooms to $199. The hotel is conveniently central and near Union Square, Chinatown, and the Financial District.

The *Nob Hill Inn* (☎ 673-6080), 1000 Pine St. at Taylor, is a pleasant 21-room hotel with prices from $90 to $200. Continental breakfast is included and some of the rooms have kitchen facilities.

Top End Nob Hill is topped by four of the city's oldest and classiest hotels; another old establishment, although only recently converted to a hotel, is on the final stretch to the top of the hill. The *Fairmont Hotel* (☎ 772-5000, (800) 527-4727), 950 Mason St., has rooms in the main building at $190 to $220 and in the tower at $250 to $300. The hotel's bars and restaurants include the New Orleans Room for jazz and the amazing Tonga Room Restaurant & Hurricane Bar complete with thunder, rain, and other special effects, all of which seem quite out of place in such discreet surroundings.

The *Huntington Hotel* (☎ 474-5400) at 1075 California St. is another of Nob Hill's seductively smooth, old-school hotels. There are just 140 rooms, 40 of them with separate parlors, at $170 to $220 for singles and $185 to $235 for doubles. The *Stouffer Stanford Court Hotel* (☎ 989-3500, (800) 622-0957), 905 California St. at Powell, is noted for the Tiffany-style glass dome over the lobby. There are 393 rooms at $205/235 up to $295/325.

The *Mark Hopkins Inter-Continental* (☎ 392-3434, (800)

327-0200), at 999 California, or as they prefer to put it "1 Nob Hill," is also right up there in price. The 390 rooms range from $190 to $270 and then up to the suites. The Top of the Mark cocktail lounge is renowned for its superb views over the Bay. The recently opened *Ritz-Carlton San Francisco* (☎ 296-7465), 600 Stockton St. at California, is on the way up Nob Hill and set in a palace-like 1909 building with a swimming pool. There are 336 rooms starting at $240, then $285 for superior rooms, $325 for deluxe rooms, and then prices head up towards the stratosphere.

Fisherman's Wharf

Only the Union Square area downtown has more big hotels than Fisherman's Wharf and this is where you'll find all the standard mid-range hotel names from Holiday Inn to Travelodge. Package tours often put their groups in these hotels.

The standard Fisherman's Wharf places include the *Travelodge* (☎ 392-6700), 250 Beach St., with rooms at $100 to $225. The *Wharf Inn* (☎ 673-7411), 2601 Mason St. at Beach, has seasonal prices ranging from $118 to $128. The big 524-room *Sheraton at Fisherman's Wharf* (☎ 362-5500), at 2500 Mason St., between Beach and North Point, has rooms at $180 to $190. Fisherman's Wharf also has a Marriott, a Holiday Inn, a Howard Johnson, a Hyatt, and a Ramada.

There are some places that break out of the cookie cutter mold like the pleasantly old-fashioned *San Remo Hotel* (☎ 776-8688, (800) 352-7366), at 2237 Mason St. between Chestnut and Francisco. Built in 1906, right after the quake, the hotel has recently been refurbished with individually decorated rooms, none of them with private bathroom facilities. Conveniently close to the Wharf, without being submerged in the tourist crush, singles are $35 to $55 and doubles are $55 to $75.

The *Tuscan Inn* (☎ 561-1100, (800) 648-4246), 425 Northpoint St. and Mason, is a luxurious hotel which is actually larger (220 rooms) than it looks and feels. There's complimentary tea and coffee in the lobby in the morning and wine in the afternoon. Costs range from $120 in the low season to $145 in the high season.

Hyde Park Suites (☎ 771-0200), 2655 Hyde St. on the corner of North Point, has 24 one and two bedroom suites, each with a full kitchen. Complimentary wine is served in the courtyard atrium in the afternoons and a continental breakfast is offered in the morning. Rooms are typically $165 to $190 but special prices are sometimes offered and this is a great place for families.

Pier 39 has an unusual variation on the B&B theme. *Dockside Boat & Bed* (☎ 392-5526) has a number of boats moored in the marina where you can have a double room for the night for $95 to $225 on weekdays and $125 to $275 on weekends – and get a wake-up call from the resident sea lions. Their office is at the C Dock on Pier 39.

The Marina

This is the real motel quarter of San Francisco. After you cross the Golden Gate Bridge from Marin, Hwy 101 becomes Lombard St. packed wall-to-wall with motels, gas stations, and fast fooderies. Turn right onto Van Ness Ave. and there are more of them. With coupons, many of these motels have rooms at $45 or less. Motels along the first stretch of Lombard are only a block south of trendy Chestnut St. in the Marina, overflowing with restaurants.

From the west there's the *Marina Motel* (☎ 921-9406, (800) 346-6118), at 2576 Lombard St.; an *Econo Lodge* (☎ 921-2505), at No. 2505, with a swimming pool; a *Ramada Limited* (☎ 775-8116), at No. 1940; and the *Rodeway Inn* (☎ 673-0691), at No.1450: all have rooms at less than $50. The *Van Ness Motel* (☎ 776-3220, (800) 422-0372), at 2850 Van Ness Ave., between Lombard and Chestnut has a quieter location than right on the highway. There are 42 rooms in this reasonably priced, basic motel; with coupons the price can be as low as $44.

Turn down Van Ness Ave. to find more motels, generally at slightly higher prices. They include the *Comfort Inn by the Bay* (☎ 928-5000, (800) 424-6423), 2775 Van Ness Ave., which has rooms from $70 to $130 depending on the time of year.

Pacific Heights

Pacific Heights has a scattering of pleasant places, including some fine B&Bs. Just off Union St. in a quiet dead-end street, the *Bed & Breakfast Inn* (☎ 921-9784), at 4 Charlton Court, is nicely furnished with some quite romantic rooms. Prices bounce up on Friday and Saturday and drop back the rest of the week, but typically cost $70 to $90 for rooms with shared bathrooms and $115 to $140 with attached bathrooms; there's also a more expensive suite. The only drawbacks to this pleasant establishment is that the breakfast is rather humdrum and they don't take credit cards.

A block south of Union St. at 2160 Green St., *Sherman House* (☎ 563-3600) is one of the most luxurious small hotels in the city with just 14 rooms in an elegant 1876

TONY WHEELER

Nob Hill's four-star Fairmont Hotel

building refurbished with all the latest modern conveniences. Some rooms have bay views – one even has a rooftop deck – and costs range from $250 to a whopping $825 a night.

The *Mansions Hotel* (☎ 929-9444), 2220 Sacramento St., is a curious place, resolutely, almost mustily, old-fashioned with a resident ghost, all sorts of curious display cases full of odds and ends, a large collection of Benjamino Bufano sculptures, and pricey rooms at $130 to $350. There's also an excellent breakfast.

The 1903 Edwardian *El Drisco Hotel* (☎ 346-2880), 2901 Pacific Ave., is in a great spot with views of the city and the Bay. No-view rooms are as low as $65; with a view, rooms are $85 and suites are $125 to $150.

Japantown

Japantown has two hotels with confusingly similar names. The *Best Western Miyako Inn* (☎ 921-4000), 1800 Sutter St., on the corner of Buchanan, adds Japanese trimmings to the Best Western formula in a comfortable hotel with rooms at $81/91. At the eastern end of the Japan Center complex, the larger and more expensive *Miyako Hotel* (☎ 922-3200), 1625 Post St., is a deluxe hotel designed with shoji screens on the windows and deep Japanese bathtubs in the bathrooms, complete with instructions on how to use them. The nightly cost is $120 to $150 for singles and $150 to $170 for doubles.

A couple of blocks east of Japantown, the *Majestic Hotel* (☎ 441-1100, (800) 869-8966), 1500 Sutter St. at Gough, survived the 1906 earthquake and despite lavish restorations retains its antique feel. The 60 rooms cost $125 to $160. Down the block at Octavia, the *Queen Anne Hotel* (☎ 441-2828, (800) 227-3970), 1590 Sutter St., is one of the most elegant B&Bs in the city, a fine 1890 building with 49 rooms and suites. They range from $99 to $120 for the standard rooms, $140 to $150 for the deluxe rooms, and $175 to $275 for the suites. A continental breakfast is included, as well as sherry and cookies in the afternoon.

Haight-Ashbury

The Haight, with its many fine old Victorian houses, has a number of interesting B&Bs and one cheaper alternative. The *Metro Hotel* (☎ 861-5364), 319 Divisadero St. between Oak and Page, is on the edge of the Lower Haight, an area very slowly on its way up in the world. The Metro offers cheap and clean rooms with attached bathroom from $45 to $55 and off-street parking just around the corner.

The *Stanyan Park Hotel* (☎ 751-1000), 750 Stanyan St., is right by Golden Gate Park, a block south of Haight St. This larger hotel in a fine old Victorian building has 36 rooms from $78 to $96 plus more expensive suites. Continental breakfast is included. Park in a well-lit area at night.

The *Red Victorian B&B* (☎ 864-1978), 1665 Haight St., offers a wonderful opportunity to relive the Summer of Love. Outside, Haight St. may be a long way from the swinging '60s but inside you can choose from the Flower Child Room, the Sunshine Room, the Rainbow Room, the Peace Room, or even the Summer of Love Room. Rates for two people range from $76 to $200; 11 of the 18 rooms are $86 or $96. Single rates are also available and a

Gay & Lesbian Accommodations

These days, most hotels are not likely to be too worried about the sexual inclinations of their guests but in San Francisco some places go out of their way to make same-sex couples welcome, and by extension, heteros not so welcome! The Castro not only has leather bars it even has a leather B&B, the *Black Stallion* (☎ 863-0131), 635 Castro St., a black-painted Victorian offering clothing optional accommodations for gay men from around $75. The *Willows Inn* (☎ 431-4770), 710 14th St., just off Market, is a 12-room B&B with shared bathrooms.

House O' Chicks (☎ 861-9849), 2162 15th St. in the Castro, offers cozy accommodations for lesbians. The two rooms are in a private home and cost $50 for single occupancy and $75 for a double. During gay celebrations such as Gay Pride week, rooms are $100.

Finding a place to stay around the Castro can be difficult and/or more expensive around the end of June (during the Gay & Lesbian Freedom Day Parade) and at Halloween. ■

complimentary continental breakfast is served in the Gallery of Meditative Art downstairs. Only the four most expensive rooms, from $120, have attached bathrooms but the Love, Starlight, Infinity, and Aquarium bathrooms are just as unique as the rooms. Every guest will want to visit the Aquarium bathroom to see if flushing the toilet will really send the goldfish, happily swimming around in the transparent toilet tank, down the gurgler.

Other B&Bs in the Haight area include the *Victorian Inn on the Park* (☎ 931-1830, (800) 435-1967), 301 Lyon St. at Fell, on the north side of the Panhandle. There are 12 rooms, all with attached bathrooms, costing from around $100 to $150. *Spencer House* (☎ 626-9205), 1080 Haight St., is just east of Buena Vista Park. The house is a superb 1887 Queen Anne Victorian mansion with six elegant guest rooms from $100 to $160. Remember the Panhandle and Buena Vista Park are not places to cruise at night.

Alamo Square, north of the Lower Haight towards Japantown, is famous for its postcard appearances, juxtaposing colorful Victorians with the city skyline. The *Alamo Square Inn* (☎ 922-2055), 719 Scott St., occupies a pair of Victorian mansions with rooms at $85 to $135. There's afternoon wine, a full breakfast, and free off-street parking. The *Archbishop's Mansion* (☎ 563-7872), 1000 Fulton St. on Alamo Square, was indeed built, back in 1904, for the city's archbishop. There are 15 rooms, all with private bathrooms, at $120 to $200, and limited off-street parking.

The Castro

There are several places to stay in the Castro, if you want to be near the gay epicenter of the city. The *Twin Peaks Hotel* (☎ 621-9467), 2160 Market St., is a basic and simple place, not notable in any way, with singles/doubles at $35/38 or at $45/50 if you want an attached bathroom. Next door, the *Perramont Hotel* (☎ 863-3222), 2162 Market St., is even cheaper with rooms at $35 a night. Continue another block south to *Beck's Motor Lodge* (☎ 621-8212), 2222 Market St., a bland motel with 57 rooms at $77 to $99 depending on the number of people, the number of beds, and the time of year.

The Mission

The Mission is a popular place to wander and admire the murals and a great place for a cheap south-of-the-border meal, but it's not a good spot for cheap accommodations. In general, cheap hotels in the Mission are places you'd rather not know about. There are, however, a couple of upscale exceptions.

The *Inn San Francisco* (☎ 641-0188), 943 South Van Ness Ave., is one of the nicest B&Bs around, housed in a fine old 1872 mansion. Rooms range from $75 to $105 for the "cozy rooms," $125 to $145 for the "spacious rooms," and $165 to $195 for the "deluxe rooms" with hot tub, spa, or fireplace. There's also an outdoor hot tub and a rooftop sundeck. Phone ahead to inquire about directions and parking.

The *Dolores Park Inn* (☎ 861-9335), 3641 17th St. at Dolores, is a small B&B between the Mission Dolores and Mission Dolores Park. There are just six rooms (only two of them with private bathrooms) but it's a relaxed, good-value spot with doubles from $75 to $160 and a pleasant garden.

San Francisco Airport

If you need to stay near the airport there are lots of possibilities along Hwy 101, from Burlingame to South San Francisco. There are direct-dial phones to many of these hotels in the baggage claim area and free shuttle buses pick up and drop off outside the terminals. There are more than 20 hotels around the airport so competition is fierce. Coupons and special deals bring many of the airport-area motels down to less than $50. For families, the Crown Sterling Suites hotels are a particularly good value.

Right at the airport, beside Hwy 101, the *San Francisco Airport Hilton* (☎ 589-0770) has 530 rooms at $140 to $180.

There's a swimming pool and if you simply want a meal before a flight, the restaurant is excellent.

Millbrae, just south of the airport, has a half dozen places, several of them with rooms in the $50 to $70 range including the *Clarion Hotel* (☎ 692-6363, (800) 391-9644), at 401 East Millbrae Ave. Burlingame is immediately south of Millbrae with more hotels from a Days Inn to a Hyatt and the all-suite *Crown Sterling Suites* (☎ 342-4600), at 150 Anza Blvd.; exit at Broadway-Burlingame. The 340 suites cost $109.

South San Francisco, just north of the airport, has plenty more including a Best Western and Days Inn. There's another *Crown Sterling Suites* (☎ 589-3400), at 250 Gateway Blvd., with 313 rooms at $93.

LONG-TERM ACCOMMODATIONS

Many cheaper places around the city offer good deals in weekly and monthly rates. Brady Acres (see Union Square) is a good example. Other central places with long-term possibilities include the *Beresford Manor* (☎ 673-3330, (800) 533-6533), 860 Sutter St., where weekly rates range from $200 to $380 and the *Harcourt Residence Club* (☎ 673-7720), 1105 Larkin St. at Sutter, west of downtown. It offers budget-priced, long-term accommodations from $130 a week (shared bathrooms) to $200 (private bathroom) and includes two meals daily. The guests are a mix of international travelers and students. The *San Francisco Residence Club* (☎ 421-2220), 851 California St., near Stockton St. atop Nob Hill, has short-term accommodations ($40 / 60 a day) but essentially it's intended for longer term visitors.

Scan the ads in the *San Francisco Chronicle* or the *San Francisco Bay Guardian* for longer term rentals. If you're planning on staying for a few months, subletting an apartment or room in the neighborhood of your choice is a good way to go. Both newspapers also list sublets.

There are a number of roommate referral services; check in the papers and under Roommate Assistance Services in the Yellow Pages. Some are neighborhood-specific and some are city-wide, and all charge a membership fee.

Places to Eat

With more restaurants per capita than any other city in the USA, San Francisco can conjure up just about every cuisine known to the world. There are a number of distinct regions for food-lovers to sample. Chinatown is, of course, the center for all the variations of Chinese cooking; North Beach is the Italian quarter; the Mission is the place for Mexican and other Latin American dishes; Japantown has some great sushi bars. Elsewhere, the ravenous can track down Afghan, Burmese, Cambodian, Creole, Cajun, Ethiopian, Filipino, French, Greek, Indian, Korean, Lebanese, Moroccan, Spanish, Thai, Turkish, and more, including of course the Bay Area's invention: California cuisine, where *fresh*, *light*, and *creative* are the key words.

San Francisco has a plethora of cutting-edge restaurants, where California cuisine gets a real run and celebrity chefs are *de rigueur*.

UNION SQUARE

Despite its limited choices for budget and moderate meals, the area around Union Square does offer three of the finest four-star dining experiences in the city: Postrio, Masa's and Fleur de Lys.

Budget Places to grab breakfast around Union Square include *Sears Fine Foods* (☎ 986-1160), at 439 Powell St., just north of Union Square. You may have to join a line for the Swedish pancakes or French toast at this popular establishment but it usually moves fast. Another city institution, a block north, is a new branch of *Lori's Diner* (☎ 981-1950), 500 Sutter St. at Powell; the original (☎ 392-8646) is at 336 Mason St. at Geary. *Yakety Yak* (☎ 885-6908), 679 Sutter St., is a curiously displaced coffeehouse, looking almost too funky and laid-back for its near-Union Square location.

At 352 Grant Ave., on the corner of Bush and right across from the Chinatown Gate, the *Cafe de la Presse* (☎ 398-2680) includes an international selection of magazines and books with breakfast dishes and sandwiches and burgers in the $7.50 to $9 range. *Franciscan Croissants* (☎ 398-8276), 301 Sutter St. on the corner of Grant, is a cozy little city center breakfast spot. A few doors down, the *San Francisco Health Food Store* (☎ 392-8477), 333 Sutter St., is like something out of the 1950s. It serves

International Post St.

The two blocks of Post St. from Taylor to Leavenworth, starting just three blocks west of Union Square, have an interesting enclave of Asian restaurants. The *China Moon Cafe* (☎ 775-4789), 639 Post St, is a modern, distinctly untraditional, Chinese restaurant which tackles Chinese food with a wholly modern perspective, in an equally modern-looking space.

Despite the mildly provocative name, the *Thai Stick* (☎ 928-7730), 698 Post St., on the corner of Jones, cooks up good basic Thai food. Cross Taylor St. to find the moderately-priced Indonesia restaurant *Borobudur* (☎ 775-1512), 700 Post St., named after the famous Javanese Buddhist temple. Finally, there's *Burma's House* (☎ 775-1156), 720 Post St., one of the city's handful of Burmese restaurants. Not that Burma has the world's most interesting cuisine but how often do you get to try it? ■

health food items and some of the best shakes ($3) around at an old-fashioned soda counter.

At lunchtime, Maiden Lane, that upscale shopping street right off Union Square, becomes the place to eat when traffic is banned and tables are put out in the street. *Mocca* (☎ 956-1188), at 175 Maiden Lane, does fancy sandwiches from $7 to $9 or try the *Nosheria* (☎ 398-3557), at 69 Maiden Lane, for more big sandwiches and strong coffee.

At 474 Geary St., *David's Delicatessen* (☎ 771-1600) is another city stalwart, noted for hefty, deli-style sandwiches. It's a good thing they're so big because they're not low-priced. At 750 Market St., on the corner with Grant and O'Farrell, *Eppler's* (☎ 392-0101), is a big bakery where you can start the day quickly and cheaply.

Food courts, with a variety of food possibilities around a common seating area, can be found in the bottom level of the *San Francisco Shopping Center* at 865 Market St. Or head for *City Eats* (☎ 393-1505), the food center on the 3rd floor of the Crocker Galleria, the shopping center between Sutter and Post, just east of Kearny.

Middle Range *Milano's Italian Kitchen* (☎ 291-8022), 341 Sutter St., is just a block from Union Square and has pizzas at $7 to $9 and pastas at $8 to $10. It's a standard place but it turns out well-prepared food and is a good choice in its handy location. A block east is the cozy little *Cafe Claude* (☎ 392-3505), 7 Claude Lane, between Sutter and Bush just west of Kearny. The menu is served French bistro-style and it's busy for breakfast, lunch, and dinner, Monday to Saturday. If it looks authentically Parisian it's because the owner stripped out a Paris bistro for it! *Anjou* (☎ 392-5373), 44 Campton Place, is a small,

PHILLIP COBLENTZ

Blow your budget at a ritzy Union Square restaurant.

moderately pricey little bistro just off Union Square with a regularly changing menu.

Looking for the latest Hard Rock? Check out the overzealous *Planet Hollywood* (☎ 421-7827) at 2 Stockton St., on the corner of Market St. There's loud music and cinema paraphernalia for tourists who really wish they were in Los Angeles but got stuck up north. The best bet is to experience it with a "specialty drink," about $6 to $8.

South of Union Square at 63 Ellis St., *John's Grill* (☎ 986-3274) has been operating since 1908 and plays up its Dashiell Hammett connections. Just a few steps from Union Square at 333 Geary St., *Lefty O'Doul's* (☎ 982-8900) does big, cheap meals like spaghetti with meat sauce, salad, and bread. The food's nothing special but the prices are encouragingly low. *Ten Thousand Buddhas* (☎ 928-2178), 610 Geary St. at Jones, prepares vegetarian Chinese-Buddhist food.

Fine Dining *Postrio* (☎ 776-7825), 545 Post St., is one of the city's prime exponents of California cuisine, as dreamed up by Wolfgang Puck, another of the West Coast's celebrity chefs. It can be hard to get reservations although it's worth trying.

Masa's (☎ 989-7154), 648 Bush St., is considered by many to be the finest restaurant in the city, and one of the finest French restaurants in the country. Chef Julian Serrano changes the menu daily, always including such haute cuisine items as foie gras, caviar, lobster, and truffles. Choose between two fixed-price menus, four courses for $68 per person, or the seven-course menu for $75, not including beverages. *Fleur de Lys* (☎ 673-7779), 777 Sutter St., is the city's other renowned French restaurant, with chef Hubert Kelly at the helm creating memorable and original dishes. The service is impeccable and the food incredible; you'll feel understandably pampered.

Teatime

Remarkably, despite the coffee craze, tea has also had a resurgence in San Francisco and a number of the ritziest hotels put on equally ritzy afternoon teas. The *Garden Court* (☎ 546-5011), in the Sheraton Palace Hotel, 2 New Montgomery St. at Market, may well be the ritziest; the full English experience, served Wednesday to Sunday from 2 to 4:30 pm, costs $15.95. The garden setting alone, complete with chandeliers and a glass ceiling, makes it worth considering.

On Union Square, or more correctly above Union Square, the *Rotunda* (☎ 362-4777), in the Neiman-Marcus department store, 150 Stockton St., does afternoon tea from 3 to 5 pm. Cross the square to the *Compass Rose* at the Westin St. Francis Hotel (☎ 774-0167), 335 Powell St., where tea is served, with musical accompaniment, from 3 to 5 pm. Close to the square, the *Campton Place Kempinski Hotel* (☎ 781-5555), 340 Stockton St., puts out the cucumber sandwiches from 2:30 to 4:30 pm.

The very ritzy *Ritz-Carlton* (☎ 296-7465), 600 Stockton St., also does very traditional English-style afternoon teas though often with some unusual variations. A classical pianist adds to the mood. Also on Nob Hill, the *Lower Lounge* at the Mark Hopkins Inter-Continental (☎ 392-3434), 999 California St., presents a pleasantly old-fashioned teatime (fruit cake and scones of course) from 2:30 to 5:30 pm. Ditto at the *Fairmont Hotel* (☎ 772-5000), 950 Mason St., where $14.50 buys enough sandwiches, pastries, and cookies to feed two.

Finally, for an open-air tea, travel west to the *Japanese Tea Garden* (☎ 752-1171) in Golden Gate Park. This is the cheapest tea you'll find at just $2 including fortune cookies, although you'll also have to pay $2 to enter the gardens. They're open daily in summer from 9 am to 6:30 pm and in winter from 8:30 am to 5:30 pm. ■

TONY WHEELER

The Palace Hotel's Garden Court is the place to satisfy that cucumber sandwich craving.

CIVIC CENTER

The Civic Center is a curious zone where San Francisco at its glossiest gets entangled with San Francisco at its worst, where opera-going crowds find themselves sharing the sidewalk with the homeless. The restaurants in this area are an equally curious blend: McDonalds and the famous Stars are almost side by side.

Just off Van Ness near the Civic Center, *Stars* (☎ 861-7827) has a front entrance at 150 Redwood Alley and a back one at 555 Golden Gate Ave. This is one of San Francisco's cutting-edge dining establishments, owned by celebrity chef Jeremiah Towers. Despite the culinary reputation (the food really is fantastic) and the prices (most main courses run from $21) this is not at all a formal place. It's a big, relaxed, stylish place, decorated with French posters. A block away, at 500 Van Ness Ave. on the corner of McAllister, *Stars Cafe* provides similar food at lower prices.

At the glossy *Max's Opera Cafe* (☎ 771-7301), 601 Van Ness Ave., right next to A Clean Well-Lighted Place for Books, the food is basic American, the servings are on the large side of big, the clientele mainly of the opera/symphony/ballet set, and the waitstaff sings for you!

Hayes Valley

The three blocks of Hayes St. between Franklin and Laguna, just west of Van Ness Ave., is a small neighborhood of shops, coffeehouses, galleries, and some good restaurants. The adjacent blocks of Market St., just to the south, are also considered Hayes Valley.

The *Hayes St. Grill* (☎ 863-5545), at 324 Hayes St. between Franklin and Gough, does upscale fish & chips like mahi mahi, tuna, swordfish, or ono for $17 to $18, followed by great desserts. Hidden away in an alley behind the Hayes St. Grill is *Vicolo Pizzeria* (☎ 863-2382), 201 Ivy St., which does designer-pizzas for the pre- and post-opera crowd. *Geva's Caribbean Cuisine* (☎ 863-1220), 482 Hayes St., is the slightly pricey Jamaican restaurant up the street where Caribbean food gets a health-conscious California twist, and it's served in elegant surroundings.

Caffe Delle Stelle (☎ 252-1110), 330 Gough St., is a reasonably priced ($8 to $11 for an entree), always-packed trattoria with simple, pleasant decor and ultra-friendly service. Aside from the delicious food, it's little things like the baskets of fresh, herbed bread with dipping sauce, the pitchers of mineral water on every table, and the restaurant's own wine label that set it apart.

The *Zuni Cafe* (☎ 552-2522), 1658 Market St., does southwestern food with a distinctly Californian touch. It's relentlessly trendy and the service and food can be up some nights and down on others but it's a great place to see and be seen. If you can't get a table and have to join the line of people waiting, don't worry; the bar is an equally popular meeting place. Right around the corner and also chic, *Floogie's Swamp Cafe* (☎ 864-3700), 1686 Market St., serves enormous platters of jazzy Cajun specialties with baskets of fresh cornbread and a variety of New Orleans beers. It's not the place for light eaters or vegetarians, and only the mighty will have room for bread pudding at the end of the meal.

The Tenderloin & Van Ness Ave.

Miss Pearl's Jam House (☎ 775-5267), in the popular Phoenix Motel at 601 Eddy St., brings Caribbean rhythms to the Civic Center / Tenderloin border region. It may not be the nicest area of San Francisco but the restaurant is fun and the food is delicious. Miss Pearl's is closed Mondays. On weekends, tables are set up around the motel pool.

Maharani (☎ 775-1988), 1122 Post St. between Van Ness and Polk, has especially good vegetarian specialties and it's very popular with the local Indian clientele – always a good sign. The tandoori dishes are terrific and when they say hot they mean it. For big meat eaters *Kublai Khan's Restaurant* (☎ 885-1378) at 1160 Polk St., has a $4.50 lunch or $6.95 dinner special. Load up your bowl with food, hand it to the chef who cooks it on a large grill, and walk away well-fed.

A block east of Polk is Larkin and *Brother Juniper's Restaurant* (☎ 771-8929), 1065 Sutter St. near Larkin, is one of the best breakfast spots in the city, with great breads and hearty organic food. It's open for lunch and dinner but closed on Sunday. Several blocks up from the Tenderloin at 1517 Polk St., between California and Sacramento, the *Swan Oyster Depot* (☎ 673-1101) serves beer, clam chowder, and sourdough bread for one of the best cheap meals in the city. It closes at 5:30 pm and all day on Sunday.

Hard Rock Cafe (☎ 885-1699), 1699 Van Ness Ave. at Sacramento, can be raucously noisy and over-energetic but it's open until all hours and the food (burgers, fries, shakes) is not a bad value. A few blocks south on Van Ness, the muralled *Tommy's Joynt* (☎ 775-4216), at the corner of Van Ness and Geary, has reasonably priced soups, stews (buffalo stew is the specialty), and an amazing list of sandwiches on superb sourdough rolls. The bar at this San Francisco institution has an equally amazing variety of beers from all over the world.

Head north to 2211 Van Ness Ave., between Broadway and Vallejo, where the *Golden Turtle* (☎ 441-4419) is reputed to have some of the best Vietnamese food in the city.

SOMA

SoMa is becoming more and more popular as a place to eat with restaurants popping up around Yerba Buena Gardens and others scattered throughout the area. A major advantage for drivers is that parking in SoMa is relatively easy at any time of day.

Budget The new SFMOMA on 3rd St. opposite Yerba Buena Gardens has the very Californian and very pleasant *Caffe Museo* (☎ 357-4500). It's open every day, including for an early breakfast on weekdays. Right in the gardens there's a branch of the popular *Pasqua Coffee Bars* with good coffee and great sandwiches.

Cafe do Brasil (☎ 626-6432), 104 7th St., close to Mission St. in the SoMa motel enclave, is a good place for breakfast or for a meal of Brazilian-style tapas. *Caffe Centro* (☎ 882-1500) is a popular little cafe at 102 South Park, that curiously London-like little patch of green just south of I-80.

For great Vietnamese food at ridiculously low prices, brave the dismally seedy neighborhood to find *Tu Lan* (☎ 626-0927), 8 6th St. at Market. Once you're inside, the atmosphere is warm and friendly. Some of the best dishes are vegetarian and there's a diner-style bar where you can watch the food being prepared at breakneck speed. It's closed Sundays.

Middle Range Several places compete for the "best burger in San Francisco" award and *Hamburger Mary's* (☎ 626-5767), 1582 Folsom St., is certainly a contender. It's a traditional noisy bar-and-diner, with burgers and sandwiches in the $6 to $8 bracket. The customers – bikers to business suits, punks to party-goers – are often as interesting as the food. Burgers and fries are also the mainstay at *Eddie Rickenbacker's* (☎ 543-3498), at 133 2nd St., south of Mission. The decor is as important as the food and you'll see a biplane hovering overhead, motorcycles flying through the air, and even an elevated model train set. It's closed Sundays.

Icon Byte Bar & Grill (☎ 861-2983) at the corner of 9th and Folsom Sts., a few blocks away from the Folsom scene, is a good restaurant and features some eclectic

JOHN ZEGART

Sipping lattes and taking in the view at Yerba Buena

local artwork. If you get a drink or a meal you can log onto their one computer and send email to your friends.

For dim sum, *Yank Sing* (☎ 541-4949), at 49 Stevenson Place, is just off Market St., between 1st and 2nd Sts. In the curious enclave of South Park the *South Park Cafe* (☎ 495-7275), 108 South Park, has a very French flavor, terrific French fries, and reasonable prices. The *Delancey Street Restaurant* (☎ 512-5179), 600 Embarcadero, has a pleasant bayside location in the shadow of the Bay Bridge and serves an interesting menu combining Mexican, Thai, Caribbean, and Cajun influences, all at reasonable prices; desserts are big.

There are some large and very popular Mexican restaurants just west of Yerba Buena Gardens. *Chevy's* (☎ 543-8060), 150 4th St., is a middle-of-the-road but high-standard Mexican eatery. They do great fajitas and their margaritas come by the pitcher. Somewhat hidden behind Chevy's is the *Cadillac Bar & Grill* (☎ 543-8226), at 325 Minna St. Head west for more Mexican food at

¡Wa-Ha-Ka! – Oaxaca Mexican Restaurant (☎ 861-1410), 1489 Folsom St. at 11th, but bring cash because they don't take credit cards.

The hard-to-find *Mission Rock Resort* (☎ 621-5538), at 817 China Basin at Mariposa, is the place for a waterfront breakfast or lunch, particularly if it's a sunny day and you can sit outside looking over the busy waterfront. At night and on weekends it's a popular bar. At *Ruby's* (☎ 541-0795), at 489 3rd St., you can't miss the huge tomato hanging out front. Inside there's big sandwiches, a so-so Caesar salad and, most importantly, knockout pizzas.

Fine Dining *Lulu* (☎ 495-5775), 816 Folsom St. at 4th, near the Moscone Center, is a modern, spacious restaurant which is currently one of the hot places to eat. It's actually three restaurants in one: Lulu is the main dining room, *Lulu Bis* is a smaller room serving a fixed price menu, and *Lulu Cafe* is good for drinks, snacks, and the raw bar. A few blocks further down, *Julie's Supper Club* (☎ 861-0707), 1123 Folsom St., has an interesting and varied menu at reasonable prices. Combined with somewhat unusual decor and live jazz on the weekends, it's one of SoMa's more popular restaurants. At 570 4th St., south of I-80, *Fringale* (☎ 543-0573) is a popular Basque bistro, crowded and noisy and a surprisingly good value for the money. It's closed on Monday.

Smoking

California is the world-center for making smokers feel uncomfortable and the Bay Area has paved the way for many anti-smoking laws. Cinemas and theaters are nonsmoking and restaurants have pretty much banned smoking altogether. Bars still allow fumes, but rumor has it this may be legislated away as well. ■

Very south of Market in China Basin is *42°* (☎ 777-5558), 235 16th St. at Illinois, serving tasty and diverse Mediterranean cuisine on the haute healthy side, with a number of vegetarian alternatives. There's live jazz and a late happy hour popular with the singles crowd. It's open daily for lunch from 11 am to 3 pm and for dinner Wednesday to Saturday from 7 pm to midnight.

FINANCIAL DISTRICT

Although the Financial District dies at night there are a surprising number of interesting dinner places around its border with the waterfront or North Beach. Plan ahead on Sunday when many places will be closed.

Budget & Middle Range Trinity Lane, between Bush and Sutter near Montgomery, is a popular place for a quick sandwich at *Kelly's* (☎ 362-4454) or a delicious frozen yogurt at *Caffe Ambrosia* (☎ 362-0538). Belden Lane between Bush and Pine near Kearny is the business favorite for more leisurely lunches. The string of restaurants includes the excellent Italian *Cafe Tiramisu* (☎ 421-7044), the Mediterranean *Cafe 52* (☎ 433-5200), *Vic's Place* (☎ 981-5222), *Cafe Bastille* (☎ 986-5673), with excellent French dishes, and the more economical *Belden Park Taquería* (☎ 989-9750).

Palio Paninoteca (☎ 362-6900), 505 Montgomery St. at Commercial, is a cafe – serving excellent coffee and focaccia sandwiches – run by the same owners of the swish (and very expensive) Palio d'Asti Restaurant. *Gourmet Burritos* (☎ 989-8077), 359 Kearny St. at Pine, does terrific burritos like Cajun chicken with prawns or sweet & hot duck.

Despite the intense competition a few blocks away in Chinatown, local food buffs claim *Yank Sing* (☎ 781-1111), 427 Battery St., has the best dim sum this side of Hong Kong. Rival foodies claim *Harbor Village* (☎ 781-8833), 4 Embarcadero Center, should be the winner. Mainly a lunchtime treat, dim sum for Sunday brunch is hugely popular (see Chinatown). At night Harbor Village metamorphoses into a more upscale establishment.

At 240 California St., right in the high-rise heart of the Financial District, the clubby but charming *Tadich Grill* (☎ 391-1849) is the oldest restaurant in San Francisco, and serves fabulous Mediterranean-style seafood (the cioppino is an experience not to be missed). Reservations are not taken, so come early if you don't want to wait long for a table; if you do have to wait, the bar is a great place to do it.

Along the Embarcadero, the very popular *Fog City Diner* (☎ 982-2000) looks like a traditional diner viewed through rose-colored glasses. The menu is on the pricey side of "diner," but the food is excellent and there's a wide variety of wines by the glass at $4.50 to $6. If you haven't made reservations, the wait can be long. Nearby is *Il Fornaio* (☎ 986-0100), in Levi's Plaza at 1265 Battery St. It's big and bright with average Italian food at reasonable prices and a good wine list.

Fine Dining The very "in" seafood restaurant *Aqua* (☎ 956-9662), 252 California St., is cool and modern with pricey, contemporary French and American dishes. More reasonably priced, *Sol y Luna* (☎ 296-8696), 475 Sacramento St. between Battery and Sansome, is a Spanish *tapas* restaurant. Tapas are hearty snacks or appetizers that you continue to order until you've had enough.

Reservations are a good idea at another neighborhood institution, the rather conservative and stuffy *Jack's* (☎ 421-7355), at 615 Sacramento St. While the food is as straightforward as the ambience, for power-lunchers this is still a powerful downtown spot. Jack's is closed on Sunday. You can also rub shoulders with the high fliers at the sky-high *Carnelian Room* (☎ 433-7500), on the 52nd floor of the Bank of America Building, 555 California St. The prices are as high as the location, the view is absolutely tremendous, and men are required to wear a jacket (tie is optional). It's open for cocktails from 4 pm, dinner from 6 pm, and Sunday brunch at 10 am.

In the fuzzy zone around Jackson Square, where the Financial District meets North Beach and Chinatown, the *Cypress Club* (☎ 296-8555), 500 Jackson St. near Montgomery, looks like it was designed by an architect moonlighting as a cartoonist. Bulbous columns, strange parachute-like lights hanging from above, and a shocking orange-and-gold color scheme all distract you from noticing that the prices are definitely steep (entrees on the high side of $20) but thankfully the food is as good as the design is weird. This is definitely a restaurant you won't forget. Nearby *Bix* (☎ 433-6300), at 56 Gold St. in Jackson Square, is a very popular and very luxurious-looking place with a mezzanine level. The prices are comparable to the Cypress Club but instead of futuristic, the style is a contrived old-fashioned look. These are two of the best dining experiences in the city.

Splendido (☎ 986-3222), on the Promenade Level of 4 Embarcadero Center, juxtaposes a rustically Mediterranean feel with its very modern Embarcadero Center setting and the see-it-all-happen open kitchen. It's a big place but the inventive food (main courses at $14 to $20) and great desserts make it a good spot for a night out. Move north along the Embarcadero to *Square One* (☎ 788 1110), 190 Pacific Ave. Mall, opposite Sydney Walton Square. California cuisine meets Mediterranean in this creative, imaginative, and, naturally, expensive restaurant.

Chef Bradley Ogden's *One Market* (☎ 777-5577) at 1 Market St. offers a fresh, seasonal menu, a fine wine list, and an array of creative side dishes, accompanied by jazz piano in the evenings; the Sunday brunch is also dynamite. Happy hour is from 5 to 7 pm on weeknights, when oysters and microbrewed beers are just $1 each.

CHINATOWN

Not surprisingly, Chinatown is packed with Chinese restaurants from tiny hole-in-the-wall places with cheap eats, to cavernous but equally economical dim sum restaurants, to pricey restaurants serving the latest Chinese haute cuisine.

Budget *Feng Haung Pastry Shop* (☎ 421-7885), 761 Jackson St., and *Garden Bakery* (☎ 397-5838), 777 Jackson St, offer traditional Chinese pastries where you can sit down and enjoy a pastry with a piping-hot cup of tea.

The line stretching outside confirms that the *House of Nanking* (☎ 421-1429), 919 Kearny St., is doing something right, although the breathless guidebook raves probably help. A couple of doors away at 925 Kearny St., *Chef Jia's* (☎ 398-1626) also turns out excellent Chinese food in hefty quantities. The *R&G Lounge* (☎ 982-7877), 631 Kearny St., serves beautifully prepared Cantonese food at low prices. The decor may be no more exciting than any other Chinatown dive but the upstairs dining room is a favorite haunt of local Chinese VIPs and visiting Hong Kong suits.

Other cheap Chinatown restaurants include *The Pot Sticker* (☎ 397-9985), 150 Waverley Place, with some of the best pot stickers (steamed or fried dumplings) in the city. The wonderfully named *New Woey Loey Goey Cafe* (☎ 399-0733), 699 Jackson St., is a popular basement restaurant that serves food at bargain-basement prices. In contrast, you have to make your way through the kitchen and proceed upstairs to feast at the long-running *Sam Wo's* (☎ 982-0596), at 813 Washington St. Sam Wo's was a favorite of the Beat writers but, curiously, it was the rudeness of the waiters rather than the quality of the food that made it so popular! Sam Wo's is a hot spot for past-midnight refueling: it's open until 7 am.

Middle Range The *Lotus Garden* (☎ 397-0707), upstairs at 532 Grant Ave., is a Chinese vegetarian restaurant with a Taoist temple above it. *Brandy Ho's* (☎ 788-7527) at 217 Columbus Ave., and the newer branch, at 450 Broadway (☎ 362-6268), are popular restaurants with food from the Hunan region. That means lots of hot red peppers but they're gracious about taking back too-spicy dishes if you ask. Two blocks off the crowded Chinatown main drag, the *Lichee Gardens* (☎ 397-2290), at 1416 Powell St., is a family-style Chinese restaurant where the crispy Peking spareribs are a must.

Fine Dining With its displays of Han Dynasty art, superb food, and prices to match the *Empress of China* (☎ 434-1345), 838 Grant Ave., is a complete contrast to Chinatown's cheap dives. If you want Chinese food at its best, then this is a place to try.

Dim Sum

For the cautious newcomer tasting unknown cuisines, *dim sum* is one of the easiest possible introductions. San Francisco rivals Hong Kong in dim sum restaurants, which are also known as *yum cha* or "drink tea," because they originated from tea houses. Chinese businessmen used to spend so many hours in tea houses – they virtually served as extensions of their offices – that the tea houses began serving snacks and lunch. Waiters roll carts among the crowds of hungry diners; on the carts are the dim sum, small individual plates of delicacies, many of them cooked in pastry. You simply select the plates you like from the passing carts. Traditionally the bill was tabulated by counting the number of empty plates on the table, but they generally keep better track now. A group is really required to tackle dim sum since you want to try as many different dishes as possible.

The *New Asia* (☎ 391-6666), 772 Pacific Ave., is a typical, big, open, noisy dim sum place with all the architectural style of an aircraft hangar. Some of the city's most popular dim sum eateries are not in Chinatown. Head towards the Financial District to find *Yank Sing*, just on the other side of the Transamerica Pyramid, or towards the Embarcadero to *Harbor Village*. There's a second *Yank Sing* in SoMa. See the appropriate sections for more details.

Jackson St. between Grant and Stockton is home to several dim sum factories that offer take-out dim sum for about 40¢ a piece. *Yung Kee Rice Noodle Co.*, 732 Jackson St., is popular with the locals. Check out the buns steaming in the back of this cramped and narrow store and ask the staff to show you what types of fillings the different buns contain. Other factories include *Delicious Dim Sum* (☎ 731-0721), 752 Jackson St., and *House of Dim Sum* (☎ 399-0888), 735 Jackon St. ■

Tommy Toy's (☎ 397-4888), 655 Montgomery St., is as much in the Financial District as Chinatown but whatever the location the elegant decor matches the equally elegant food which manages to bring a French flavor to Chinese cuisine. The service is excellent, the prices are sky-high, and reservations are a must.

NORTH BEACH

The transition from Chinatown to North Beach is a curious one. Columbus Ave. is clearly the demarcation line but while no Chinese restaurants creep north of the line, the odd Italian restaurant does trickle over to the south side. North Beach is, however, *the* neighborhood for choice Italian food and drinks, from an espresso to kick-start your morning to a plate of pasta to satisfy late-night hunger pangs.

Budget For breakfast or a snack along Columbus Ave., start with *Cornucopia* (☎ 398-1511), at No 114. The *Stella Pastry* (☎ 986-2914) at No. 446 is a nice little cafe where you can start the day with an orange juice, a cappuccino or espresso, and a croissant or Danish for just $4.

Pizza and pasta are, of course, North Beach specialties and *North Beach Pizza* (☎ 433-2444), 1499 Grant Ave. and Union, is one of the best-known pizzerias in the city. It's so popular they have a second branch *North Beach Pizza Too* (same number), two blocks south at 1310 Grant Ave. Pizza costs range from $7 to $18.

Next door to North Beach Pizza Too, *Mo's Burgers* (☎ 788-3779), 1322 Grant Ave., is the place to go when you need a real burger fix. *Mario's Bohemian Cigar Store* (☎ 362-0536), 566 Columbus Ave., is an inexpensive cafe/bar/restaurant that looks out onto Washington Square and serves focaccia sandwiches and tiramisu.

Middle Range On the north side of Washington Square, *Mama's Girl* (☎ 362-6421), 1701 Stockton St., is a great place for a filling, if slightly pricey, breakfast. It's closed Monday.

L'Osteria del Forno (☎ 982-1124), 519 Columbus Ave., is a tiny place run by two Italian women who make wonderful handmade raviolis and pizzas. It's closed on Tuesdays. *Basta Pasta* (☎ 434-2248), 1268 Grant Ave. at Vallejo, is a long-running pasta restaurant that is not only reasonably priced but serves some of the best Italian food in the city; it's open until late into the evening. The *Stinking Rose* (☎ 781-7673), 325 Columbus Ave., proclaims itself as a "garlic restaurant" although it does admit to serving some food with its garlic.

KITTI HOMME

In North Beach "si mangia bene".

North Beach is not 100% Italian and there are interlopers like *Helmand* (☎ 362-0641), 430 Broadway, serving excellent Afghani food. While this usually means a heavy emphasis on meat, they offer a number of vegetarian dishes.

At *Anthony's* (☎ 391-4488), 1701 Powell St., pasta meets seafood (steamed Maine lobsters in particular), although the fried calamari is also delicious. What's really remarkable about this spot is that it's not some flashy restaurant – the food is cheap!

Fine Dining Washington Square has two of San Francisco's prime power-lunching restaurants. The *Washington Square Bar & Grill* (☎ 982-8123), 1707 Powell St., is something of a city institution – solid, professional, and it's been around forever. On the other side of the square, *Moose's* (☎ 989-7800), 1652 Stockton St., has a great people-watching view and good food. At lunchtime, you can get the Mooseburger, a Caesar salad, or pizza for less than $10. There's a good selection of wines by the glass and an elegant bar. Also on the square, the *Fior D'Italia* (☎ 986-1886), 601 Union St., claims to be the oldest Italian restaurant in the entire country.

Tucked behind the cable cars, *Zax* (☎ 563-6266), 2330 Taylor St. near Columbus, is a well-kept secret. This California bistro serves its cosmopolitan crowd stupendous food from a small but inventive menu.

Vegetarian Food

These days, more folks are eating vegetarian than ever before, and almost every restaurant will have some vegetarian dishes. Certain places, however, stand out, like the pricey but superb *Greens* in Fort Mason. They're so dedicated to preparing the absolute best in vegetarian food they even grow their own vegetables at the Green Gulch Farm & Zen Center at Muir Beach in Marin County. *Amazing Grace* in the Mission is another excellent vegetarian eatery.

Chinese cuisine, usually dedicated to eating the most unimaginable parts of anything that moves, also has its vegetarian side and you can sample it at the *Lotus Garden* in Chinatown or at the *Ten Thousand Buddhas Restaurant*, in the Financial District.

For cheap eats vegetarian-style, it's hard to beat the Vietnamese restaurant *Tu Lan*, even if it is in one of the rougher parts of SoMa. It's not a strictly vegetarian restaurant but some of the best dishes are the non-meat ones. *Truly Mediterranean* in the Mission has some great Middle Eastern vegetarian dishes while *Ganges* is an excellent Indian vegetarian restaurant in the Haight-Ashbury. ■

NOB HILL & RUSSIAN HILL

Right in the heart of Nob Hill, *Hyde Street Bistro* (☎ 441-7778), 1521 Hyde St. between Pacific and Jackson, has a seasonally changing menu based on Austrian and northern Italian cuisine. For good made-to-order sandwiches and Middle Eastern food, try *R.J.'s* (☎ 567-6091), 1609 Polk St. between Sacramento and Clay.

The casual *Le Petit Cafe* (☎ 776-5356), 2164 Larkin St. at Green, has great breakfasts of fresh-squeezed orange juice, scones, eggs, and french toast. If the weather is pleasant, it's a treat to sit outside.

I Fratelli (☎ 474-8240), 1896 Hyde St., has large portions of wonderful Italian fare, Chianti, and a very friendly atmosphere. *Zarzuela* (☎ 346-0800), 2000 Hyde St. at Union, is an authentic Spanish tapas place where the prices are reasonable but the dishes a bit skimpy. Tapas are around $4 to $7 and more substantial meals are $10 to $15.

FISHERMAN'S WHARF

You shouldn't come to Fisherman's Wharf looking for cheap eats. There are no undiscovered restaurant bargains but fresh seafood is a Fisherman's Wharf specialty from the takeaway food stalls around the waterfront parking lot and along Jefferson St. If you're here during the mid-November to June crab season, enjoy Dungeness crab and sourdough bread – which is about as San Franciscan as you can get.

Despite appearances, Pier 39 – at least in terms of restaurants – isn't solely a tourist creation. At the beginning of the pier, the *Eagle Cafe* (☎ 433-3689) looks like it's half-a-century old because indeed it is. In 1978 it had been run by the same owners for over 50 years when it was picked up and moved two blocks to its present location. It's your basic diner serving basic diner food. The views are nice and at night it's just a bar.

The *Buena Vista Cafe* (☎ 474-5044), 2765 Hyde St., near the cable car turntable, serves sandwiches and burgers and is a popular bar. The '50s-style diner *Johnny Rocket's* (☎ 693-9120), 81 Jefferson St., turns out burgers and fries that stand up well against the neighboring fast food outlets.

There are better seafood restaurants in other parts the city but if you decide to eat here, *Alioto's* (☎ 673-0183), 8 Fisherman's Wharf, has great views of the boat basin and entrees at $14 to $20. *Tarantino's* (☎ 775-5600), 206 Jefferson St., dates back to long before the Wharf became a tourist trap and has more great views and fresh fish at $13 to $19. Ghirardelli Square has some interesting restaurants including *McCormick & Kuleto's* (☎ 929-1730) at the Beach and Larkin corner, with an extensive seafood menu.

Cafe Pescatore (☎ 561-1111), 2455 Mason St. at North Point, is part of the Tuscan Inn and just far enough from the heart of the area to stand on its own merits as an excellent restaurant noted for its seafood, pasta, and pizza.

THE MARINA & FORT MASON

Where to stay and where to eat in the Marina are two wholly different games. Lombard Street's wall-to-wall generic motels are where you stay; yuppified Chestnut St. is where you eat. Lombard St. does, however, have fast food places and *Mel's Drive-In* (☎ 921-3039), at 2165 Lombard St., an authentic-looking '50s diner with burgers and fries.

The pleasant *Chestnut St. Grill* (☎ 922-5558), 2231 Chestnut St., has a huge choice of sandwiches and burgers at $4.50 to $6, and tables out on the sidewalk. *World Wrapps* (☎ 563-9727), 2257 Chestnut St., takes the idea of burritos one step further, wrapping tortillas around an international choice of ingredients from Thai chicken to curried vegetables.

Bepple's Pies (☎ 931-6226), 2142 Chestnut St., serves sandwiches and tempting dessert pies until late at night. The *Andalé Taquería* (☎ 749-0506), 2150 Chestnut St., offers the standard Bay Area Mexican dishes or, around the corner, *Sweet Heat Restaurant* (☎ 474-9191), 3324 Steiner St., fixes innovative and healthy Californian/ Mexican food (the chicken, wild mushroom, and veggie taco, for example) at reasonable prices.

If you're looking for a hearty meal, *Izzy's* (☎ 563-0487), 3345 Steiner St., is the place to go for steak, chops, and seafood. Over at Fort Mason is *Greens Restaurant* (☎ 771-6222), Building A, one of the city's best-known vegetarian restaurants. There's real imagination at play in the dishes and the results can be terrific. It's open for lunch Tuesday to Saturday, brunch on Sunday, and dinner Monday to Saturday. On Friday and Saturday they serve a fixed price dinner, typically for about $36. There's also a bakery and takeout counter so if you can't afford a full meal you can still enjoy a picnic on the waterfront.

At 2942 Lyon St., at the main gate to the Presidio and within walking distance to the Palace of Fine Arts, *Liverpool Lil's* (☎ 921-6664) is a small neighborhood dive with reasonable prices, a seafood and burgers menu, and an English pub-style atmosphere.

PACIFIC HEIGHTS

Move away from the Bay and three blocks up the hill from Lombard St. in the Marina to find Union St., the main drag of Pacific Heights, still referred to as Cow Hollow, since this was once dairy farming country. Singles cruising the bars have replaced the cows and *Perry's* (☎ 922-9022), 1944 Union St., has a crowded bar and good burgers and salads. *Doidge's Kitchen* (☎ 921-2149), 2217 Union St., is another Pacific Heights institution although here the main feature is breakfast and lunch; it's not cheap but the food is great.

Prego (☎ 563-3305), 2000 Union St., is a modern, mid-priced Italian restaurant with a popular bar. *Pasand Madras Cuisine* (☎ 922-4498), 1875 Union St., manages to combine jazz and Indian food.

Yoshida Ya (☎ 346-3431), 2909 Webster St. just off Union, is pleasant-looking but pricey with main courses at $16 to $18. Tempura and yakitori (Japanese-style kebabs) are specialties. Also just off Union St. is *Pane e Vino* (☎ 346-2111), 3011 Steiner St., with an open kitchen and excellent pasta dishes.

Plump Jack (☎ 563-4755), 3127 Fillmore St., has reasonably priced burgers, sandwiches, and pastas at lunchtime in elegant yet friendly bistro surroundings. At night reservations are recommended, and they serve more sophisticated fare with an emphasis on seafood and a superb wine-by-the-glass list.

JAPANTOWN

The three interconnected shopping centers – the Tasamak Plaza, Kintetsu Restaurant Mall, and the Kinokuniya Building – are packed with restaurants, particularly the Kintetsu Building. More Japanese restaurants can be found along Post St. and in Buchanan Mall.

Floating sushi bars like *Isobune* (☎ 563-1030), at 1737 Post St. in the Kintetsu Mall, are very popular in Japan but slightly unusual here. The sushi chefs stand in the center of the room, fenced off by an oval bar around which the customers sit. The chefs prepare food, load it onto small dishes and place the dishes on wooden boats that sail in a canal around the inner perimeter of the bar. Patrons simply lift the dishes they want off the bobbing boats. Dish prices range from $1.20 to $2.50. When you've eaten your fill, the bill is calculated by adding up your empty dishes. It's fun and cheap and the sushi is delicious. Also in the Kintetsu Mall, *Mifune* (☎ 922-0337), 1737 Post St., offers popular Japanese dishes, particularly noodles, at moderate prices.

Sanppo (☎ 346-3486), 1702 Post St., is a down-home, cheap Japanese restaurant. In the Kinokuniya Building, *Isuzu* (☎ 922-2290), 1582 Webster St., is a more upscale restaurant specializing in seafood.

Much more expensive Japantown restaurants include the pricey, seafood-oriented *Elka Restaurant* (☎ 922-7788) in the Miyako Hotel at 1625 Post St. The menu is an accomplished, eclectic blend of Pacific Rim cooking styles. *Benihana of Tokyo* (☎ 563-4844), 1737 Post St., in the Kintetsu Mall, is a large chain restaurant where the chefs prepare your food at the table; dishes start from $20.

THE FILLMORE

The restaurant stretch of Fillmore St., between Sutter and Jackson just north of Japantown, blends Japanese restaurants with other national cuisines.

The *Hillcrest Bar & Cafe* (☎, 563-8400), 2201 Fillmore at Sacramento, is a smooth, relaxed spot perfect for sipping drinks and munching on fancy burgers and sandwiches.

The popular *Jackson Fillmore* (☎ 346-5288), 2506 Fillmore St. at Jackson St., is set in an old-fashioned diner and serves fine southern Italian food at reasonable prices. The *Elite Cafe* (☎ 346-8668), 2049 Fillmore St., is an informal and extremely popular Cajun and Creole seafood restaurant with a relaxed atmosphere, and a great bar. *Pacific Heights Bar & Grill* (☎ 567-3337), 2001 Fillmore St., is a bright, cheery neighborhood restaurant with California cuisine, a great oyster bar, and an excellent menu with daily specials. *Osome* (☎ 346-2311), 1923 Fillmore St., has some of the best Japanese food in the city.

Neecha (☎ 922-9419), 2100 Sutter St., is a pleasant local Thai restaurant that serves quality food. If you're craving sushi, try *Godzilla Sushi* (☎ 931-1773), 1800 Divisadero at Bush. Sit at the bar or one of the few tables (the place is tiny) and listen to contemporary alternative music rather than the usual Japanese soothing strands. *Toraya Sushi Bar & Grill* (☎ 931-9455), 1914 Fillmore, is also tasty, and a fun late-night stop (it's open until 11 pm except Sunday when it's open to 10 pm); it's closed on Monday.

HAIGHT-ASHBURY

The '60s may be long gone but the Haight is still a youth zone and the emphasis here is definitely on cheap eats, in a decidedly hip setting.

Upper Haight

Budget You can start your day with great bagels at *Holey Bagel* (☎ 626-9111), 1206 Masonic Ave. Later, fill up on spicy Cajun and Creole vittles at the *Crescent City Cafe* (☎ 863-1374), 1418 Haight St., or satisfy carnivorous instincts at the *Pork Store Cafe* (☎ 864-6981), 1451 Haight St., where they serve heaping, delicious breakfast platters.

KITTI HOMME

Hanging out in the Haight

Zona Rosa (☎ 668-7717), at the corner of Haight St. and Shrader St., serves good, cheap Mexican food and their black bean vegetarian burrito can't be beat. *Double Rainbow* (☎ 668-6690), 1724 Haight St. sells hefty pizza slices and dishes out some unusual ice cream flavors. Vermont-based *Ben & Jerry's* (☎ 249-4685) at the corner of Haight and Ashbury serves their excellent ice cream and yogurt.

All You Knead (☎ 552-4550), 1466 Haight St., is very much part of the Haight-Ashbury scene and is open from breakfast until late with a vigorously healthy menu that is slightly at odds with the often washed-out clientele!

Middle Range *Kan Zaman* (☎ 751-9656), 1793 Haight St., is a perfect Haight-Ashbury restaurant, with Middle Eastern food (entrees are $8 to $10) and a funky Arabian nights decor with cushion-on-the-floor seating along one wall. After the meal, enjoy a hookah pipe for $7. Note that credit cards are not accepted.

Tapas, that Spanish plan to make an entire meal out of starters, make their Haight appearance at the Caribbean-influenced, lively, immensely popular *Cha Cha Cha* (☎ 386-5758), 180 Haight at Shrader St. The tapas (try the fried plantains with black beans) and sangria are excellent; credit cards are not accepted. Be prepared to wait at peak dinner hours.

Massawa (☎ 621-4129), 1538 Haight St., does East

Breakfast in San Francisco

In general, San Francisco restaurants are updated and recycled as fast as the latest software from Silicon Valley. Breakfast spots, however, are an exception; they all seem to have been around for 100 years. Prime places include *Sear's* and *Lori's*, traditional diners just a stone's throw from Union Square. In North Beach, where late nights are the norm, *Mama's Girl* is a great place for a late-morning start, and *Le Petit Cafe* on Russian Hill is a good place for noisy mid-morning gatherings. In SoMa the new *Caffe Museo* in the Museum of Modern Art serves interesting breakfast goodies as does South Park's *Caffe Centro*. Fisherman's Wharf offers the half-century old *Eagle Cafe*.

Two of the city's prime breakfast spots are *Brother Juniper's*, near Van Ness, and *Doidge's Kitchen*, in Pacific Heights. Surprisingly, Haight-Ashbury slackers seem to retain enough energy to get up for a hearty breakfast because the Haight is prime breakfast territory including *All You Knead*, the *Pork Store*, or *Spaghetti Western* in the lower Haight. *Zazie* in Cole Valley is known for gingerbread pancakes, hefty omelettes and lattes served in huge ceramic bowls. *Aunt Mary's* in the Mission serves traditional breakfast fare, although here you ask for *huevos revueltos* instead of scrambled eggs. ■

African and Eritrean/Ethiopian food. It's fun to sample with a big, friendly group since everyone digs in to a central supply – and with their fingers, no less. There's also a selection of African beers. It's closed on Monday. *Dish* (☎ 431-3534), 1398 Haight St., on the corner of Masonic, takes its name from the collection of mismatched plates on the wall. It's popular for breakfast and lunch, but is chiefly famed for its earlier incarnation as the flower-power era Drugstore Cafe.

Two blocks south of Haight St., at 775 Frederick St. by Golden Gate Park, *Ganges* (☎ 661-7290) is a terrific Indian vegetarian restaurant, but it's closed on Sunday and Monday.

Cole Valley

A couple of blocks south of Haight St., Cole Valley's laid-back restaurants and cafes are a haven for twenty-somethings. Part cafe, part French bistro, *Zazie* (☎ 564-5332), 941 Cole St., is a terrific spot for breakfast or brunch in the tiny flower-filled patio. They're also open for lunch and dinner. *Crepes on Cole* (☎ 664-1800), 100 Carl St. at Cole, serves a variety of savory or sweet crepes ($3 to $6) inspired by international cuisines, from Indian to Hawaiian to Greek, as well as soups, sandwiches, and salads.

A couple of quick stops for a do-it-yourself lunch in Golden Gate Park include the famous *Tassajara Bakery* (☎ 664-8947), 1000 Cole St. where you can stock up on fresh bread, cakes, and other baked goods; *Say Cheese* (☎ 665-5020), 856 Cole St., with a huge variety of, you guessed it, cheeses; and *Real Foods Market*, (☎ 564-2800), 1023 Stanyan St., a small gourmet grocery with a deli and organic produce.

Lower Haight

Ten blocks east of the Haight-Ashbury, the lower Haight is bar-central, but when the party crowd needs sustenance they can turn to *Ya Halla* (☎ 522-1509), at 494 Haight St., or *Nargeleh Cafe* (☎ 255-7820), at 531 Haight St., for Middle Eastern food.

Spaghetti Western (☎ 864-8461), 576 Haight St., is the lower Haight's – if not the city's – most popular breakfasting spot, serving heaping platters of down-home eats amid a funky paint scheme. Try the Spuds O' Rama, a piled-high plate of home-fried potatoes with all the fixings. *Kate's Kitchen* (☎ 626-3984), just down the street at 471 Haight St., is another lower Haight favorite for breakfast, serving inventive pancake and egg dishes with southern influences. Around the corner, the large, laid-back *Squat & Gobble Cafe* (☎ 487-0551), 237 Fillmore St., is the perfect spot for a hearty breakfast with 40 or 50 of your closest friends.

A block south of Haight St. off Fillmore is *Thep Phanom* (☎ 431-2526), 400 Waller St., hailed as one of San Francisco's best Thai restaurants. Specials change nightly but the coconut soup is a must.

THE CASTRO & NOE VALLEY

The Castro's most popular pastime is people-watching so, naturally, the most popular restaurants tend to be ones with good vantage points. Heading the list is *Cafe Flore* (☎ 621-8579), 2298 Market St., a popular coffeehouse with a large outside patio that is packed on sunny days. For a cafe, their menu of breakfast specials, lunch sandwiches, and simple pasta dishes is excellent. At the gourmet grocery/deli *Harvest Ranch Market* (☎ 626-0805), 2285 Market St. at 16th, there are no tables, but their outdoor sidewalk benches provide a perfect resting spot while you indulge in their amazing assortment of improv edibles. You can choose between sandwiches, trays of sushi, fresh produce, bins of dried fruit, vegan baked goods, salads, and much more; it's open to 11 pm nightly.

The *Patio Cafe* (☎ 621-4640), 531 Castro St. between 18th and 19th, with a big, noisy, covered patio tucked away in the back, is a fun place for big sandwiches, burgers, and pastas. *Hot 'n' Hunky* (☎ 621-6365), 4039 18th St., just off Castro, is a strong contender in the "best burger in San Francisco" contest. Naturally, the "macho man" burger is a big favorite.

While waiting in the long lines at the Castro Theater, the key places to run to across the street for a bite to eat are *Marcello's Pizza* (☎ 863-3900), at 420 Castro St., mainly a takeout, and *Noah's Bagels* (☎ 552-2256), 400 Castro St.

RICK GERHARTER

RICK GERHARTER

Cruising the Castro with the top down

Pozole (☎ 626-2666), 2337 Market St., serves Latin American food in a zany pink world of religious art, and hand-painted tables and walls. It feels a bit like a hallucination, but it's hip and therefore the burritos tend to cost a few dollars more than the norm. If you want to sample Middle Eastern eats, try the popular and excellent *La Méditerranée* (☎ 431-7210), at 288 Noe St. It's closed on Mondays. *Orphan Andy's* (☎ 864-9795), 3991 17th St., a Castro institution, is a popular burger-and-fries diner open 24 hours.

The Castro's proximity to the Mission means you'll find a host of decent Mexican taquerías like *Taquería Zapata* (☎ 861-4470), at 4150 18th St., and the small *Bad Man José's* (☎ 861-1706), at 4077 18th St.

In nearby Noe Valley, *Firefly* (☎ 821-7652), 4288 24th St. at Douglass, advertises "home cooking with no ethnic boundries." The shrimp and scallop potstickers are delicious! It's upscale but affordable; reservations are recommended.

Tom Peasant Pies (☎ 642-1316), 4108 24th St., makes an assortment of sweet and savory tarts, a great light snack.

THE MISSION

While the Mission doesn't offer a wide choice of "fine dining," for a cheap, filling, and often surprisingly high-quality meal it's hard to beat. The city's best Mexican food is not the sole culinary possibility; the Mission boasts a wide range of Latino dining opportunities from Spanish tapas to Cuban, Guatemalan, Nicaraguan, Salvadoran, Peruvian, and Puerto Rican. Fast food, pizzerias, and Chinese restaurants also pop up and there are a handful of classier establishments. But the prime Mission delight is the eclectic selection of weird and wonderful cafes. Note that credit cards are usually not accepted at any of the cheaper places or even at many of the pricier ones.

Latino Restaurants

The junction of 16th and Valencia is a hot restaurant corner in the Mission with more than 10 interesting restaurants within one block. *Taquería La Cumbre* (☎ 863-8205), 515 Valencia St. at 16th, satisfies big appetites with excellent low-priced food served cafeteria-style. Burritos range from $2.75 to $5.25; just make sure you've decided if you want your beans (black or pinto), whole or refried when you place your order. The *carne asada* (chopped steak) burrito is the house specialty. A few doors down *Puerto Alegre* (☎ 626-2922), 546 Valencia St., is another cheap, excellent Mexican eatery.

The extremely popular *Cafe Macondo* (☎ 863-6517), 3159 16th St., decked out with comfortable couches and tables with reading lamps, serves strong coffee and some Central American dishes. Across the road, *Cafe Picaro* (☎ 431-4089), 3120 16th St., is a colorful, Spanish tapas restaurant. Get a group together to sample the wide variety of dishes like the *tortilla de patatas* (potato omelette) and *pollo al ajillo* (garlic chicken).

Head south from Mexico to Central America via restaurants like the inexpensive Salvadoran *Panchita's* (☎ 431-4232), 3091 16th St. A couple of doors away is *Taquería Pancho Villa* (☎ 864-8840), 3071 16th St., another place that tries to rise above the basic level with a wider

Mexican Food

San Francisco's cheapest restaurants? Mexican. San Francisco's original cuisine? Mexican. Mexican food is pretty simple: you take beans, cheese, meat, chicken, seafood, or a combination thereof, spice it up with chiles or salsa, and then serve it up in some form of a *tortilla* (a thin pancake made of pressed corn or wheat flour). *Salsa* (a chunky sauce of tomatoes, onions, peppers, and cilantro sauce) is the zingy spice of life in any Mexican meal. Beans, a long-time basic staple in Mexican cooking, are often served whole or refried, which means they've been boiled, mashed, and then fried.

Mexican dishes you'll find at almost every restaurant for *el desayuno* (breakfast), *la comida* (lunch), or *la cena* (dinner) include:

burrito – a flour tortilla filled with ingredients.

chile relleno – a fried, stuffed green pepper.

enchilada – take a burrito, dip it in sauce, and then bake it.

huevos rancheros – the most Mexican of breakfasts: fried eggs with spicy tomato sauce on a tortilla.

quesadilla – a flour (or corn) tortilla filled with cheese and heated

taco – a corn tortilla fried crisp and folded and filled, or the "soft taco," a flour tortilla warmed but not fried.

tamale – steamed, stuffed cornmeal wrapped in corn husks.

tostada – a flat, crisp corn tortilla topped with the usual ingredients.

Mexican food is best accompanied with a *cerveza*, a Mexican beer. The popularity of Mexican beer in the USA is a fairly vivid indictment of the wishy-washy standard of most American beers. That said, order a *Corona*, a *Dos Equis*, or a *Tecate*. ■

variety of only marginally more expensive dishes. Try dinner No. 4, garlic shrimp and chicken asada.

La Rondalla (☎ 647-7474), 901 Valencia St. at 20th, is brave enough to escape from the standard tacos and enchiladas to tackle more adventurous Mexican fare. A mariachi band performs in the evening and, in case you were confused, their glittery Christmas decorations stay up year round. It's closed Monday and they don't take credit cards. Assemble a collection of tapas ($4 to $5) at the tasty, popular *Esperpento* (☎ 282-8867), at 3295 22nd St., just off Valencia. It's closed Sunday and they also don't take cards.

La Taquería (☎ 285-7117), 2889 Mission St., just south of the 24th St. BART, claims to be the Mission's original taquería. There are no surprises here but it's very popular and also surprisingly comfortable. Nearby is *La Taquería San José* (☎ 282-0203), 2830 Mission St., another popular budget-priced spot with terrific burritos and tacos.

Cross South Van Ness to find *El Nuevo Frutilandia* (☎ 648-2958), 3077 24th St. They serve up huge Cuban and Puerto Rican meals, accompanied by guitar music on the weekend.

Restaurants – the Rest of the World

In that restaurant-packed block of 16th at Valencia, *Pastaio* (☎ 255-2440), 3182 16th St., is a cozy little pizzeria and Italian restaurant with reasonably priced meals. A few doors down, cross the border into France where *Ti Couz* (☎ 252-7373), 3108 16th St., turns out a huge variety of sweet ($2 to $5) and savory ($3 to $5) crepes. In between, *Abbondante* (☎ 626-5523), 3122 16th St., cooks up basic, down-home food including hearty breakfasts like huevos rancheros ($4).

On the other side of the street, *Truly Mediterranean* (☎ 252-7482), 3109 16th St., serves terrific shwarmas, falafels, and other eastern Mediterranean delicacies, including many vegetarian dishes. Turn the corner to *Cafe Istanbul* (☎ 863-8854), 525 Valencia St., a tiny cafe that pumps out ultra-strong Turkish coffee and filling Middle Eastern dishes. Go north to *Pauline's Pizza* (☎ 552-2050), 260 Valencia St., for great gourmet pizzas heavy with imaginative toppings. At the northern edge of the Mission, just off Market St., *Amazing Grace* (☎ 626-6411), 216 Church St., is a cafeteria-style vegetarian restaurant with a great salad bar.

Not all of the Mission's dining possibilities are necessarily cheap. *Le Trou* (☎ 550-8169), 1007 Guerrero St., is a traditional French restaurant with simply prepared but consistently good food. The prices are very reasonable and there's a three-course fixed price menu; it's closed on Monday. Across the road, *Flying Saucer* (☎ 641-9955), 1000 Guerrero St., is a tiny restaurant that serves sophisticated and innovative cuisine amid its off-the-wall decor. Although it's much cheaper than downtown restaurants, it's pricey for the Mission and they don't take credit cards. *Woodward's Garden* (☎ 621-7122), 1700 Mission St., is an intimate and unpretentious place with delicious Californian cuisine. You know it has to be good when the owners used to be chefs at Greens and Postrio.

There are a number of good restaurants on nearby Potrero Hill. *Goat Hill Pizza* (☎ 641-1440), 300 Connecticut St. at 18th, is a long-time neighborhood favorite. There's a great view and local art hangs on the walls. Monday is all-you-can-eat pizza and salad night ($7.95); get there early if you don't want to wait. *Asimakopoulos Cafe & Deli* (☎ 552-8789), 288 Connecticut St., is one of the best Greek restaurants in town, with entrees from $9.

THE RICHMOND

The inner Richmond, on the east side of Park Presidio Blvd. (Hwy 1), has become "New Chinatown" with a slew of Chinese restaurants. You'll also find a scattering of Burmese, Cambodian, Japanese, Thai, Vietnamese, and other Asian restaurants as well. Clement St., east of Park Presidio Blvd and again between 20th and 25th Sts., has a wide selection.

If hunger strikes you on the way to the Richmond, stop at 3300 Geary Blvd., where the *Straits Cafe* (☎ 668-1783) cooks up Singaporean or Nyonya food. Singapore is a bit of a melting pot and their own cuisine blends Chinese cooking with the spicier curries of Malaysia to produce unique, flavorful dishes.

More than a few sushi enthusiasts have proclaimed *Kabuto* (☎ 752-5652), 5116 Geary Blvd., the best sushi bar in the city. It's closed Monday and Tuesday and can be crowded on weekends but is open late. *Angkor Wat* (☎ 221-7887), 4217 Geary Blvd., has terrific Cambodian food in a very friendly atmosphere. *Tommy's Mexican Restaurant* (☎ 387-4747), 5929 Geary Blvd., specializing in Yucatan cuisine, has been run by the same family for over 30 years. The service is as good as the food is tasty. Fresh-squeezed lime margaritas are a specialty.

The best known Thai restaurant in the area, *Khan Toke Thai House* (☎ 668-6654), 5937 Geary Blvd., has a romantic but casual atmosphere; wear loose-fitting clothing and make sure there are no holes in your socks, as you'll be asked to remove your shoes and sit at low tables.

Le Soleil (☎ 668-4848), 133 Clement St. between 2nd and 3rd Aves., is an outstanding Vietnamese restaurant with friendly service, reasonable prices, and delicious, light but satisfying food. Try the shrimp wrapped around sugar cane, the grilled beef (cooked at your table), and the fried banana dessert.

Laghi (☎ 386-6266), 1801 Clement St., at 19th Ave., is a popular little Italian restaurant, known for its regularly changing menu of consistently good pastas and veal dishes. It's closed on Monday. The *Grapeleaf* (☎ 668-1515), 4031 Balboa St., is a small Lebanese restaurant with great Middle Eastern food and a belly dancer some evenings. It's closed Monday and Tuesday. One of the few kosher delis in San Francisco, *Shenson's Delicatessen* (☎ 751-4699), 5120 Geary St., caters to the large Orthodox Jewish population that lives in the avenues.

Keep heading east and Geary become Point Lobos Ave. Right at the end, the *Cliff House* (☎ 386-3330), 1090 Point Lobos Ave., is known for its colorful history and great views (if you can snag a window seat) but not for the food, which consists of ordinary sandwiches and burgers from $8. But, the setting is superb and a drink at sunset is a real San Francisco experience. Just in back of the Cliff House, you can get the same superb views, and a peek at the foundations of the Sutro Baths, from *Louis' Restaurant* (☎ 387-6330), 902 Point Lobos Ave., where the burgers are only $5.50.

THE SUNSET

South of Golden Gate Park, the Sunset district also has a large collection of budget ethnic eating places, particularly along Irving Ave. from 5th all the way to 25th. The star of the inner Sunset is *PJ's Oyster Bed* (☎ 566-7775), 737 Irving St., a Cajun/Creole seafood restaurant and fish market. In addition to a good selection of oysters ($8.95 a half dozen, $15.95 a dozen), the menu includes classics like gumbo, crab cakes, jambalaya, alligator filets, and crawfish for $15 to $20. It's casual, raucous, and popular, so call ahead.

There's also a concentration of middle-range restaurants along 9th Ave. between Lincoln and Irving. *Ya Ya Cuisine* (☎ 566-6966), 1220 9th Ave., is perhaps the only place in the world where you can get Iranian-Californian food. This merging of cuisines makes for an interesting blend of spices: try the ravioli appetizers filled with pureed dates spiced with cardamom and cinnamon.

Just down the block, *Stoyanoff's* (☎ 664-3664), 1240 9th Ave., serves some of the best Greek food in the city. Selections are limited, but the vegetarian moussaka, fashioned out of a light pastry with a subtle touch of dill, is a sure bet. *Peppers* (☎ 566-7678), 1290 9th Ave., is a tiny Mexican restaurant known for its fresh ingredients and mesquite-grilled meat. There is sit-down service, but the real treat is to order takeout and wander down the block to Golden Gate Park.

Noriega St. between 19th and 26th Aves. has another concentration of ethnic restaurants. A few worth the trip into the Sunset are *Fujiyama-ya* (☎ 665-1772), 1234 Noriega St., a great value for sushi and other Japanese dishes and, next door, the highly-praised *Casa Aguila* (☎ 661-5593), 1240 Noriega St., an authentic Mexican restaurant.

Entertainment

San Francisco's nightlife doesn't hinge on huge, hyperfashionable nightclubs but rather on its eclectic bars, hopping dance clubs, and cutting-edge concert spaces – most of which cater to every sexual preference imaginable. There are a number of theater venues, a renowned opera house, a symphony, and a ballet company. Sporting events are also important.

COFFEEHOUSES

Coffeehouses sometimes straddle several categories: they may be a bar and restaurant as much as a cafe. The following listings are essentially cafes where you go to sip coffee and sit around – reading, doodling, watching the world go by, or simply daydreaming. See the following Bars section for places where the alcohol is as important as the coffee, or the Places to Eat chapter for places where the food gets equal billing.

Union Square & Civic Center

Cafe de la Presse (☎ 398-2680), 352 Grant Ave., in a corner of the Triton Hotel and right across the street from the Chinatown gate, is a popular, European-style cafe with an international selection of newspapers and magazines.

Two of downtown's coolest casual hangouts are in Hayes Valley, near the Civic Center. At funky little *Momi Toby's Revolution Cafe* (☎ 626-1508), 528 Laguna St., you will never be bored. If the piles of magazines and the eclectic CD collection don't keep you entertained, have a seat at the piano. They serve beer and wine in addition to snacks and coffee drinks.

Mad Magda's Russian Tea Room & Cafe (☎ 864-7654), 579 Hayes St., with its candles, painted tables, and a giant silk Kremlin on the wall, is the perfect place for tea, coffee, or an inexpensive lunch. There's a patio and a psychic on duty at all times ($13 for a sitting). They're open until midnight Wednesday through Saturday.

North Beach

It's the North Beach cafes that really give the neighborhood its laid-back, European character. To nurse a coffee in leisure day or night, Grant Ave. is the ideal cafe thoroughfare.

Coffee: The Chains & Local Roasters

San Francisco may not quite rival Seattle – the USA's coffee capital – but caffeine enthusiasts will not be disappointed. Apart from individual outlets the city also has a number of coffeehouse chains. Lonely Planet's opinion on the chains and local roasters are:

Java City This chain labels itself a bakery and cafe but it has even more of a mass-produced, Taco Bell-coffeehouse feel than Starbucks; to-go plastic and styrofoam cups abound.

Muddy Waters This neighborhood coffeehouse has expanded to a small chain. All serve strong coffee and are strewn with newspapers and fliers and filled with coffee hounds reading (or pretending to read and really just eaves-dropping on conversations). Some outlets loan out chess boards and they also serve soy milk lattes.

Peets This Bay Area institution started in Berkeley and also sells excellent tea. They serve Noah's bagels although their pastry selection is overpriced. Compared to rival Starbucks, the coffee is stronger, the decor woodsy rather than marble, and the service less snooty.

Pasqua Delicious sandwiches, an excellent Caesar salad, tasty pastries, and decent coffee. They're always easy to find since most are near heavy foot-traffic.

Spinelli Eight in San Francisco; good coffee, boring atmosphere, but usually a bench out front.

Royal Grounds Not the most inviting atmosphere but they offer a good assortment of pastries.

Starbucks This chain originated in Seattle and is now extending nationwide. Starbucks is the McDonald's of espresso. The staff is pretty and pretentious, the coffee is good, the pastries run out by noon, and it always closes too early. They pride themselves on training and repeating cutesy names, like "double cap." ■

Caffe Trieste (☎ 392-6739), 601 Vallejo St. at Grant, is one of the most popular in the city. Long-time cafe fanatics report that it's the best spot in the city for engaging in intellectual conversation. Other good places to try include the popular little *North End Caffe* (☎ 956-3350), 1402 Grant Ave., and the equally small *Gathering Caffe* (☎ 433-4247), 1326 Grant Ave., which often features jazz. The large, inviting *Savoy Tivoli* (☎ 362-7023), 1434 Grant Ave., is as much a bar as a cafe, and is filled day and night.

The immensely popular *Vesuvio Cafe* (☎ 362-3370), 255 Columbus Ave., is as much a bar as a cafe but whether alcohol or caffeine is your poison, Vesuvio is the place to imbibe.

JAMES LYON

Street life in the Haight

Haight-Ashbury

Upper Haight This neighborhood overflows with comfortable cafes where you can enjoy a strong coffee while watching the entertaining street action. The *People's Cafe* (☎ 553-8842), 1419 Haight St., and *Cafe Paradiso* (☎ 221-5244), 1725 Haight St. both serve quality coffee and snacks. *Blue Front* (☎ 252-5917), 1430 Haight St., serves coffee until late at night and often has live music.

Up the hill from the Haight-Ashbury in Cole Valley, the *San Francisco Coffee Company* (☎ 242-0200), 848 Cole St., specializes in gourmet espresso drinks. Try out the house speciality, the "Cole Valley," a latte sweetened with almond syrup. *Jammin' Java* (☎ 668-5282), 701 Cole St., is a pleasant spot.

Lower Haight This area offers its youthful, cafe-bound residents a host of possibilities, particularly as a late-night alternative to bars. The sprawling *Horse Shoe* cafe (☎ 626-8852), 556 Haight St. between Steiner and Fillmore, attracts the laid-back slacker crowd. It's open until 1 am nightly and is crowded with people who look like they'll still be there at 1 am the next day. *Cafe International* (☎ 552-7390), 508 Haight St, draws a quieter, more introspective clientele and serves salads, sandwiches, and light Middle Eastern meals.

Open-Mic Poetry
Open-mic ("mic" is short for microphone) poetry readings – open to anybody who wants to get in front of a crowd and versify – are surprisingly popular in San Francisco. Most usually have a featured reader followed by a host of other brave souls. Popular venues for these spoken-word performances include the *Paradise Lounge* (☎ 861-6906), 1501 Folsom St. in SoMa, during their "Poetry above Paradise" evenings on Sundays nights at 8 pm. In the Lower Haight, *Cafe International* (☎ 552-7390), 508 Haight St., has open-mic on Fridays at 9 pm. *Owl & the Monkey Cafe* (☎ 665-4840), 1336 9th Ave. in the Sunset, hosts their open-mic night on Thursdays at 8 pm. The *Chameleon* (☎ 821-1891), 853 Valencia St. in the Mission, presents open readings on Mondays at 9 pm. Also in the Mission, there's the women-only open-mic "Sister Spit" night at *Blondies* (☎ 864-2419), 540 Valencia St., on Sundays at 9:30 pm. Men are graciously invited – but only as observers. ■

The Castro

The Castro has a number of the coffee chain outlets, like Spinelli on Castro St. and Pasqua on 18th, but *Cafe Flore* (☎ 621-8579), 2298 Market St., has an outdoor patio and really capitalizes on the chic Castro ambience. Not known as "Cafe Hairdo" for nothing, this is the number one beauty-flaunting spot in the neighborhood. Or, for less attitude, cross Market St. to the low-key *Jumpin' Java* (☎ 431-5282), 139 Noe St., between 14th and 15th.

The Mission

The Mission may be best known for its huge selection of Latino restaurants but it's also got a weird and wonderful collection of coffee bars. The very popular *Cafe La Boheme* (☎ 285-4122), 3318 24th St., turns out a huge variety of coffees. *Muddy's* (☎ 647-7994), 1304 Valencia at 24th St., is a large, cluttered cafe littered with newspapers, and chess and backgammon games for patrons. *Muddy Waters* (☎ 863-8006) at 521 Valencia St. at 16th St. is a smaller, less inviting version but worth stopping by.

Red Dora's Bearded Lady Cafe & Gallery (☎ 626-2805), 485 14th St. near Guerrero, is a lesbian coffeehouse that doubles as a gallery, and hosts various readings and events on weekend evenings (call for information).

On Potrero Hill, *Farley's* (☎ 648-1545), 1315 18th St., is a true neighborhood joint with weekly poetry readings, local art displays, and good people- and dog-watching opportunities. It's one of the last places in the city to refuse to offer lowfat milk in their lattes.

The Richmond & the Sunset

At the very end of Muni's N-Judah line, *Java Beach* (☎ 665-5282) is the local hangout for surfers, beachcombers, and other sun lovers, with outdoor tables right across from the beach. It's a wonderful place to join the locals for a game of speed chess or just to people-watch.

Walking into the wonderful *Owl & the Monkey Cafe* (☎ 665-4840), 1336 9th Ave, is like entering your grandmother's kitchen; it's homey and old-fashioned, and the garden patio offers a soothing escape from city sounds. On Friday and Saturday evenings they put on a diverse mix of live acoustic music, and on Thursday nights, open-mic poetry readings.

Across the park in the Richmond, *Simple Pleasures* (☎ 387-4022), 3434 Balboa St., is a funky, cluttered cafe with a garage-sale furniture collection, comfy couches, big tables, and live music. Evening entertainment varies from live jazz to open-mic nights to piano lounge music.

BARS & CLUBS

Prime areas include downtown for history, Nob Hill for the views, North Beach for those with literary pretensions, Pacific Heights for swinging singles, the Castro for gay nightlife, the Lower Haight for bar-hoppers with a punk sensibility, and SoMa for late-night carousing.

Free Eats

Happy hour appetizers continue to be a strong tradition in San Francisco. At the turn of the century the bar Martin & Horton's provided drinking patrons with a free meal of soup, boiled salmon, roast beef, bread and butter, potatoes, tomatoes, crackers and cheese – and a Brandy Smash only cost a quarter to start with! Nowadays you won't find anything like this, but there are happy hour bargains, when drinks are cheaper and free snacks are sometimes doled out.

Places to try include the Mexican *Cadillac Bar* (☎ 543-8226), 325 Minna St., near Yerba Buena Gardens and the Moscone Center in SoMa, where Mexican snacks are offered weekdays from 4 to 6:30 pm. Also in SoMa, *Eddie Rickenbacker's* (☎ 543-3498), 133 2nd St., has some great taste treats weekdays from 5 to 7 pm.

On the borderland between Union Square and the Financial District, the *Iron Horse* (☎ 362-8133), 19 Maiden Lane and Kearny, puts out appetizers weekdays from 5 to 7 pm. Atop Nob Hill the over-the-top *Tonga Room* (☎ 772-5278) in the Fairmont Hotel, 950 Mason St., goes dim sum happy weekdays from 5 to 7 pm. Or, head to the Mission for oysters on Fridays from 5 to 7 pm at *El Rio* (☎ 282-3325), 3158 Mission St. ■

Licensing laws in California are comparatively liberal (you can get a drink almost anywhere) but you have to be 21 and if you look at all youthful you may well be asked to prove your age.

It's often a fuzzy line between bars, clubs, and concert venues, with many night spots playing alternate or dual roles on various nights of the week. SoMa has the biggest concentration of clubs and music venues and the Mission and the Haight-Ashbury are lined with bars that are especially popular with the twenty-something crowd.

Union Square

Downtown bars neatly divide into bars on the street and hotel bars, some of which offer great views or interesting histories. However, aside from a couple of dives and the expensive hotel lounges, there's just not much here and those seeking nightlife would do best to head across Market St. into SoMa, or up into North Beach.

In the theater district, the *Mason St. Wine Bar* (☎ 391-3454), 342 Mason St., has live jazz and a wide selection of wines by the glass. Heading west from Union Square, the *Blue Lamp* (☎ 885-1464), 561 Geary St., is a neighborhood-style bar with live jazz and blues most nights. From Thursday to Saturday, the cover charge is just a couple of bucks.

In the hotels, start at the warmly atmospheric *Compass Rose* (☎ 774-0167), in the Westin St. Francis Hotel on Union Square, one of the city's most romantic and historic bars. In the opulent Sheraton Palace Hotel (☎ 392-8600), the *Pied Piper Bar*, with its huge 1909 Maxfield Parrish painting, the *Pied Piper*, is another must-see, but

Karaoke Craze

Karaoke, the "empty orchestra" sing-along Japanese craze, is alive and well in San Francisco, and particularly, of course, in Japantown. On weekend nights crowds warble along in Japanese and English, and sometimes a number of other Asian languages. There's often a $5 to $10 cover charge or minimum. Close to Union Square are *Oiri* (☎ 989-9760), 120 Cyril Magnin, and *Hime* (☎ 441-4756), 336 O'Farrell St., which has sushi and sing-alongs in a number of languages. *Ichirin* (☎ 956-6085), 330 Mason St., features a wide Japanese menu and late night noodles. *Izakaya & Murasake* (☎ 921-0720), 422 Geary St., has a menu which includes izakaya, small Japanese appetizers. *Club La Dor Karaoke* (☎ 777-3238), 839 Howard St. in SoMa, features small private rooms and also karaoke in a number of languages. ■

Pool & Billiards
Eager to catch up on your misspent youth? San Francisco's pool-hall possibilities include *Chalkers* (☎ 512-0450), 1 Rincon Center, 101 Spear St. at Mission, close to the Embarcadero. This civilized pool parlor even offers "informal instruction from a roving pro." *Hollywood Billiards* (☎ 252-9643), 61 Golden Gate St., is not the nicest part of the Tenderloin but there are no less than 37 billiard tables and a full bar. It's open 24 hours from Wednesday through Saturday. In the upper Haight, *Park Bowl* (☎ 752-2366), at 1855 Haight St., is a grungy, old-fashioned-style bowling alley with a billiards room.

There's free pool every day from 3 to 7 pm at the popular *Paradise Lounge* (☎ 861-6906), 1501 Folsom St. in SoMa. You can combine pool with jazz at *Cafe du Nord* (☎ 861-5016), 2170 Market St. at the Mission/Castro border, or at the *Elbo Room* (☎ 552-7788), 647 Valencia St. in the Mission. ■

the nearby airy *Garden Court* is an even nicer place for a drink. The Clift Hotel's Art Deco *Redwood Room* (☎ 775-4700), 496 Geary St. at Taylor, is open to midnight every night except Friday and Saturday, when there's live jazz until 1 am. The *Starlight Roof* at the Sir Francis Drake Hotel (☎ 392-7755), 450 Powell St., just off Union Square, has wonderful views.

Civic Center & Tenderloin

Devotees of the grape must check out *Hayes & Vine* (☎ 626-5301), 377 Hayes St., a beautiful, sophisticated wine bar with a selection of international wines available by the bottle, by the glass, or by the "flight" (including themes such as the "Tuscan classics").

Despite its questionable Tenderloin address *Club 181* (☎ 673-8181), 181 Eddy St. at Taylor, is a slick supper club and nightclub with some of the hottest jazz in town. It's pricier than other jazz clubs although without dinner and just a $5 to $10 cover charge, it's not so bad. The *Edinburgh Castle* (☎ 885-4074), 950 Geary St., has a big selection of British (and more importantly, Scottish) beers on tap. If you have a hankering for a Tartan Bitter and a game of darts, this is the place.

SoMa

San Francisco's hip South of Market district, with the greatest concentration of bars and clubs in the city, is definitely the place to go for late-night entertainment. SoMa bars cater to several distinct clienteles including the suits, local barflies, and trendy folks decked out in rave outfits. The SoMa dance and live music clubs are scattered along Folsom and 11th Sts.

Under 21
The drinking age in California is 21 so most bars and clubs deny entry to those under 21. There are, however, some bars that cater to this set. The *Trocadero* (☎ 495-6620), 520 4th St. at Bryant in SoMa, often puts on an all-ages dance club on Wednesday nights. Other SoMa clubs occasionally open their doors to those under 21 so call ahead to inquire. The *Palladium* (☎ 434-1308), 1031 Kearny St. at Columbus in North Beach, is a big, all-ages dance club open from Thursday to Saturday. *Cobb's Comedy Club* (☎ 928-4320), 2801 Leavenworth St., in the Cannery at Fisherman's Wharf is open to those under 21 all week. ■

Bars The Bay Bridge sails right over the top of the *Gordon Biersch Brewery* (☎ 243-8246), 2 Harrison St., an immensely popular after-work gathering place. They serve a broad range of microbrews and you can eat beer-battered appetizers and other dishes in the upstairs restaurant. If they haven't escaped this far from the Financial District it's likely that the suits have been waylaid at *Harry Denton's* (☎ 882-1333), in the Harbor Court Hotel, at 161 Steuart St., which also serves varied selection of microbrews and features live music from Wednesday to Saturday.

Continue along the waterfront to the *Mission Rock Resort* (☎ 621-5538), 817 China Basin at Mariposa. It can be hard to find but once located there are a couple of outdoor decks where you can watch the waterfront activity and on weekend afternoons there's live blues from about 1 to 7 pm.

In the Folsom St. nightclub strip *Kate O'Brien's* (☎ 882-7240), 579 Howard St, is a comfortable Irish pub. On 11th St. is *20 Tank Brewery* (☎ 255-9455), 316 11th St., a microbrewery bar popular for sinking a few between clubs.

The Eagle (☎ 626-0880) at 12th and Harrison is the quintessential leather bar, and a good place to find out about leather happenings.

Live Music SoMa is a prime hunting ground for blues and jazz, particularly for "new jazz" (also called "jazz fusion"), a mix of jazz and rock or blues. *Julie's Supper Club* (☎ 861-0707), 1123 Folsom St. at 7th, is a bustling restaurant with live blues and jazz on Friday and Saturday night. *Eleven* (☎ 431-3337), 374 11th St. at Harrison, serves reasonably priced Italian cuisine, an assortment of microbrews on tap, and presents live loft jazz nightly. *330 Ritch* (☎ 541-9574), at 330 Ritch St., off Townsend near 3rd St. and the CalTrain station, serves inventive tapas and hosts live jazz and dancing most nights; it's closed Sunday and Monday.

The *Hotel Utah Saloon* (☎ 421-8308), 500 4th St. at Bryant, in the shadow of the freeway, has bands several nights a week, and the *Covered Wagon Saloon* (☎ 974-1585), 911 Folsom St. at 5th, evolves from an afternoon and early evening bar to live music and dancing at night; their funky theme nights are always popular. You can also dance at the *Cat's Grill & Alley Club* (☎ 431-3332), 1190 Folsom St. near 8th, a trendy "in" spot where the fashionable grind to DJs or live bands. The decor is surreal, and they also serve tapas and light meals until late. Music varies nightly, from '70s retro to hard-core industrial, so call first.

The two-story *Up & Down Club* (☎ 626-2388), 1151 Folsom St. between 7th and 8th, is a hip spot to hear local jazz bands and is open Monday to Saturday. Though it's co-owned by supermodel Christy Turlington, it's pleasantly low on price and attitude.

Slim's (☎ 621-3330), 333 11th St., is an authentic R&B club partly owned by '70s rock star Boz Scaggs. Opening days and showtimes vary but it's strictly standing-room-only if a popular show is on. Check BASS for advance tickets.

Right on the corner of 11th at 1501 Folsom St. is the *Paradise Lounge* (☎ 861-6906), a noisy, crowded, youthful hangout. There may be as many as five different shows on some nights, ranging from rock to jazz to poetry readings. Earlier in the afternoon, from 3 to 7 pm, there's free pool for all. There's no sign to proclaim the name at *Holy Cow* (☎ 621-6087), 1535 Folsom St., but it's hard to miss a life-size plastic cow suspended over the sidewalk. A young SoMa crowd flocks here nightly and the music is mainstream. The *Ace Cafe* (☎ 621-4752), 1539 Folsom St., is a pleasantly relaxed bar and restaurant with live jazz most nights.

Dance Clubs SoMa nightclubbing requires some local, underground knowledge. Trendy clubs constantly fade in and out and even when they're hot, it may only be for certain nights of the week since many clubs host different theme nights along the lines of organized public parties. A happening club, for example, may cater to a hip-hop crowd one night and the bondage-and-fetish set the next. To find out what's going on, check the weekly *Bay Guardian* Calendar section.

Towards the bay end of Howard St., *DV8* (☎ 777-1419), 55 Natoma St., boasts four floors of music, drinking, and dancing in an urban derelict zone of freeway overpasses, warehouses, and parking lots. The action continues until

4 am from Thursday to Sunday, and you'll often face long lines.

Next door, *The Caribbean Zone* (☎ 541-9465), 55 Natoma St., is someone's fully realized fantasy of a tropical getaway in SoMa. Tables are tucked amid lagoons and trickling waterfalls, ferns sprout in dark corners, and reggae rhythms set the tone. Climb upstairs into the hull of a crashed airplane, where synchronized video monitors in the windows simulate low flight over lush islands. It's open for dinner, but the dance floor and late-night cocktails are the real draw.

The *DNA Lounge* (☎ 626-1409), 375 11th, is a big, mass-market dance club. It hit its heydey in the '80s and, after a few slow years, seems to be making a comeback. The DNA Lounge is open every night until 4 am with nightly DJs or live bands.

The crowd at the *Trocadero* (☎ 495-6620), 520 4th St. between Bryant and Brannan, varies with the theme for the evening. Once a week is "Bondage a Go-Go," a soft-core S&M party, but on the other nights of the week they present loud live rock and punk music and it's sometimes open to all ages. The dance floor is as big as a roller rink, and the disco balls were salvaged from an old Rolling Stones tour.

The *End Up* (☎ 543-7700), 995 Harrison St. at 6th, underneath the freeway, is one of the most popular dance clubs in the city, particularly on its gay and lesbian nights. *The Stud* (☎ 863-6623), 399 9th St. at Harrison, is another gay and lesbian dance club. While it was once exclusively a club for gay men, it now attracts a more varied crowd, depending on the night.

The *Sound Factory* (☎ 543-1300), 525 Harrison, is the amusement park of dance clubs, with 15,000 sq. feet of dance space in many rooms on many levels. *Ten15* (☎ 431-1200) at 1015 Folsom, is another biggie with a fluctuating music menu.

Financial District

In the heart of skyscraperland, the *London Wine Bar* (☎ 788-4811), 415 Sansome St. at Sacramento, is a cozy English pub-style bar with an extensive wine list.

The 52nd-floor *Carnelian Room* (☎ 433-7500), atop the Bank of America Building, 555 California St., has the best views in the city. Drink prices are as high as the viewpoint but it's elegant as well as spectacular. It's open for cocktails from 4 pm and dinner from 6 pm. The circular bar at *Equinox* (☎ 788-1234), at top of the bayfront Hyatt Regency Hotel, rotates the full 360°, showing off San Francisco from every conceivable angle.

TONY WHEELER

Sex & Sin

With the old guard of the porn industry slowly fading from view, San Francisco's formerly underground subcultures are beginning to take over the vacated spotlight. The bars and clubs of SoMa, the Mission, and the Castro are the latest focus of the city's continuing fascination with transgression. There you may find weekly gatherings ranging from cross-dressing dances to ritualized blood-lettings. Listings for the tamest of these events, as well as truly inventive personals ads, can be found in the back pages of the *SF Weekly* and the *Bay Guardian*.

Meanwhile, downtown, hints of the Barbary Coast still exist. A survivor of the city's days of gay excess is the *Nob Hill Cinema* (☎ 781-9468), 729 Bush St., near Powell, just a few blocks from Union Square, where you can see "big nude men" perform. The entry fee is $20; phone inquiries elicit an amazing recorded message about what you're going to see.

A long wildlife mural along Polk St. doesn't hint at what goes on in the adjacent *O'Farrell Theater* (☎ 776-6686), at 895 O'Farrell St. Actually, not much goes on: it quickly all comes off and then it's just lots of nude dancing women.

The O'Farrell Theater has had a colorful history even for an x-rated spot. The Mitchell Brothers learned their craft at the San Francisco State University's film department and struck it lucky in 1972 when Marilyn Chambers, the star of their first big-budget porn flick, *Behind the Green Door*, simultaneously managed to become the picture-of-innocence loving mother on a million Ivory Snow detergent boxes. Her soapbox career was quickly terminated but neither Marilyn nor the Mitchell brothers looked back. Until 1991˙that is, when one Mitchell brother shot and killed the other one. Sentenced to six years for voluntary manslaughter, he's currently out on a half-million dollars' bail while the appeals go through. ■

Nob Hill & Russian Hill

Topping the list of Nob Hill bars is the *Top of the Mark* (☎ 392-3434), the rooftop bar atop the Mark Hopkins Hotel, at 999 California St. While the view is tremendous, stuffy coats and ties are the norm for men and it's more a tourist attraction than anything else. Ride the glass elevator to the *Oak Room* in the Fairmont Hotel (☎ 772-5000), down an $8 bottle of beer, dig the view, visit the free hors d'oeuvres table often, and remember to tip big. The Fairmont's *Tonga Room* is wacky fun and definitely worth seeing, although the drinks are expensive. Hurricanes blow through the artificial lagoon every half hour after 5 pm from Tuesday to Saturday. The *New Orleans Room*, also in the Fairmont, is one of the city's best jazz venues.

Johnny Love's (☎ 931-6053), 1500 Broadway at Polk, is the city's most notorious singles bar and restaurant – a true clichéd pick-up scene – and the cover charges are outrageous.

North Beach

North Beach cafes and bars often overlap and sometimes a restaurant is thrown into the mix. The *Vesuvio Cafe* (☎ 362-3370), 255 Columbus Ave., looks across Jack Kerouac St. to City Lights Bookstore. Vesuvio's history as a Beat hangout may make it a tourist attraction but it continues to be a popular neighborhood bar.

Two other historic bars sit directly across Columbus Ave. *Tosca Cafe* (☎ 391-1244 or 986-9651), 242 Columbus Ave., is as famous for its people-watching opportunities as it is for the arias that emanate from the all-opera jukebox. Their mixed-drink menu offers a plethora of choices including a delicious white nun (kahlua, brandy and steamed milk). Local literati are known to unwind here in the red vinyl diner booths. Next door, across the tiny Adler Plaza, is the dark, cavernous *Specs'* (☎ 421-4112). Also known as the "Adler Museum," this amusing bar has a hodge-podge of memorabilia plastered on the walls and ceiling.

A block south, at 155 Columbus Ave., the *San Francisco Brewing Company* (☎ 434-3344) is a modern establishment with a microbrewery turning out its own beer on the premises. There's live music (jazz to blues to zydeco) several nights a week. At 1434 Grant Ave. the *Savoy Tivoli* (☎ 362-7023) is a spacious bar and cafe that pulls in the masses on weekend nights; it's closed Monday.

Finally, or more correctly firstly, there's the *Saloon* (☎ 989-7666), 1232 Grant Ave., just above Columbus.

Go to Church

The *Glide Memorial United Methodist Church* (☎ 771-6300), 330 Ellis St., puts on an all-inclusive service featuring a bumpin' gospel choir, jazz band, and an acid-casualty slide show. *St. Mary's Cathedral* (☎ 567-2020), 1111 Gough St. at Geary, near Japantown, has free concerts every Sunday at 3:30 pm.

On Wednesdays at 6 pm and Sundays at 11:45 am, *St. John's African Orthodox Church* (☎ 621-4054), 351 Divisadero at Oak, popularly known as the "Church of St. John Coltrane," holds its services in a converted storefront hung with Byzantine-style paintings of the jazz master with his sax in one hand and holy scriptures in the other. Lovers of jazz and Jesus pack the place and music reaches a devotional high as the entire congregation jams to Coltrane's *A Love Supreme* and other religious tunes. ■

This worn-looking old bar has been around since before the 1906 quake. Despite its wooden construction, it was one of only two buildings in North Beach to survive the fire which followed the tremblor. Dating from 1861 (or so the owners say), it looks like it hasn't had a coat of paint since the day it was built. Blues and '60s rock names often perform here.

Fisherman's Wharf

Buena Vista Cafe (☎ 474-5044), 2765 Hyde St., is ideally located near the cable car turntable and is so popular you may have to wait in line to get in. Try an Irish coffee as they claim to have introduced it to San Francisco. On Pier 39, the *Eagle Cafe* (☎ 433-3689) is an authentic old bar that especially stands out amidst the hokey Wharf madness.

Lou's Pier 47 (☎ 771-0377), 300 Jefferson St., is another refreshing curiosity in this mass-market tourist zone. Real blues seven nights a week is what's on the menu.

Pacific Heights

Pacific Heights is famous as singles' bar territory. *Perry's* (☎ 922-9022), 1944 Union St., is the number-one cruising spot and is featured in Armistead Maupin's *Tales of the City* novels as the archetypal San Francisco "breeder" bar. Just off Union St., the *Pierce St. Annex* (☎ 567-1400), 3138 Fillmore St. between Greenwich and Filbert, has an equally strong reputation as one of the prime pick-up spots in the city. You'll find 21 different beers on tap at the hugely popular and noisy *Union Ale House* (☎ 921-0300), 1980 Union St.

TONY WHEELER

Vesuvio Cafe was a favorite Beat hangout in the '50s.

One of the city's most infamous yuppie cruising spots is the intersection of Fillmore and Greenwich Sts., known as "the Triangle." A trio of bars, the *Balboa Cafe* (☎ 921-3944), the *Golden Gate Grill* (☎ 931-4600), and the *Baja Cantina* (☎ 885-2252) make up the points of the triangle where hordes of tipsy suburban singles congregate. Just up the street on Lombard, *Blues* (☎ 771-2583), 2125 Lombard St., has live music and dancing and is often packed.

Japantown & the Fillmore

Jack's Bar (☎ 567-3227), 1601 Fillmore St., is oddly located in the shadow of the Japan Center, but it's been a popular blues hangout since the 1930s so they must be doing something right. There's live jazz or blues every night and it's open until 2 am. *Harry's Bar* (☎ 921-1000), 2020 Fillmore St., is a smoothly traditional bar with live music.

Big with the just graduated crowd, *Frankie's Bohemian Cafe* (☎ 621-4725), 1862 Divisadero at Pine, is an eclectic bar/cafe usually packed with twenty-somethings enjoying the beer selection, salads, and vegetarian dishes.

Haight-Ashbury

In keeping up with its eclectic roots, the Haight-Ashbury boasts a collection of varied bars and clubs that continue on down to the Lower Haight.

Upper Haight The *Persian Aub Zam Zam* (☎ 861-2545), 1633 Haight St., has achieved cult status namely due to Bruno, the ornery bartender, who, on some nights, will only serve martinis, and then only if you ask nicely.

RICK GERHARTER

Drag queens at a benefit for the film *Priscilla Queen of the Desert*

The motorcycles lined up outside the *Nightbreak* (☎ 221-9008), 1821 Haight St., are a strong hint of what you'll find inside. The *Gold Cane* (☎ 626-1112), 1569 Haight St., is your basic bar with little atmosphere but cheap drinks. If you feel like donning the '40s outfit you just bought at one of the Haight's slew of vintage stores, head to the distinctly retro *Club Deluxe* (☎ 552-6949), 1511 Haight St., where the crowd dresses the part, enjoying the swing and big band tunes.

Club Boomerang (☎ 387-2996), 1840 Haight St. is a small, crowded venue where up-and-coming bands perform.

If you're tired of the Upper Haight bustle of shops and tie-dyed panhandlers and just want to relax to some smooth jazz or feel-good surfabilly, head to the *Kezar Bar & Restaurant* (☎ 681-7678), 900 Cole St. at Carl where you can down a big burger with a cool martini. This neighborhood spot attracts a crowd of friendly locals.

Lower Haight Ten blocks from the corner of Haight and Ashbury, the three blocks of Haight St., between Pierce and Webster, is a jumping enclave of noisy bars where young crowds pass the evening hours.

The start of this bar quarter is marked by *Don's Different Ducks* (☎ 431-4724), 668 Haight St., but the real concentration begins across Steiner. The appropriately dark *Midtown Bar* (☎ 558-8019), 582 Haight St., starts to fill up early in the evening and throbs with action throughout the night. Across the street are two post-industrial bars, *Noc Noc* (☎ 861-5811), at 557 Haight St., and *Toronado* (☎ 863-2276), at 547 Haight St. How do you recognize a post-industrial bar? Well, Noc Noc, with its space-age, curving metal bar and light fixtures, is the place where the spaceship crew from *Alien* hang out when they're earthside.

Head back across Haight St. to the *Mad Dog in the Fog* (☎ 626-7279), at 530 Haight St., a popular British-style pub with dart boards, soccer on TV, lots of beer varieties, pub grub, and a young, heavy-drinking crowd. In keeping with the British tradition, on Monday and Thursday they host "Quiz Night," where groups of friends compete over trivia questions thrown out by a witty emcee. Continuing along Haight St. past Fillmore St. brings you to *The Top* (☎ 864-7386), at 424 Haight St., and *Nickie's* (☎ 621-6508), at 460 Haight St., two noisy, hopping joints packed most nights of the week. At The Top, the DJ's music of choice is punk and reggae while at Nickie's, the tunes range from hip hop and world music to funk and jazz.

The Castro

Cruising the Castro is a time-honored activity for the city's large gay community. The *Twin Peaks Tavern* (☎ 864-9470), 401 Castro St. at Market St., was the first to have large bay windows so the patrons could watch the passing scene. Nicknamed the "Glass Coffin," this bar caters to an older crowd.

Gay & Lesbian Nightlife

San Francisco's gay nightlife scene extends beyond the Castro's borders and a number of mainstream clubs feature a weekly gay and lesbian night. On Sundays, the *Covered Wagon Saloon* hosts its "Muffdive" night for women only. *Club Townsend* (☎ 974-6020), 177 Townsend St. at 3rd, and the *End Up* (☎ 543-7700), 995 Harrison St. at 5th, feature gay and lesbian dance nights on different evenings of the week. To zero in on the current hotspot, ask around at some of the established Castro bars and cafes.

A Different Light Bookstore (☎ 431-0891) at 489 Castro St. is a veritable fountain of information and an excellent place to find out about the night's happenings. Pick up the free gay papers, the *Bay Area Reporter* and the biweekly *San Francisco Bay Times*, for bar and club listings. *On-Q* and *Odyssey* magazines are also good bets. A terrific and fun-to-read source of information is *Betty & Pansy's Severe Queer Review of San Francisco*, available at A Different Light. ■

The Detour (☎ 861-6053), 2348 Market St., offers great drink bargains, with $1 beers and shots on Sunday, and the longest happy hour around from 2 to 8 pm. *The Cafe* (☎ 861-3846), 2367 Market St., has a large deck overlooking Market St., an outdoor garden patio, and a pool table. Once a women's bar, it's now mixed. Other bars include *Castro Station* (☎ 626-7220), 456 Castro St., and the *Phoenix Club* (☎ 552-6827), 482 Castro St.

As far as straight / mixed bars go, the '30s-style *Cafe du Nord* (☎ 861-5016), 2170 Market St. at Sanchez, is a former speakeasy that combines jazz and West Coast blues at its best. Tuesday is Latin music night, with free salsa dancing lessons at 9 pm.

The Mission

The Mission's bars are, like most everything else about the Mission, an eclectic, funky mix. *El Rio* (☎ 282-3325), 3158 Mission St., is a large, cheerful bar and dance club with a popular Friday night happy hour, and a unique, spacious outdoor garden patio strung with lights. The crowd from night to night, from gay to lesbian to straight, with a large Latino presence. On Sunday afternoons, a live salsa band performs.

The always-packed *Elbo Room* (☎ 552-7788), 647 Valencia St., is dominated by a long bar (serving cheap drinks) and pool tables, and a dance floor and stage where many of San Francisco's new jazz bands get their start.

Slow Club (☎ 241-9390), 2501 Mariposa St., is a hip and mellow hang-out spot set in a deserted neighborhood, with a few sidewalk tables for sipping espresso, a dimly lit restaurant that serves "Continental" cuisine, and a bar tucked away in back.

At the crowded 16th and Valencia St. junction, *Esta Noche* (☎ 861-5757), 3079 16th St, is a Latino gay bar, especially popular with cross-dressers. *Zeitgeist* (☎ 255-7505), 199 Valencia St., is the "in" spot for bikers – from bicycle messengers to motorcyclists. The *Rite Spot* (☎ 552-6066), 2099 Folsom St. at 17th, is a true local haunt with inexpensive drinks. *Dalva* (252-7740), 3121 16th St., serves spicy glasses of sangria (their house specialty) and other cheap drinks, and is especially conducive to a long evening of intense conversation or a romantic tête-à-tête. Across the street, *Kilowatt* (☎ 861-2595), 3160 16th St., is a new hot venue for local bands.

The Mission also manages to harbor a couple of Irish bars. The down-to-earth *Original McCarthy's* (☎ 648-0504) is at 2329 Mission St. and the *Dovre Club* (☎ 552-0074) hides in a corner of the Women's Building at 3541 18th St.

On the eastern outskirts of the Mission, at the base of Potrero Hill, the aptly-named *Bottom of the Hill* (☎ 626-4455, 621-4455 for show information), 1233 17th St., presents live music seven nights a week ranging from jazzy funk to folky punk. A small patio and a late-night kitchen ensure a good crowd at this otherwise out-of-the-way hotspot.

The Richmond

If you're out in the Richmond district sampling the bargain-priced restaurants, you can get a post-dinner drink at *Pat O'Shea's Mad Hatter* (☎ 752-3148), 3848 Geary Blvd. Bands perform on weekends but the prime attraction here are the plethora of TVs tuned to a true international melange of sporting events. *The Plough & the Stars* (☎ 751-1122), 116 Clement St., takes top honors as one of the most popular Irish bars in the city with cheap beers and occasional live bands.

CONCERT VENUES

The *Fillmore Auditorium* (☎ 346-6000), 1805 Geary Blvd at Fillmore, is back in action with a broad range of live music from big-name rock bands to wild punk gigs. In keeping with the tradition Bill Graham began in the '60s, free apples and psychedelic posters are handed out to everyone attending a concert.

The stylish, old bordello-turned-concert hall, the *Great American Music Hall* (☎ 885-0750), 859 O'Farrell St., between Polk and Larkin, puts on a true mix of acts from acoustic folk to African rhythm to rock & roll. The *Warfield* (☎ 775-7722), 982 Market St., between 5th and 6th, near the Civic Center, hosts headliners and up-and-coming local groups. Most huge concerts are usually held outside San Francisco at the *Oakland Coliseum*, the *Shoreline Amphitheater* in Mountainview, or a number of other stadium-size venues.

COMEDY & CABARET

A number of bars occasionally feature comedy nights, but for the real thing, San Francisco has two immensely popular comedy clubs: The *Punchline* (☎ 397-4337) at 444 Battery St. in Maritime Plaza in the heart of the Financial District and *Cobb's Comedy Club* (☎ 928-4320), 2801 Leavenworth St., in the Cannery at Fisherman's Wharf. Cobb's has a showcase night on Mondays with 12 to 15 up-and-coming comics performing and a cover of $5. Both clubs usually have two performances, one around

8 pm and one around 11 pm, with a cover charge ranging from $5 to $15 and a two-drink minimum.

Along comedic lines is the everlasting *Beach Blanket Babylon* extravaganza in North Beach (see the Theater section for more information). Also in North Beach is *Finocchio's* (☎ 982-9388), 506 Broadway, where female impersonators engage in a "been-there, seen-that" type of comedy routine.

In the Castro, *Josie's Cabaret & Juice Joint* (☎ 861-7933), 3583 16th St., puts on gay and lesbian comedy and cabaret performances nightly, and has a great backyard patio for balmy afternoons.

CINEMA

Forget those modern multi-screen theaters – San Francisco boasts a bunch of great, old, single-screen dinosaur theaters. The Bay Area is a terrific region for movie-goers with wonderful old cinemas, discerning local film buffs, and lots of foreign and art house venues. Typically it costs $7.50 to see a movie. See the *Bay Guardian* and the *SF Weekly* for schedules.

Topping the list for cinemas where the building is as interesting as the film is undoubtedly the *Castro Theatre* (☎ 621-6120), 429 Castro St. just off Market. A magnificent Wurlitzer organ rises out of the stage and the theater has as much plush velvet, Grecian columns, and fake plants as any vintage cinema buff can take.

TONY WHEELER

The *Alhambra* (☎ 775-2137), 2330 Polk St. at Union in the Polk Gulch is a general release cinema and it nonetheless looks fantastic.

In business since 1913, the *Clay Theater* (☎ 346-1123), 2261 Fillmore St. at Clay, is the longest continuously operating cinema in the city. It still looks magnificent, if a little careworn.

RICK GERHARTER

The *Roxie* (☎ 863-1087), 3117 16th St. at Valencia, in the Mission, screens an adventurous, eclectic selection of films although the space itself is pretty featureless. At the small *Red Vic* (☎ 668-3994), 1727 Haight St. in the Haight-Ashbury, you can see rare cult films and other interesting oldies. The *Lumière* (☎ 885-3200), 1572 California St. at Polk, has three screens and shows a mix of art house films and new releases. Out in the Richmond District, the Art Deco *Balboa* (☎ 221-8184), 3630 Balboa St., has been operating since 1926 and screens new releases.

The *Casting Couch* (☎ 986-7001), 950 Battery St. near Levi's Plaza and the Embarcadero, is a tiny theater with luxury loveseat couches seating just 46 people. Gourmet snacks are delivered to your seat; admission is $8.50 and American Express is accepted. The *San Francisco Cinematheque* (☎ 978-2787) is in the Center for the Arts, 701 Mission St in Yerba Buena Gardens.

The better multiplex cinemas include the eight-screen *Kabuki 8 Theater* (☎ 931-9800), 1881 Post St. in Japantown. They show a good mix of blockbusters and special interest films, and offer validated parking. Or, there's the towering glass-and-steel *Galaxy* (☎ 474-8700), 1285 Sutter St. and Van Ness, which has been provoking pro and con arguments ever since it opened in 1984. *Opera Plaza* (☎ 771-0102), 601 Van Ness Ave., is another modern complex, with four screens and an interesting program of film releases.

The city hosts the San Francisco Film Festival (☎ 931-3456) in April (mainly at the Kabuki), the Lesbian & Gay Film Festival in June (at the Castro Theatre), the Asian American Film Festival (☎ 863-0814) in March (at the Kabuki cineplex), and the Jewish Film Festival (☎ (510) 548-0556) in July / August (at the Castro).

Finally, one of the best film venues in the Bay Area is not in San Francisco at all but across the Bay in Berkeley at the *Pacific Film Archive*.

PERFORMING ARTS

Theater

San Francisco is not a cutting-edge city for theater, but it has one major company, the American Conservatory Theater (ACT) that sponsors the big hits a season or so after they've opened in New York and London. The city is also home to a variety of smaller alternative theater companies, and there's always some worthwhile performance going on.

You can reserve tickets directly with the theater, through BASS (☎ (510) 762-2277), or go for same-day half-price tickets at the Tix Bay Area booth (☎ 433-7827) in Union Square.

Big Houses ACT's (☎ 749-2228) *Geary Theater*, 450 Geary St., is its main performance space and is newly rebuilt after being damaged in the 1989 earthquake. They also put on performances at the *Marines Memorial Theatre*, 609 Sutter St., and at the mid-sized *Stage Door Theatre*, 420 Mason St., both in the Union Square-area theater district.

The big spectacular shows – like the Andrew Lloyd-Webber musicals – show at the *Curran Theatre* (☎ 474-3800), 445 Geary St., between Mason and Taylor.

The *Magic Theater* (☎ 441-8822) at Building D, Fort Mason Center, is probably the city's most adventurous large theater. The *Golden Gate Theater* (☎ 474-3800), 1 Taylor St. at Golden Gate and Market, also puts on larger shows, although generally they're more mainstream.

Many of the jokes will go straight over non-San Francisco residents' heads, but *Beach Blanket Babylon* at *Club Fugazi* (☎ 421-4222), 678 Green St. in North Beach, is San Francisco's longest-running comedy extravaganza, now into its third decade and still packing them in (over 21 years of age, except at matinees, please!). There are shows Wednesday to Sunday and cleaned-up matinee performances on Saturday and Sunday. Watch for the hats.

Alternative Theater There are many small theater spaces like *The Marsh* (641-0235),1062 Valencia St., around the city that host experimental shows If you're in town in September, check out the *Fringe Festival* (☎ 931-1094), when a number of theaters put on new plays and solo performances for a ticket price of only $7. Some of the more active smaller theaters in San Francisco include:

Bay Front Theater	☎ 776-8999	Building B, Ft Mason
Cable Car Theatre	☎ 982-5463	430 Mason St.
Exit Theater	☎ 673-3847	156 Eddy St.
Mason St. Theatre	☎ 982-5463	340 Mason St.
Theatre on the Square	☎ 433-9500	450 Post St.
Phoenix Theatre	☎ 721-1717	301 8th St. at Folsom
Theater Rhinoceros	☎ 861-5079	2926 16th St.
Theater Artaud	☎ 621-7797	450 Florida St.

Classical Music

The *San Francisco Symphony* performs September to May in the Davies Symphony Hall (☎ 431-5400), Van Ness Ave. at Grove St. Tickets are typically $24 to $68 but

What's Happening & Where to Get Tickets
The daily *San Francisco Chronicle* has fairly extensive movie and theater listings and the Sunday "pink section" of the *Examiner-Chronicle* is even more complete, especially for the established symphony, ballet, and opera events. However, for the city's most extensive run-down on entertainment possibilities – from stadium-size rock acts to obscure open-mic poetry readings – check the weekly free papers: the *San Francisco Bay Guardian* and the *San Francisco Weekly*. The *San Francisco Arts Monthly* covers music, theater, dance, art films, and the visual arts. For gay and lesbian entertainment listings, pick up the *San Francisco Bay Times* in the Castro.

For theater tickets and tickets to the big rock acts and other shows call BASS (☎ (510) 762-2277), or visit their outlets at The Wherehouse or Tower Records stores. TIX Bay Area (☎ 433-7827) at 251 Stockton St. in Union Square sells half-price same-day tickets for musical performances, opera, dance, and theater. The booth is open Tuesday to Thursday from 11 am to 6 pm and Friday and Saturday from 11 am to 7 pm. They take cash only and there's a $1 service charge. ■

cheap seats go on sale two hours before the performance for $10 to $12, cash only.

There are also performances at the Herbst Theatre (☎ 392-4400), Veterans Building, 401 Van Ness Ave. The *San Francisco Conservatory of Music* (☎ 759-3475) puts on a variety of performances at Hellman Hall, 1201 Ortega Ave. at 19th.

Opera

The acclaimed *San Francisco Opera* performs from early September to mid-December and briefly during the summer. Ticket prices range from $21 for the cheapest, side balcony seats to $135 for a box seat, and sell out well ahead. Student tickets are a great deal: for only $20, students with a valid student ID will get to sit in the $100 orchestra section. These tickets go on sale two hours before the performance. Standing-room tickets, available for some shows, are $8 and go on sale two hours before the performance. The opera performs at the War Memorial Opera House (☎ 864-3330), 301 Van Ness Ave. at Grove St.

Dance

The *San Francisco Ballet* (☎ 703-9400), the oldest ballet company in the USA, also performs at the opera house or at the Center for the Arts Theater (☎ 978-2787), 700 Howard St. at 3rd, in the Yerba Buena Gardens in

SoMa. Tickets are typically $7 to $100 but senior/student tickets are sometimes available for half price. Other dance performances take place at a variety of venues around the city including the Herbst Theatre.

Free (or Cheap) & Outdoors

Free (or cheap) outdoor entertainment abounds in San Francisco. The big performance companies sponsor numerous concerts in historic or open-air venues, particularly in the summer but also during other times of the year. There are also many small performing troupes and special annual festivals and events.

The *Noontime Concert Series* (☎ 255-9410) puts on a varied repertoire of free classical music performances in Old St. Mary's Church, at Grant Ave. and California St. in Chinatown, every Tuesday at 12:30 pm; donations are appreciated. Fridays during the summer, there are lunchtime jazz concerts in Justin Herman Plaza downtown.

The *San Francisco Symphony* and the *San Francisco Ballet* hold free performances in the Sigmund Stern Grove at Sloat Blvd. and 19th Ave. on summer Sundays. This open-air auditorium, sunken into an amphitheater of eucalyptus and redwood trees, is a beautiful spot for a picnic. Call ☎ 252-6252 for schedule information.

One of the city's most popular outdoor events is *Shakespeare in the Park* (☎ 666-2222) in Golden Gate Park's Liberty Tree Meadow behind the Conservatory of Flowers. The San Francisco Shakespeare Festival performs one play each fall, opening Labor Day weekend and running for five weekends. It's free and starts at 1:30 pm but fills up much earlier. The second Sunday in September, also in Golden Gate Park, is *Opera in the Park*, a free non-costumed concert celebrating the opening of the opera season. It runs from 1:30 to 3:30 pm and draws huge crowds; it's held in Sharon Meadow.

The *San Francisco Mime Troupe* (☎ 285-1717, 285-1720 for schedule information) performs at parks throughout San Francisco all summer. Don't expect any silent, white-faced mimes – this is "political musical theater" in the *commedia dell'arte* tradition. It's big, it's loud, it's free (donations accepted), and it's a lot of fun.

SPECTATOR SPORTS

San Francisco's NFL (National Football League) team, the *San Francisco 49ers* (☎ 468-2249), have been regular Super Bowl champions, while the National League baseball team the *San Francisco Giants* (☎ 467-8000) have slugged their way into the hearts of local fans. Both teams play at the cold and windy Candlestick Park, south of the city. There's a long-running argument over building a new, more user-friendly downtown stadium for the two teams and, at the same time, drawing in the *Golden State Warriors* (☎ (510) 638-6300) NBA basketball team, who play at the Oakland Coliseum.

The *Oakland A's* (☎ (510) 638-0500), the American League baseball team, have won more games than the Giants, but aren't as sentimentally popular. Recently recovered from the depths of L.A., the *Oakland Raiders*, another NFL team, is back to play at the Coliseum. The bruisers of the National Hockey League are teamed up as the *San Jose Sharks* (☎ (408) 287-4275).

Tickets Regardless of the team you want to see and whether they're in Oakland or San Francisco, sporting event tickets are available through BASS (☎ (510) 762-2277, in San Jose call (408) 998-2277) – you can either call and order tickets by credit card or go to a BASS outlet, which include the Wherehouse and Tower Records chains.

You can also order them through the telephone numbers of the organizations themselves, or visit their ticket offices (weekdays 9 am to 5 pm, Saturday 9 am to 1 pm) to avoid the BASS service charge (usually around $3 a ticket) and handling fees.

If you have your heart set on seeing a game – *call ahead for tickets!* That said, due to the sheer number of games, baseball tickets are usually easy to come by – you can turn up at the stadium and get good seats for only $7 to $15. For hockey, which isn't as popular in sunny Cal as it is back east, tickets are also usually easy to get the day of the game but are costlier. Football and basketball, however, are expensive local favorites: count on forking over $25 to $100, and if you haven't booked well ahead, you probably won't get in. Ticket brokers, who sometimes charge astronomical prices, include Just Tix (☎ (510) 838-0193) and Mr. Ticket (☎ (415) 292-7328).

Getting There & Away If you drive, get directions by calling the team's phone number.

To get to the "Stick," CalTrain runs reasonably close but Muni also operates special bus services to the stadium when games are on. For Oakland Coliseum, take BART – it's got a stop on the Fremont line ("Coliseum") and is easily the fastest way in and out of the East Bay during an event. For multiple public transportation options to the San Jose Arena, call the Sharks.

Shopping

San Francisco's shopping, like its nightlife, is best when the words "small", "odd", and "eccentric" come in to play. Sure, there are big department stores and an international selection of name brand boutiques, but the oddities of the Castro, Haight-Ashbury, or Pacific Heights are a lot more fun.

Most city shops are open Monday to Saturday, typically 9 or 10 am to 5 or 6 pm. Bookstores are often an exception, some of which are open daily, until late. Tourist oriented shops, like the Grant Ave. in Chinatown and Pier 39 at Fisherman's Wharf are places also open daily.

For foreign visitors US prices are competitive with those anywhere in the world, particularly for electronics, cameras, computer equipment, and clothes. Visitors should not forget the 8.5% sales tax which is lumped on to everything and is not, like European VAT (value added tax), refundable to foreign visitors. A price 10% lower than back home is going to be as expensive when sales tax is added.

WHERE TO SHOP

Union Square

San Francisco's downtown shopping concentrates around Union Square and nearby Market St. Macy's (☎ 397-3333), Neiman-Marcus (☎ 362-3900), and Saks Fifth Avenue (☎ 986-4300) make up the square's trio of plush department stores. Nordstrom (☎ 243-8500) occupies the top several floors of the stylish San Francisco Shopping Center (☎ 495-5656), 865 Market St. at Powell and 5th; where you can also find clothing boutiques, novelty shops, and the Emporium. Rumor has it Bloomingdales may be ousting out Emporium though.

In the surrounding streets you'll find the fashion world well represented by the likes of Chanel, Ralph Lauren, Gianni Versace, and Gucci. At the Emporio Armani boutique (☎ 677-9400), 1 Grant Ave. just off Market, you can select from the designer's exclusive shoes and clothes, and have lunch or espresso at the cafe in the center of the store.

Gump's (☎ 982-1616), 135 Post St., is a San Francisco institution, half museum and half home furnishings store with some wonderful Asian art pieces.

SoMa

The big deal in SoMa is outlet shopping. Yerba Buena Square (☎ 974-5136), 899 Howard St. at 5th, and the 660 Center (☎ 227-0464), 660 3rd St. at Townsend, both house a variety of outlet operations and are open daily. The Esprit Factory Outlet (☎ 957-2550), 499 Illinois St. at 16th, Potrero Hill, is a big warehouse with 30% to 50% discounts on Esprit apparel.

Hayes Valley

Hayes St., between Franklin and Laguna near the Civic Center, has experienced a newfound commercial boom in the years following the 1989 earthquake and subsequent demolition of Hwy 101 over Gough St. When the debris was cleared away galleries, boutiques, and cafes began to appear, turning it into a new, though still little-known, hotspot.

Chinatown

Only Fisherman's Wharf rivals Chinatown for sheer quantity of tourist junk. If you want a cheap souvenir then you've come to the right place and a stroll down Grant Ave. will supply all the postcards, Golden Gate snowstorms, and questionable T-shirts you could want. Explore the back streets and alleys and you'll find all sorts of less-touristy goods like bargain priced dishes and bowls or weird herbal pharmaceuticals.

TONY WHEELER

A Chinatown apothecary

Haight-Ashbury

The Haight has a fine collection of strange shops. It's particularly good for music, especially older and second hand records, and used clothing, though it also has its share of pricey shops. 683 Haight St. (☎ 861-1311) has '60s rock & roll memorabilia, and Comic Relief (☎ 552-9010) at 1597 Haight St. is the place for off-the-wall comic books. In the Lower Haight it's hard to pass by a shop with a name like Used Rubber (☎ 626-7855), 597 Haight St. at Steiner. It's dedicated to proving what a multitude of things you can find to do with old truck tires and fan belts.

KITTI HOMME

A wacky storefront in the Haight

Fisherman's Wharf

If you really need a San Francisco souvenir, you'll find what you're looking for at Fisherman's Wharf. Of course there are fun shops, even on Pier 39, the Fisherman's Wharf centerpiece. The Cannery, Ghirardelli Square, and the Anchorage are other wharf-front shopping centers.

Union St. & the Marina

Union St. in Pacific Height's 'Cow Hollow' is dotted with interesting boutiques, antique stores, and trendy little galleries. Only a few blocks down towards the Bay is Chestnut St. in the Marina, an equally upscale little enclave tending toward the twenty-something crowd.

Fillmore St.

Filled with cafes, restaurants, and home-furnishing stores Fillmore St. north of Geary St. and Japantown is not for the budget-conscious. Enjoy the gorgeous views from the top of the hill overlooking the Bay and stop to get a bite to eat before heading in to view the mansions of Pacific Heights.

The Castro & Noe Valley

Just south of Market St., and barely off the new F Muni line, four blocks of Castro St. are the center of the busy neighborhood, housing numerous shops and restaurants. For fun, check out Cliff's Variety (☎ 431-5365), 479 Castro, where you can find anything from housewares and Play-Doh to that three-penny nail you need to hang your SFMOMA poster.

Follow Castro south, over a hill, and below lies Noe Valley. 24th St. is the main shopping street. This haven is for those looking to get away from the tourist throng and browse a thoroughly San Francisco street with the usual fine selection of art and clothes, coffee and books.

Museum Stores

San Francisco's varied collection of museums have some great stores with interesting items. The new SFMOMA Museum Store (☎ 357-4035), 3rd St. by Yerba Buena Gardens, has a superb selection of books on modern art and arty items relating to the museum collection. This is the place to buy a "fog dome." In Golden Gate Park the museums all have interesting stores: the Academy Store (☎ 750-7330) at the California Academy of Sciences, the Museum Store (☎ 750-3642) at the M.H. de Young Memorial Museum, and the Asian Art Museum's store (☎ 668-8921). Naturally the Exploratorium Store (☎ 561-0390) has instructional toys and games. ■

WHAT TO BUY

Antiques & Art

The Jackson Square area, a small enclave at the borderland between the Financial District and North Beach, and appropriately one of the few parts of downtown to survive the 1906 quake and fire, is one of the city's prime shopping areas for antiques and furnishings. The Jackson Square Art & Antique Dealers Association (☎ 296-8150), 414 Jackson St., is an umbrella organization for 25 of these dealers. Union St. in Pacific Heights is another good hunting ground.

Streets going west out of Union Square are home to many galleries. On Geary St. you'll find a run of galleries on the south side of the street between Powell and Mason; one of the better is Caldwell Snyder (☎ 296-7896) at 357 Geary. Others include the Nevska Gallery (☎ 392-4932), right next door, focusing on Russian art, and Galerie Adrienne (☎ 288-6575) with a modern mix.

A few blocks north on Sutter St., starts another line of galleries and shops. Right on the corner of Powell and Sutter is the Martin Lawrence Gallery (☎ 956-0345) with contemporary graphics. Cross the street to a line of small spaces focusing on the European classics, including Eleonore Austerer Gallery (☎ 986-2244) and Cobra Fine Art (☎ 397-2195). Across the street is one of the three Academy of Art College galleries.

In the vicinity of SFMOMA, South of Market, are some great galleries that give a decent perspective on the alternative San Francisco art scene. Among the many are Acme Gallery (☎ 896-2263) at 667 Howard St., and 111 Minna St. Gallery (☎ 974-1719) with a small coffee bar. Vision Gallery (☎ 621-2107) at 1155 Mission, between 7th and 8th Sts, is one of the city's larger photography galleries with four shows going on at once. Admission is usually free to the above places.

Most galleries are open weekdays to 5 or 6 pm. The first Thursday of each month galleries stay open late and often have small receptions. Check out the *Bay Guardian* or the *SF Weekly* to find out about openings and receptions.

Bicycles

Bicycle stores to try include Start to Finish (☎ 202-9830), 2530 Lombard St. in the Marina, and (☎ 243-8812), at 599 2nd St. at Brannan in SoMa. They rent and repair bicycles and will ship overseas. Avenue Cyclery (☎ 387-3155), 756 Stanyan St., by Golden Gate Park in the Haight-Ashbury, and City Cycle (☎ 346-2242), 3001 Steiner St. in Pacific Heights, are other stores to try.

Books

San Francisco is a bookish city – the Bay Area is one of the biggest reading markets in the USA and topped only by New York City as a publishing center. Bookstores include many interesting specialty stores but true bibliophiles should also venture to the East Bay to explore Berkeley's superb selection of bookshops.

General Bookstores Many city bookshops are open late, often every night of the week. Borders (☎ 399-1633) is a huge and glossy bookshop with a cafe on the northwest corner of Union Square. A Clean Well Lighted Place for Books (☎ 441-6670), 601 Van Ness Ave. in Opera Plaza near the Civic Center, is a good place to hear author readings. The Booksmith (☎ 863-8688), 1644 Haight St., is a general bookstore in the most ungeneral of neighborhoods.

Green Apple Books (☎ 387-2272), 506 Clement St., between 6th and 7th in the Richmond district, is one of the best bookstores in the city.

San Francisco's most famous bookstore, City Lights (☎ 362-8193), 261 Columbus Ave., North Beach, was the first paperbacks-only bookshop in the USA and has always been at the cutting edge of writing and literature. It was the center of the Beats in the '50s and is still owned by its founder, poet Lawrence Ferlinghetti. It's a wonderful place to book browse late at night – the poetry room upstairs has hands down the best selection anywhere.

Specialty Bookstores Rand McNally (☎ 777-3131), 595 Market St. at 2nd, has a superb selection of travel books and maps. On the other side of the Financial District Thomas Bros. Books & Maps (☎ 981-7520), 550 Jackson St. in Jackson Square, also specializes in travel and maps. Sierra Club Bookstore (☎ 923-5600), 730 Polk St., between Eddy and Ellis, has their full line and material on the natural environment.

The Mission is the place for all sorts of interesting bookshops with a mission. Once upon a time if you wanted a copy of Mao's little red book, China Books (☎ 282-2994), 2929 24th St. in the Mission, was where you got it, and this is still the place for Chinese publications. Modern Times Bookstore (☎ 282-9246), 888 Valencia St., has strong sections on feminism and other contemporary issues, and Old Wives Tales Book Store (☎ 821-4575), 1009 Valencia St., is a woman-oriented bookshop.

In Japantown the Kinokuniya Bookshop (☎ 567-7625), Kinokuniya Building, 1581 Webster St., has a great collection of books in Japanese including plenty of

TOM SMALLMAN

SCOTT SUMMERS

Farmers' Markets at Civic Center (top) and the Ferry Building (bottom)

Toys, Games & Weird Stuff
Close to Union Square, FAO Schwartz (☎ 394-8700), 48 Stockton St., is the San Francisco branch of the major upscale toy store chain. Toys for much bigger boys can be found at the Sharper Image (☎ 398-6472), 532 Market St.

In North Beach Quantity Postcards (☎ 986-8866), 1441 Grant Ave., is dedicated to weird, OK sometimes very weird, postcards. It's impossible to visit this shop without developing an overwhelming urge to send a card to some long lost friend. Just north of Washington Square in North Beach, Rock Posters & Collectibles (☎ 956-6749), 1851 Powell St., has a great collection of rock memorabilia, particularly from San Francisco's psychedelic heyday. Similar memorabilia including '60s rock posters and cards can be found at 683 Haight St. (☎ 861-1311), 683 Haight St., Haight-Ashbury. ■

manga, Japanese comic books. Try the European Book Company (☎ 474-0626), 925 Larkin St. at Geary, for foreign books and magazines. Marcus Books (☎ 346-4222), 1712 Fillmore St., specializes in African and African-American issues.

A Different Light Bookstore (☎ 431-0891), 489 Castro St. in the Castro, is America's largest gay and lesbian bookseller.

Periodicals Harold Newsstand (☎ 441-2665), 524 Geary St. has the best choice of out-of-town newspapers in the city. Cafe de la Presse (☎ 398-2680), 328 Grant Ave., has European papers and magazines. Both places are near Union Square.

Cameras & Photography

Adolph Gasser (☎ 495-3852), 181 2nd St., south of Market, has a huge range of new and used photographic and video equipment, and also processes film. Downtown, Brooks Camera (☎ 392-1900), 45 Kearny St., sells new cameras and does repairs and rentals, as does Camera Boutique (☎ 982-4946), 342 Kearny St.

For cheap film and developing, call 334-2020 for the nearest Walgreens Drugs. For quickie one-hour jobs, Fox Photo and Ritz Camera each have several local labs with a decent selection of films. Check the Yellow Pages for locations.

Cars & Motorcycles

This is not Los Angeles, but it's still California, and a car is still a birthright. Of course there will be a dealer for every brand of car on sale in California – you want a

Ferrari, try Ferrari of San Francisco (☎ 380-9700) at 595 Redwood Highway, Mill Valley, just north of the Golden Gate Bridge and the Marin Tunnel.

Dawdyiak Cars (☎ 928-2277), 1450 Franklin St., has examples of European exotica and some very nice classic examples of Detroit iron. Classic means from the era when the quality of a car was gauged by the height of its tail fins. Fantasy Junction (☎ (510) 653-7555), 1145 Park Ave., across the Bay in Emeryville, will satisfy your curiosity as to what a half-a-million-dollar car looks like.

Motorcycles get a go as well. Dudley Perkins (☎ 703-9494), 66 Page St., close to Market, is the place for Harley-Davidson enthusiasts with new bikes and some fine vintage Harleys on display at the world's oldest Harley dealership. Magri Motorcycles (☎ 285-6735), 1220 Pennsylvania Ave., between 25th St and Army on Potrero Hill, specializes in British motorcycles. It's closed Sunday and Monday.

Fashion

San Francisco is a stylish city, but the great thing about it is the style spectrum is so far-ranging and diverse – in San Francisco, anything goes, from sharp tailored suits to retro to drag extravagance, and everything in between.

San Francisco is hometown to two internationally known clothing chains quite apart from Levi's jeans. The Gap has half a dozen city locations and Banana Republic can be found at 256 Grant Ave. and 2 Embarcadero Center.

Wilkes Bashford (☎ 986-4380), 375 Sutter St, carries high-quality men's clothes, if price is no object. Nomads (☎ 864-5692), 556 Hayes St., features casual menswear by local designers with a European touch. There are many great women's clothing stores in San Francisco – a few favorites are Ambiance (☎ 552-5095), 1458 Haight St.,

Levi Strauss

San Francisco's contribution to sartorial elegance is a straightforward one: Levi's jeans. A German gold rush immigrant, the 21-year-old Levi Strauss arrived from New York in 1850, burdened with materials from his brothers' store. When he'd sold everything else except the sailcloth he struck on the idea of using it to make indestructible pants for hard working miners. With his brothers he founded Levi's in 1853. The riveted pockets idea was patented in 1873 and the word denim was also a Levi invention. When serge from Nîmes in France was substituted for sailcloth the "serge de Nîmes" became denim. ■

and Solo (☎ 621-8579), 2298 Haight St., with casual and dressy women's clothing plus vintagey hats and jewelry.

Villains (☎ 626-5939) at 1672 Haight St. sells alternative shoe styles, including Doc Martens and Converse. For more shoes of the übermod, hip hop variety, try Urban Outfitters (☎ 989-1515) at 80 Powell St. or X-Large (☎ 626-9573), the store started by members of the Beastie Boys, at 1415 Haight St.

For athletic shoes, good places to look for brand names are: First Step at 57 Powell St. (☎ 986-5947) and 216 Powell St. (☎ 989-9989).

Food & Drink

There's a Saturday farmers' market, from 8:30 am to 2:30 pm, at the Embarcadero by the Ferry Plaza Building, offering locally grown and organic produce, fresh baked breads, and other local items.

If you don't leave San Francisco with an appreciation for **sourdough bread** you haven't tried enough. Boudin Bakery (☎ 928-1849), 156 Jefferson St., Fisherman's Wharf, is still the best place for classic sourdough. There's another Boudin in the basement of the Macy's in Union Square (☎ 296-4740), one in Ghirardelli Square (☎ 928-7404), and a number of others throughout the city.

Freed, Teller & Freed (☎ 673-0922), 1326 Polk St. is a specialty tea store featuring every conceivable **tea** creation, including tea ice cream. For a run-down of local **coffee** roasters see the Entertainment chapter.

Ghirardelli, of course, is the name in **chocolate**. You can find Ghirardelli treats all over the city and beyond, but to make an experience of it, go to their stores, Ghirardelli's Premium Chocolates (☎ 474-3938), which sells ice cream and fountain drinks, and Ghirardelli Too (☎ 474-1414), which has gifts, espresso, and frozen yogurt, in the namesake square. Both are usually open past 9 pm.

In the Castro, a different kind of decadence can be found at RoCocoa Faerie Queene Chocolates (☎ 252-5814) at 415 Castro; the diverse and international selection here is sure to delight even the most depressed. Joseph Schmidt Confections (☎ 861-8682), 3489 16th St., is another locally famous chocolatier.

For overseas visitors, taking back a few bottles of Napa or Sonoma Valley **wine** is a great idea but check your home country's import regulations before loading up.

The Napa Valley Winery Exchange (☎ 771-2887), 415 Taylor St., downtown, has small production and specialist wines. K & L Wines & Spirits (☎ 896-1734), 734 Harrison St. near the Moscone Center, also has a wide selection of Californian wines. Plump Jack Wines (☎ 346-9870) at 3201 Fillmore can give you excellent recommendations. Trader Joe's (☎ 863-1292), 555 9th St., and Cost Plus (☎ 928-6200), 2552 Taylor St., both have excellent deals. Beverages & More (☎ 648-1233) 201 Bayshore Blvd, is a veritable warehouse of liquors and wines.

Music

For a huge selection of CDs and great prices go by Tower Records. There are a few outlets around the city including Tower Outlet (☎ 957-9660), 660 3rd St. in the SoMa outlet zone but Tower Records (☎ 885-0500), Columbus Ave. and Bay, close to Fisherman's Wharf, is one of the best. The Wherehouse (☎ 751-3711), 3301 Geary Blvd also has a big selection.

For used records, CDs, and tapes try Rough Trade Absolute Music (☎ 543-7091), 695 3rd St., best known for launching punk and alternative music in the '70s and '80s, both on indie labels and its own. This San Francisco legend has recently moved from the Haight to new digs South of Market. Other places for off-the-wall records are Recycled Records (☎ 626-4075), 1377 Haight St., for second hand CDs and vinyl; and Reckless Records (☎ 431-3434), 1401 Haight St., for indie releases and imports.

And, of course, the largest music store in the world has recently opened its doors in San Francisco, the Virgin Megastore (☎ 397-4525), 2 Stockton St. at Market, complete with listening stations and a cafe.

Further afield Berkeley has a number of interesting music stores, particularly Amoeba and Rasputin on Telegraph Ave.

Outdoor Gear

Many of these stores sell not only clothing but the necessaries for outdoor adventure, including travel guides. They can give good advice, and have bulletin boards full of information.

The North Face (☎ 433-3223), 180 Post St., has its headquarters in the area and has a good selection of high quality outdoor and adventure travel gear. Try their factory outlet store in SoMa (☎ 626-6444), 1325 Howard St., for discounted styles. Patagonia (☎ 771-2050), 770 North Point, Fisherman's Wharf, is another respected name in outdoor gear. Eddie Bauer (☎ 986-7600), 220 Post St., has three floors of outdoor equipment and clothing.

Adults Only
In the heart of the Mission there's a shop providing means for adult entertainment. Good Vibrations (☎ 974-8980), 1210 Valencia St., specializes in vibrators of all types and sizes, as well as other paraphernalia. This tasteful sex shop has sex toys, books, and videos.

If you're into the leather subculture, do your shopping in the Castro and SoMa. Image Leather (☎ 621-7551), 2199 Market St., is a hard-core leather and fetish gear shop; descend into the "dungeon" where there's a . . . well, a museum of sorts. ■

Over in the East Bay, REI (☎ (510) 527-4140), 1338 San Pablo Ave., is a supermarket-size shopping (and rental) center for outdoor clothing and equipment. Marmot, the top-quality mountaineering outfitter is also locally based, with their full line represented at their flagship store (☎ (510) 849-0735) in Berkeley at 3049 Adeline St., just off Ashby Ave.

Piercings & Tattoos

Getting a pin through it is a San Francisco specialty; numerous specialist body piercers will pierce parts of your body that go way beyond those mundane ears. Bejeweled noses, eyebrows, lips, and tongues are frequently seen, and nipples and navels are the most popular "below the neck" piercings, though men can consider a half a dozen different ways of putting a pin through their genitals: choose between a Prince Albert, a frenum, a dydoe, an ampallang, an apadravya, or a guiche. There aren't quite so many genital possiblities for women but for the very brave even a clitoral piercing is possible.

Piercing specialists start with The Gauntlet (☎ 431-3133), 2377 Market St. at Castro; one glance at their staff will tell you they know all about piercing. In the Haight-Ashbury there's Anubis Warpus (☎ 431-2218), 1525 Haight St., and in the Lower Haight, Body Manipulations (☎ 621-0408), 254 Fillmore St.

Tattoos are what you need to go with your piercings and the Lyle Tuttle (☎ 775-4991) tattoo parlor, at 841 Columbus Ave. in North Beach, also has a small tattoo museum.

Excursions

MARIN COUNTY

☎ AREA CODE: **415**

Across the Golden Gate Bridge from San Francisco, Marin County is wealthy, laid back, and right in tune with every trend that comes by. From hot tubs and cocaine to New Age spiritualism, mountain biking, and designer pizzas, Marin was there first. It's a wonderfully varied peninsula with fashionable Sausalito and Tiburon on the bay side and the wild Pacific coastline stretching north to Stinson Beach, hideaway Bolinas and Point Reyes National Seashore. Between bay and ocean the central hills rise to Mt. Tamalpais, overlooking the redwood stand of Muir Woods.

Getting There & Away

Highway 101 cuts directly through Marin County; Hwy 1 branches off at Mill Valley and heads to the coast. Golden Gate Transit (☎ 332-6600) operates buses from San Francisco to Marin; Golden Gate Ferries (same number) run from Fisherman's Wharf to Sausalito and Larkspur; and the Red & White Fleet (☎ 546-2896) goes to Sausalito and Tiburon, as well as Angel Island.

The Marin Headlands

The most dramatic and instantly recognizable post card shots of San Francisco are taken from the Marin Headlands, the rolling hills above the Golden Gate Bridge. The US military controlled the Headlands for over a century, leaving its mark with a number of forts and garrisons, but meanwhile keeping the area blessedly free of development. When they vacated the site, concerned citizens were able to create the Golden Gate National Recreation Area (GGNRA).

Once across the Golden Gate Bridge, exit on Alexander Ave. and turn left under the freeway. Follow winding Conzelman Rd. along the ridges of the hills; it passes Fort Spencer, which dates to the Spanish-American War and rises to Hawk Hill, where in the fall hundreds of migrating birds of prey can be seen. At the end of the road is a short trail down to **Point Bonita Lighthouse**, built in 1877.

JOHN ZEGART

The slopes of Mt. Tamalpais

JOHN ZEGART

The Golden Gate Bridge from the Headlands

The visitors center (☎ 331-1540) is off Bunker Rd., north of Conzelman Rd. From here there are many opportunities for hiking and biking. Rodeo Lagoon is a home to many species of birds, and **Rodeo Beach** is a secluded place to enjoy the rugged Pacific. You can't get any further by car, but there's an extensive trails system that links up to Mt. Tam, Muir Beach and other sites to the north.

The **Marine Mammal Center** (☎ 289-7325), north of the lagoon, rehabilitates injured and orphaned sea creatures. The **Discovery Museum** (☎ 332-7674) at 557 East Fort Baker in a converted military barracks, is a kid's paradise, with hands-on exhibits from arts & crafts to biology to photography.

The *Marin Headlands Hostel* (☎ 331-2777) is housed in former officer's quarters at Fort Barry. Call the GGNRA office (☎ 331-1540) for camping information.

TONY WHEELER

Point Reyes Lighthouse

Sausalito

Once a small seafaring center populated by fisherfolk, the tiny bayside community of Sausalito is now fiercely expensive and fashionable, a tourist haven with a curious mix of junky souvenir shops and costly galleries and boutiques. Still, there's no denying Sausalito's beauty, stretched along the water's edge with uninterrupted views of Angel Island and San Francisco. It makes a great day out from San Francisco and the ferry connection is a good alternative to the community's parking problems. The main street of town is Bridgeway, and the visitors center (☎ 332-0505), upstairs in the Village Fair at 777 Bridgeway, has a walking guide booklet to make wandering the Sausalito waterfront more interesting.

The Army Corps of Engineers' **Bay Model** (☎ 332-3871), 2100 Bridgeway, is a large, scale model of the San

Francisco Bay, built in 1954 to study the complex waterflows of the bay. In the same center are displays on the history of Marinship, the WWII shipbuilding yard that once occupied the site, turning out a completed ship every 13 days at the height of the war.

Mill Valley & Mt. Tamalpais

If Sausalito is too touristy for your taste, head inland to Mill Valley. This town in the redwoods has the feel of an artist's retreat. It began as a redwood logging center, and the town square was once the station for a scenic railway that carried visitors up Mt. Tamalpais (Mt. Tam). The *Depot Bookstore & Cafe* (☎ 383-2665), 87 Throckmorton, now occupies the old depot building, a perfect spot for coffee and people watching. Aside from having excellent restaurants and shopping, Mill Valley is also a point of departure for hiking and biking on Mt. Tam.

Mt. Tamalpais State Park (☎ 388-2070) includes Mt. Tam itself and the Muir Woods National Monument. The panorama from the 2571-foot peak of Mt. Tam is a breathtaking 360° of ocean, bay, city, and hills rolling into the distance. Over 200 miles of hiking and biking trails wind around the mountain, and deer, fox, bobcat, and even the occasional mountain lion dwell in the forests and dells.

Muir Woods is the 550-acre remnant of the vast redwood forests that once covered the area. President Theodore Roosevelt made it a national monument in 1908 and named it after Sierra Club founder John Muir. It's open from 8 am to sunset; the visitors center (☎ 388-2595) is at the main entrance.

For detailed information on hiking and biking in the area, check out the selection of trail guides and maps at the Depot Bookstore. The San Francisco Bay chapter of the Sierra Club leads an array of free hikes on weekends – call ☎ 776-2211, ext 6884 for recorded information.

The Coast

Point Reyes National Seashore Divided from the mainland by Tomales Bay, the triangular peninsula of Point Reyes National Seashore comprises 110 sq. miles of long fog-swept beaches, lagoons, rough-hewn rock formations, and forested cliffs. Extensive inland and coastal hiking trails and hike-in camping areas make this a perfect destination for wilderness seekers, despite the damage caused by a 1995 fire that consumed some 13,000 acres when campers failed to extinguish an illegal fire.

The westernmost point of the peninsula, the Point Reyes Headlands, is crowned by the Point Reyes Light-

The San Andreas Fault
The San Andreas fault follows Hwy 1 along the coast before heading out to sea via Tomales Bay. Point Reyes lies to the west of the faultline, which means it's slowly heading northward at a rate of about three inches a year, leaving the rest of California behind.

The area's claim to fame, in fact, is that it was the epicenter of the devastating 1906 quake – the peninsula shifted 16 feet north. There's a half-mile interpretive earthquake trail that leaves from the visitors center. ■

house, the best spot in the Bay Area for whale watching. To the north a long strand of beach stretches for miles. To the south is Drakes Bay, with Drakes Estero and Limantour Estero Reserve branching off into saltwater lagoons.

The visitors center (☎ 663-1092) is on Bear Valley Rd. – turn off Hwy 1 just north of Olema; here you can get maps to the area as well as camping permits and information on flora and fauna. Beyond the center the road branches. Limantour Rd. turns off to the west and Sir Francis Drake Blvd. continues on to the Point Reyes Headlands.

The *Point Reyes Hostel* (☎ 663-8811) is off Limantour Rd., and there are four hike-in campgrounds for backpackers. Car campers should head inland on Sir Francis Drake Blvd. to *Samuel P. Taylor State Park* (reserve through Destinet (☎ (800) 444-7275), with secluded riverside campsites. The town of Olema has a little grocery store and a restaurant.

Bolinas The pretty little beachside community of Bolinas became famous for its disappearing direction signs, removed by locals intent on hiding from the outside world as it passed by on Hwy 1. So be alert if you're looking for it – the sometimes-signposted turn-off is immediately north of Audubon Canyon Ranch on Hwy 1. The cliff-backed beach and quiet lagoon are lovely, and the town itself charming, if sometimes inhospitable.

The Bolinas Museum (☎ 868-0330), 48 Wharf Rd., has changing exhibits on the art and history of coastal Marin. There are tide pools at Duxbury Reef Nature Reserve, round the end of Duxbury Point. The Audubon Canyon Ranch (☎ 868-9244) is a major nesting ground for herons and egrets, and at the Point Reyes Bird Observatory (☎ 868-0655), off Mesa Rd. west of Bolinas, there are bird banding and netting demonstrations, a visitors center, and nature trail. The Coast Trail into Point Reyes National Seashore begins at the Palomarin Trailhead at the end of Mesa Rd.

Stinson Beach Stretching for three miles, Stinson Beach is the most popular beach along Hwy 1. Despite its freezing waters and frequently overcast skies, it still draws crowds of surfers, hikers, and Sunday drivers, especially on weekends. There are a couple of cafes and breakfast spots, and that's about it.

Muir Beach Muir Beach is more remote than Stinson Beach. Just north on Hwy 1 there are superb views at the Muir Beach Overlook. The Green Gulch Farm & Zen Center (☎ 383-3134) at 1601 Hwy 1, is in the hills above the ocean, and has a Buddhist retreat, Sunday morning meditation sessions, and study programs.

Places to Eat

A good breakfast stop before a day of hiking is the *Dipsea Cafe* (☎ 381-0298), 200 Shoreline Hwy, on the water in Mill Valley; they also serve lunch. Or pick up your provisions at *Whole Foods Market* (☎ 381-1200), 411 Miller Ave, Mill Valley.

There are a number of overpriced restaurants on the waterfront in Sausalito; a better alternative is Tiburon's *Sam's Anchor Cafe* (☎ 435-4527), 27 Main St., which has an unbeatable view. It's worth a stop for daiquiris on the deck even if you aren't hungry.

In Mill Valley, *Jenny Low's* (☎ 388-8868), 38 Miller Ave., has delicious, inventive Chinese food, and the *Buckeye Roadhouse* (☎ 331-2600), 15 Hwy 1, offers a versatile menu from barbecued chicken to linguine with clams.

The *Lark Creek Inn* (☎ 924-7766), 234 Magnolia Ave. in Larkspur, is a four-star dining experience in an old Victorian home in the redwoods. Chef/owner Bradley Ogden's specialty is "American" food, but with the freshest ingredients and a flair. *Marin Joe's* (☎ 924-2081), 1585 Casa Buena Drive, Corte Madera, is one of Marin's oldest restaurants and a local favorite, serving great steaks and burgers – you'll never find goat cheese or sun-dried tomatoes here!

Entertainment

If you find yourself in Marin in the evening, *Sweetwater* (☎ 388-2820), 153 Throckmorton Ave. in Mill Valley, is Marin's finest spot for jazz and blues. *New George's* (☎ 457-8424), 842 4th St. in San Rafael, has a wide variety of live music. If you're into microbreweries, the *Marin Brewing Company* (☎ 461-4677) at Larkspur Landing, fits the bill; this is the twenty-something hangout of choice.

THE WINE COUNTRY

☎ AREA CODE: **707**

Northern California's glorious Wine Country is a feasible day trip from San Francisco but an overnight stay will give you a much better taste of the vineyards. The best time to visit is autumn harvest when the grapes are on the vine, or spring when the hills are brilliant green.

Wine has been produced in this region since 1857, but setbacks early this century, such as deadly phylloxera blights and Prohibition, slowed things down for a time. Beating the French in a blind tasting in Paris in 1976 put California on the international wine map and it's never looked back.

The two valleys, Napa and Sonoma, lie between one and 1 1/2 hour's drive north of San Francisco. Napa Valley, further inland, has 200 or more wineries. Sonoma

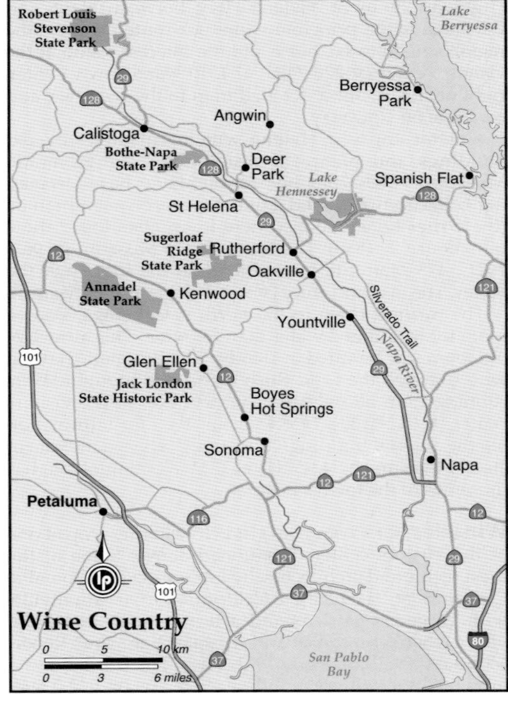

Valley is low key and less commercial, with only about 30. Both offer the same rustic beauty of vineyards, wildflowers, as well as green and golden hills.

Getting There & Away

You pretty much need a car to get to and around the Wine Country, though with planning and patience you may negotiate the bus system. Napa Valley Transit (☎ 255-7631, (800) 696-6445) runs buses from the Vallejo BARTlink bus stop through the Napa Valley to Calistoga. Golden Gate Transit (☎ (415) 332-6600, (707) 576-7433) has buses from San Francisco to Sonoma and Sonoma County Transit (☎ 576-7433, (800) 345-7433) covers the Sonoma Valley.

Napa Valley

Highway 29, or St. Helena Hwy, between Napa and Calistoga is the principle wine-tour route. **Napa** is the region's main town, but is of little interest – stop at the visitors center (☎ 226-7459) at 1310 Napa Town Center, right off 1st St., for a detailed map to the wineries, and continue on your way.

A better stop is **St. Helena**, with lots of interesting old buildings and plenty of restaurants. The Silverado Museum (☎ 963-3757), 1490 Library Lane, has a fascinating collection of Robert Louis Stevenson memorabilia (the writer honeymooned here in an abandoned mine bunkhouse in 1880). The Napa Valley Museum (☎ 963-7411), 473 Main St., has exhibits on the history of the valley. The visitors center (☎ 963-4456) is at 1080 Main St.

The furthest town to the north is **Calistoga**, known more for its mineral water than for wine. This attractive old town was founded in 1859 by Sam Brannan, the man who sounded the Gold Rush alarm that brought '49ers running from all over the country. Stop at the visitors center (☎ 942-4123), 1458 Lincoln Ave., for information on the town's buildings and many spas. The Sharpsteen Museum (☎ 942-5911) at 1311 Washington St., has dioramas of the town's history.

Wineries For a complete guide to wineries stop at one of the visitors centers mentioned above. Some of the most scenic and architecturally interesting are: Domaine Chandon (☎ 944-2280), 1 California Drive, Yountville, with gorgeous gardens and a terrace with knock-out views where you can sit and sip sparkling wine; Robert Mondavi (☎ 226-1395), 7801 Hwy 26, fronted by a mission-style winery building; Sterling (☎ 942-3344),

1111 Dunaweal Lane, Calistoga, where a cable car ride carries you up to the hilltop winery; Clos Pegase (☎ 942-4981), 1060 Dunaweal Lane, Calistoga, where architecture, art, and wine form an alliance; and Inglenook Vineyards (☎ 967-3300), 1991 Hwy 26, Rutherford, with its romantic ivy-covered stone chateau.

Other wineries of interest include: Beaulieu (☎ 963-2411), 1960 Hwy 26, founded in 1900 and one of the few wineries to still offer free tastings; Beringer (☎ 963-4812), 2000 Main St., St. Helena, the oldest continuously operating winery in the valley (it survived Prohibition by manufacturing sacramental wine!); St. Supéry (☎ 963-4507), 8440 Hwy 29, Rutherford, with the most interactive and innovative displays on wine making in the valley; Stag's Leap (☎ 944-2020), 5766 Silverado Trail, Napa, the winery whose cabernet sauvignon won the famous 1976 Paris taste test; and the Hess Collection Winery (☎ 255-1144), 4411 Redwood Rd., Napa, with an extensive private art collection.

Activities Bicycle riding is a favorite way to see the valley. The Silverado Trail is a quieter road than Hwy 29. Getaway Bicycle Tours (☎ 942-0332), in Calistoga, runs half- and full-day bicycle tours of the valley. If you'd prefer to look down on the valley from above, try a hot-air balloon or glider trip. Calistoga Gliders (☎ 942-5000) operates from the gliderport at 1546 Lincoln Ave. in Calistoga; trips are between $80 and $150. There are lots of hot-air balloon operators including Above the West (☎ (800) 627-2759) and Napa Valley Balloons (☎ 944-0228, (800) 253-2224), both in Yountville.

Places to Stay Accommodations range from camping to motels to lovely B&Bs. Call the Napa Valley B&B Referral Hotline at ☎ 257-7733 for information. Campers will find the most options in the Calistoga area, with tent sites at the *Napa County Fairgrounds* (☎ 942-5111), 1435 Oak St. and at *Bothe-Napa Valley State Park* (☎ 942-4575), three miles south on Hwy 29. The *Calistoga Ranch Club* (☎ 942-6565) has cabins ($45) as well as tent sites. The *Travelodge* (☎ 226-1871) at the corner of 2nd and Coombs in Napa is affordable. In Calistoga many places combine accommodations with spas. Call the visitors center for referrals.

Places to Eat There are some truly deluxe destination restaurants in the Napa Valley where the rule is fresh, creative, and expensive cuisine accompanied by magnificent wines. *Ristorante Tra Vigne* (☎ 963-4444), 1050 Charter Oak Ave., St. Helena, is one of the finest

TONY WHEELER

Clos Pegase Winery

and it also has the Cantinetta in its courtyard, a deli, and wine shop where you can get a quicker, cheaper meal. *Mustards Grill* (☎ 944-2424), 7399 Hwy 29 in Yountville and the *Auberge de Soleil Restaurant* (☎ 963-1211), 180 Rutherford Hill Rd. in Rutherford, are also quintessential Wine Country dining experiences.

Piatti (☎ 944-2070), 6480 Washington St., Yountville, is a favorite Italian restaurant, and *Stars Oakville Cafe* (☎ 944-8905), 7848 Hwy 29, is a humbler country version of San Francisco's Stars restaurant.

For a less ostentatious experience but an equally fabulous meal, *Pairs Parkside Cafe* (☎ 963-7566), 1420 Main St., St. Helena, is simple, reasonably priced, and memorable – a real find.

The *Napa Valley Wine Train* (☎ 253-2111), (800) 427-4124) serves daily brunch ($52), lunch ($55), and dinner ($64) in a 1917 Pullman Dining Car. The 36-mile trip between Napa and St. Helena takes three hours and it's a beautiful ride.

Sonoma Valley

The unassuming Sonoma Valley is actually the birthplace of California wine. Hungarian Count Agoston Haraszthy started producing wine here in 1857, and by the late 1860s there were already 50 vintners operating in the area.

The town of **Sonoma** at the southern end of the valley is surrounded by vineyards and has a fascinating history

TONY WHEELER

Inglenook Vineyards' elegant chateau

as the site of an 1846 uprising of US settlers against the Mexican military command. The resulting "Bear Flag Republic" was short-lived; when the Mexican-American War broke out a month later, it was absorbed into the expanded US territory. The revolt did, however, give California its state flag.

The 1834 Mission San Francisco Solano de Sonoma (☎ 938-1519), 114 E. Spain St., was the last of the California missions and the only one built under Mexican rule (the rest were built by the Spanish). For other sites in town, stop by the visitors center (☎ 996-1090), 453 E. 1st St., for a copy of the *Sonoma Walking Tour* booklet.

North on Hwy 12 are the sleepy small town of **Glen Ellen** and the Jack London State Historic Park (☎ 938-5216), formerly the novelist's 800-acre ranch.

Wineries Unlike Napa Valley, free tastings are still the norm in Sonoma Valley. Wineries include the historic *Buena Vista* (☎ 938-1266), 18000 Old Winery Rd., which was Haraszthy's original vineyard; and the *Gundlach-Bundschu* winery (☎ 938-5277), 2000 Denmark St., another oldie, dating to 1858. In Glen Ellen, try *Sebastiani* (☎ 938-5532), 389 4th St. E.; *Glen Ellen Winery* (☎ 935-3000), 1883 London Ranch Rd.; and *Valley of the Moon* (☎ 996-6941), 777 Madrona Rd.

Places to Stay & Eat B&Bs close to the center of town include the *Thistle Dew B&B* (☎ (800) 382-7895), 171 W. Spain St., and the *Victorian Gardens Inn* (☎ 996-5339), 316 E. Napa St. The cheapest option in the area is *El Pueblo Motel* (☎ 996-3651), 896 W. Napa St., and the most expensive may be the *Sonoma Mission Inn & Spa* (☎ 938-9000), 18140 Sonoma Hwy at Boyes Hot Springs, the perfect spot for an indulgent weekend getaway. Non-guests can also take advantage of the spa facilities on weekdays and Sunday afternoon.

If you're stocking up for a Sonoma Valley picnic, *Good to Go* (☎ 938-0301), 603 Broadway in Sonoma, has everything you'll need. *Della Santina's* (☎ 935-0576), 101 E. Napa St., is a small restaurant cooking up very well prepared Tuscan food; there's also a branch of the wonderful *Piatti* chain (☎ 996-2351) at 405 W. 1st St. The Mexican roots of the region show through at *La Casa* (☎ 996-3406), 121 E. Spain St., a popular restaurant near the mission.

THE EAST BAY

☎ AREA CODE: **510**

Linked to San Francisco by the Bay Bridge, the East Bay is mostly covered with dense suburbs ranging from the sordid to the elite. Gritty Oakland and opinionated Berkeley dominate the sprawl while the hills that rise behind them are surprisingly pristine with miles of park land at their ridgeline and towering Mt. Diablo in the background. To find out about the East Bay Regional Parks, call the Parks District at ☎ 562-7275.

Getting There & Away

BART links San Francisco with the East Bay. If you're headed into downtown Oakland, disembark at the 12th or 19th St. Stations; both emerge onto busy Broadway.

For Berkeley, continue on the Richmond line and exit at the Berkeley Station; it's a few blocks walking from there to Telegraph Ave. and the university campus.

AC Transit (☎ 839-2882, (800) 559-4636) has transbay bus service.

Oakland

Oakland has always languished in San Francisco's shadow, but it has enough attractions to justify a foray across the bay. It's a city of remarkable racial and economic diversity encompassing a busy harbor, a frenetic Chinatown, the popular shops and restaurants of Piedmont and College Aves., and the vast Regional Parks along the hills. Oakland is well known for its enduring progressive jazz and blues scene. Stop into the visitors center (☎ 893-9000), 1000 Broadway, Suite 200, for more information.

There's nothing dazzling about **downtown Oakland**, but amid the slightly decrepit old buildings there are some surprises, such as the mosaic-fronted 1931 Paramount Theater at Broadway and 21st, home of Oakland's ballet and symphony, and the abandoned 1928 Fox Oakland Theater at Telegraph and 19th, an Art Deco beauty. Among the crumbling filigree, modern buildings are cropping up, like the imposing double-towered Federal Building and its surrounding City Center complex of shops and restaurants, on 14th St. off Broadway. Oakland's untouristy **Chinatown** is focused on Franklin and Webster Sts.

Jack London Square, on the waterfront at the end of Broadway, is a converted industrial zone now stuffed with restaurants; in the neighboring Jack London Village, the **Jack London Museum** (☎ 451-8218) has exhibits about the native author.

Downtown Oakland's visual centerpiece is **Lake Merritt**, a salt-water lake that was the nation's first wildlife refuge. The sternwheeler *Merritt Queen* (☎ 444-3807) paddles around the lake on weekends for $1.50/75¢. The **Oakland Museum** (☎ 238-3401), 1000 Oak St., isn't far. Its terrific collection focuses on California art and history.

Places to Eat There's a collection of restaurants in Jack London Square and lots of inexpensive authentic Asian places in Chinatown. Outstanding restaurants in Oakland include *Spettro* (☎ 465-8320), 3355 Lake Shore Ave., near Lake Merritt, with excellent value and service and very creative cuisine. *Bay Wolf Restaurant* (☎ 655-6004), 3853 Piedmont Ave., is Oakland's contribution to California cuisine; *Creme de la Creme* (☎ 420-8822), 5362 College Ave. in Rockridge, is a romantic little French restaurant; *Zachary's Chicago Pizza* (☎ 655-6385), 5801 College Ave., makes superb "stuffed" pizza; and *Rick & Ann's* (☎ 649-8538), 2922 Domingo Ave. by the Claremont Hotel, has phenomenal breakfasts and brunches.

Entertainment *Merchant's* (☎ 465-8032), tucked in a warehouse at 3rd and Franklin Sts., is a seedy dive featuring up-and-coming alternative rock bands on Friday and Saturday nights, cheap drinks, and minimal cover. *Eli's Mile High Club* (☎ 655-6661) at 3629 Martin Luther King Jr. Way is a renowned East Bay blues center with music Wednesday to Sunday and a $4 to $8 cover charge. *Yoshi's* (☎ 652-9200) at 6030 Claremont Ave. manages to combine jazz and Japanese food in a big 300-seat club. Yoshi's will be moving at the end of '96, so be sure to call ahead to find out the new location. Big-name jazz headlines at *Kimball's East* (☎ 658-2555) at 5800 Shellmound St. in Emeryville. Downstairs is *Kimball's Carnival* where the music takes a Latin and Caribbean flavor.

Berkeley

Berkeley – "Bezerkeley" – erstwhile seat of radical student politics, has mellowed since its '60s heyday but is still considered a mecca of liberalism and the bizarre. Centered around the campus of the University of California, it sprawls from the bay all the way to the crest of the East Bay hills. **Telegraph Ave.** is the center of South Side, Berkeley's colorful student zone, where street vendors hawk their tie-dyed wares among mohawked urban urchins and the down-and-out homeless. The visitors center (☎ 549-7040) is at 1834 University Ave.

TONY WHEELER
Sather Tower

The oldest of the **University of California** campuses, "Cal" first opened its doors in 1873, and today there are over 1000 professors to some 30,000 students, and enough Nobel laureates to necessitate designated Nobel-only parking spaces on campus!

From Telegraph Ave. the tightly packed campus is entered via Sproul Plaza, center for people watching and soapbox oration. Also of interest on campus is Sather Tower, the 307-foot campanile modeled on St. Mark's in Venice; you can ride the elevator to the top for 50¢. The

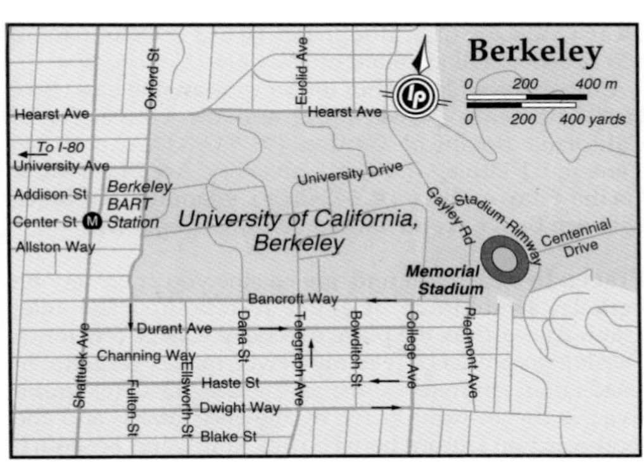

TONY WHEELER

Self-expression in "Bezerkeley"

Hearst Museum of Anthropology (☎ 643-7648) is in room 103 Kroeber Hall, on Bancroft Way near College Ave.

University-affiliated but off campus are the Lawrence Hall of Science (☎ 642-5132) and the University of California Botanical Garden (☎ 642-3343), both on Centennial Drive, and the University Art Museum & Pacific Film Archive (☎ 642-0808), spanning the block between Bancroft and Durant below College Ave.

Places to Eat You'll find any cuisine you crave among Berkeley's multitude of ethnic restaurants. The Telegraph Ave. area is the place for cheap eats. A few hints: *Cafe Intermezzo*, 2442 Telegraph Ave., makes gargantuan salads and sandwiches; *Blondie's Pizza*, 2340 Telegraph Ave., is the institution for by-the-slice pizza; and the food court on Durant between Telegraph and Bowditch has a selection of Asian take-out joints. For a more serious, sit-down meal, *The Blue Nile* (☎ 540-6777), 2525 Telegraph Ave., is a popular Ethiopian restaurant and the *Bateau Ivre* (☎ 849-1100), 2629 Telegraph Ave., is a classy French cottage with rich, wonderful food.

One of the Bay Area's finest restaurants is *Chez Panisse* (☎ 548-5525), 1517 Shattuck Ave., where chef Alice Waters created "California cuisine." It's a different fixed menu every day, ranging from $35 to $65. Reservations are a must. Upstairs is a more relaxed cafe where you can order à la carte. Down the street a little way is *Cha-Am* (☎ 848-9664), 1543 Shattuck Ave., for fantastic Thai food.

The blocks around Shattuck and University Aves. are also restaurant-filled; the '50s-style *Original Mel's Diner* (☎ 540-6351), 2240 Shattuck Ave., a popular after-movie place for burgers and shakes – it's open to midnight.

Entertainment Berkeley's streets are lined with coffeehouses, mostly filled with studying students. The most popular are *Caffe Strada* (☎ 843-5282) at 2300 College Ave., with a tree-shaded patio; *Cafe Milano* (☎ 644-3100) 2522 Bancroft Way, with a sky-lit loft; *Wall Berlin* (☎ 540-8449) at 2517 Durant, with some of the strongest java around; and the cafe at the *International House* (☎ 642-9932), at Bancroft and Piedmont Aves., where the university's foreign students hang out.

On Telegraph Ave., *Larry Blake's* (☎ 848-0886), 2367 Telegraph, is noisy and lively with bars on three floors and live music downstairs. *Raleigh's Pub* (☎ 848-8652), 2438 Telegraph, is a frat-boy hangout, but it has a nice outdoor patio. *Bison Brewery* (☎ 841-7734), 2598 Telegraph, brews its own beer and has live music on weekends. Over on Shattuck Ave., *Jupiter* (☎ 843-8277) is the best bar in town, with a big outdoor beer garden, a huge selection of microbrews, good pizza, and live jazz.

There are many movie theaters in Berkeley, but the unusual ones are *UC Theater* (☎ 843-6267), 2036 University Ave. and the *Pacific Film Archive* (PFA) (☎ 642-1124), 2621 Durant Ave., both of which play classic and obscure films. To see what's going on in the way of university performing arts events, read the flyers on bulletin boards around town, or get a copy of the *Daily Californian* from the kiosks in Sproul Plaza.

THE PENINSULA

☎ AREA CODE: **415**

San Francisco is the tip of a 30-mile-long peninsula, sandwiched between the Pacific Ocean and the Bay. Interstate 280, running along the San Andreas fault, is the dividing line between the densely populated South Bay and the rugged and remarkably lightly populated coast. The city of Palo Alto is distinguished from other South Bay suburbs as the home of Stanford University. The main coastal community between San Francisco and Santa Cruz is Half Moon Bay, a beach escape with a number of festivals to attract day-trippers.

Getting There & Away

CalTrain (☎ (800) 660-4287) runs between San Francisco and Palo Alto daily; it's $3.25. Or take SamTrans (same number) bus Nos. 7F and 16F for $2.

Palo Alto

Though Stanford University may be the centerpiece of Palo Alto, the town's toney 'downtown' and Stanford Mall shops, excellent restaurants, and pubs are away from the campus, and offer an unsurpassed suburban variety that attracts an upscale crowd of its own. Palo Alto is 30 miles south of San Francisco via I-280 or Hwy 101; the chamber of commerce (☎ 324-3121) is at 325 Forest Ave.

You can rent a bike (try Bike Connection, ☎ 424-8034, 2086 El Camino Réal), to get a feel of the town, mall, and campus.

Endowed and built by robber baron Leland Stanford, **Stanford University** opened in 1891. The Stanford Univeristy Information Booth (☎ 723-2560) is in Memorial Hall just east of the Main Quad, where Auguste Rodin's *Burghers of Calais* mill about. Surrounding the Main

Quad are the original 12 campus buildings, in a mix of Romanesque and Mission Revival styles. They were joined in 1903 by the mosaic-fronted Memorial Church. East of the quad is the 285-foot Hoover Tower; the ride to the top costs $2/1.

Free walking tours depart from the information booth daily at 11 am and 3:15 pm. A free pamphlet, a *Guide to Outdoor Sculpture* is available here. Parking for those without a permit (a one-day pass is $4 from the information booth) is extremely difficult.

Places to Eat Visit the Stanford Mall on El Camino Réal for one of the best outdoor produce and garden markets in the Bay Area.

Try the *Peninsula Creamery Fountain & Grill* (☎ 323-3131) at the corner of Hamilton and Emerson Sts. *Miyake Sushi* (☎ 323-9449), 261 University Ave., has been a local favorite for years. For popular pub and grub, go to *Blue Chalk* (☎ 326-1020), 630 Ramona St. or *Gordon Biersch* (☎ 327-4475), 604 Emerson St., an arm of San Francisco's upscale brewpub.

Half Moon Bay

Half Moon Bay developed as an escape from the big city back in the Victorian era. The long stretches of beach still attract weekenders, and there are a host of rather upscale B&Bs. Main St., with shops, cafes, and restaurants, is the main drag. Visitor information is available at the chamber of commerce (☎ 726-8380), 520 Kelly Ave.

Pumpkins are a major crop, and the Halloween harvest is celebrated with an annual Pumpkin Festival. Inland there are trails through Purissima Creek Redwoods for hiking and biking.

If you're looking to stop for dinner along the coast, the *Moss Beach Distillery* (☎ 728-5595), at Beach Way and Ocean Blvd. in Moss Beach, sits on a cliff and claims to be haunted by the "Blue Lady," who wanders the cliffs awaiting the return of her piano-playing lover.

Index

Maps

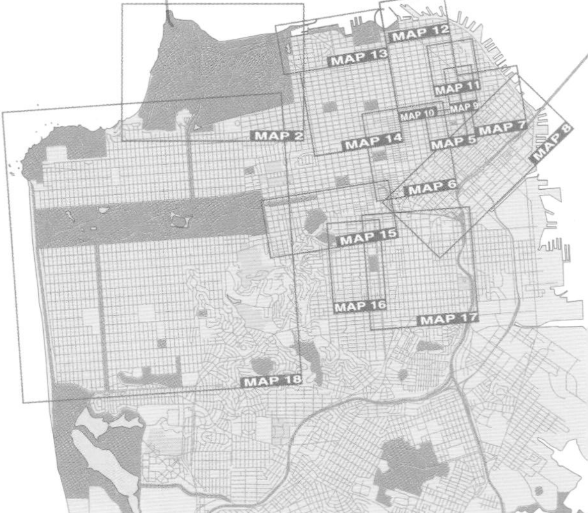

MAP 12
MAP 13
MAP 11
MAP 10
MAP 9
MAP 2
MAP 14
MAP 5
MAP 7
MAP 8
MAP 6
MAP 15
MAP 16
MAP 17
MAP 18

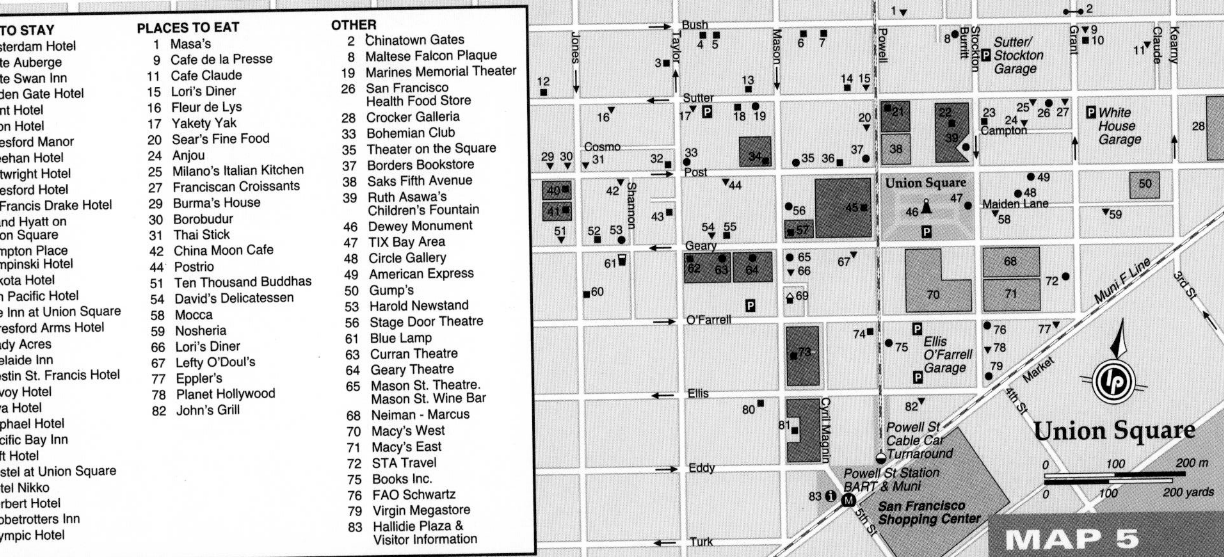
MAP 5
Union Square
PLACES TO STAY
3 Amsterdam Hotel
4 Petite Auberge
5 White Swan Inn
6 Golden Gate Hotel
7 Grant Hotel
10 Triton Hotel
12 Beresford Manor
13 Sheehan Hotel
14 Cartwright Hotel
18 Beresford Hotel
21 Sir Francis Drake Hotel
22 Grand Hyatt on Union Square
23 Campton Place Kempinski Hotel
32 Dakota Hotel
34 Pan Pacific Hotel
36 The Inn at Union Square
40 Beresford Arms Hotel
41 Brady Acres
43 Adelaide Inn
45 Westin St. Francis Hotel
52 Savoy Hotel
55 Diva Hotel
57 Raphael Hotel
60 Pacific Bay Inn
62 Clift Hotel
69 Hostel at Union Square
73 Hotel Nikko
74 Herbert Hotel
80 Globetrotters Inn
81 Olympic Hotel
PLACES TO EAT
1 Masa's
9 Cafe de la Presse
11 Cafe Claude
15 Lori's Diner
16 Fleur de Lys
17 Yakety Yak
20 Sear's Fine Food
24 Anjou
25 Milano's Italian Kitchen
27 Franciscan Croissants
29 Burma's House
30 Borobudur
31 Thai Stick
42 China Moon Cafe
44 Postrio
51 Ten Thousand Buddhas
54 David's Delicatessen
58 Mocca
59 Nosheria
66 Lori's Diner
67 Lefty O'Doul's
77 Eppler's
78 Planet Hollywood
82 John's Grill
OTHER
2 Chinatown Gates
8 Maltese Falcon Plaque
19 Marines Memorial Theater
26 San Francisco Health Food Store
28 Crocker Galleria
33 Bohemian Club
35 Theater on the Square
37 Borders Bookstore
38 Saks Fifth Avenue
39 Ruth Asawa's Children's Fountain
46 Dewey Monument
47 TIX Bay Area
48 Circle Gallery
49 American Express
50 Gump's
53 Harold Newstand
56 Stage Door Theatre
61 Blue Lamp
63 Curran Theatre
64 Geary Theatre
65 Mason St. Theatre. Mason St. Wine Bar
68 Neiman - Marcus
70 Macy's West
71 Macy's East
72 STA Travel
75 Books Inc.
76 FAO Schwartz
79 Virgin Megastore
83 Hallidie Plaza & Visitor Information
Bush
Sutter
Post
Geary
O'Farrell
Ellis
Eddy
Turk
Jones
Taylor
Mason
Powell
Stockton
Burritt
Grant
Claude
Kearny
Cosmo
Shannon
Campton
Maiden Lane
Cyril Magnin
Market
4th St
5th St
3rd St
Muni F Line
Sutter/ Stockton Garage
White House Garage
Ellis O'Farrell Garage
Union Square
Powell St Cable Car Turnaround
Powell St Station BART & Muni
San Francisco Shopping Center
0
100
200 m
0
100
200 yards

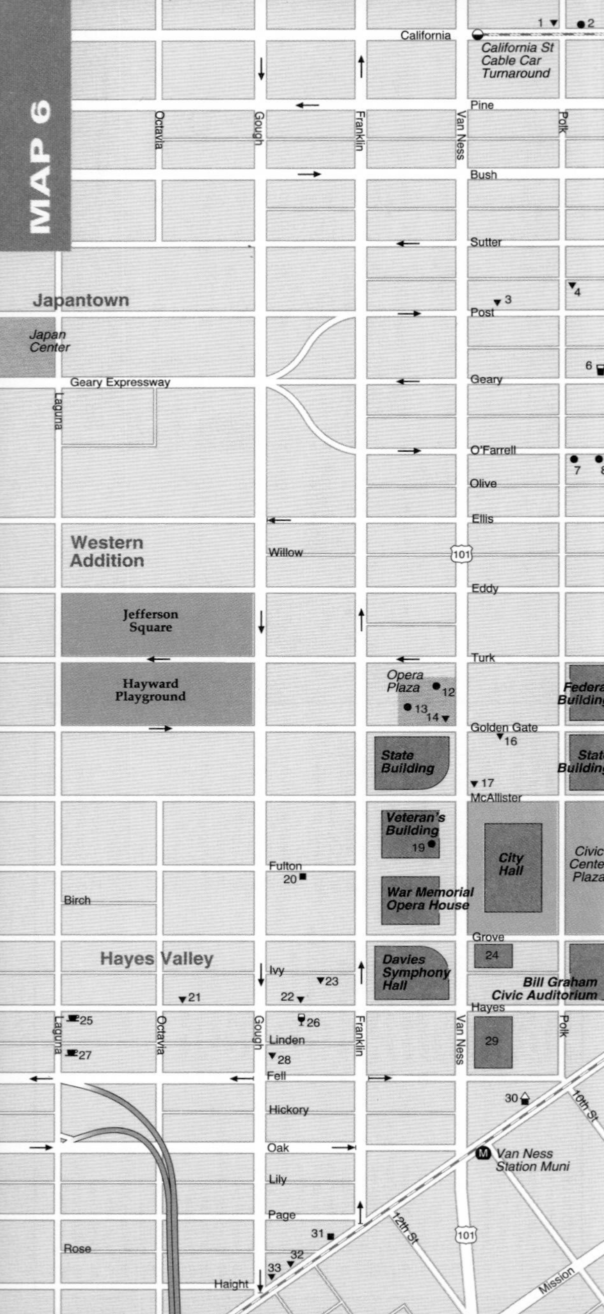
MAP 6
California
California St Cable Car Turnaround
Pine
Bush
Sutter
Post
Geary
O'Farrell
Olive
Ellis
Willow
Eddy
Turk
Golden Gate
McAllister
Fulton
Grove
Ivy
Hayes
Linden
Fell
Hickory
Oak
Lily
Page
Rose
Haight
Birch
Octavia
Gough
Franklin
Van Ness
Polk
Laguna
Geary Expressway
Japantown
Japan Center
Western Addition
Jefferson Square
Hayward Playground
Opera Plaza
Federal Building
State Building
Veteran's Building
City Hall
Civic Center Plaza
War Memorial Opera House
Davies Symphony Hall
Bill Graham Civic Auditorium
Hayes Valley
Van Ness Station Muni
10th St
12th St
Mission
101

Nob Hill
Pine
Bush
Sutter
Post
Geary
O'Farrell
Ellis
Eddy
Larkin
Hyde
Leavenworth
Jones
Taylor
Mason
Shannon
Cyril Magnin
Tenderloin
6th St
Stevenson
Jessie
Mission
7th St
8th St
Market
Muni F Line
SF Main Library
Federal Building
UN Plaza
New Public Library
Civic Center Station BART & Muni
Civic Center & Tenderloin
0 100 200 m
0 100 200 yards
PLACES TO STAY
10 Phoenix Motel
15 Central YMCA Hotel
20 Inn at the Opera
30 Grand Central Hostel
31 Pensione San Francisco
PLACES TO EAT
1 Swan Oyster Depot
3 Maharani
4 Kublai Khan's Restaurant
5 Brother Juniper's Restaurant
14 Max's Opera Cafe
16 Stars
17 Stars Cafe
21 Geva's Caribbean Cuisine
22 Hayes St. Grill
23 Vicolo Pizzeria
28 Caffe delle Stelle
32 Zuni Cafe
33 Floogie's Swamp Cafe
OTHER
2 Lumiere Theater
6 Edinburgh Castle
7 Mitchell Brothers O'Farrell Theater
8 Great American Music Hall
9 Exit Theater
10 Miss Pearl's Jam House
11 Club 181
12 A Clean Well Lighted Place for Books
13 Opera Plaza Cinema
18 Hollywood Billiards
19 Herbst Theater
24 San Francisco Art Commission Gallery
25 Mad Magda's Russian Tea Room
26 Hayes & Vine
27 Momi Toby's Revolution Cafe
29 AAA Office

MAP 7
Pacific
Jackson Square
Gold
Jackson
Hotaling
Custom House
Front
Bostonship Plaza
Washington
Transamerica Pyramid
Redwood Plaza
Merchant
Mark Twain
Maritime Plaza
Clay
Leidesdorff
Commercial
Sacramento
Kearny
Spring
Montgomery
Sansome
Battery
California
Bank of America Building
Pine
Belden
Russ Building
Bush
Trinity
Citicorp Center
Sutter
Crocker Galleria
Montgomery Station BART & Muni
Stevenson
Jessie
1st St
Ecker
Post
Maiden Lane
Muni F Line
2nd St
New Montgomery
Anthony
Geary
Minna
Natoma
Market
3rd St
San Francisco Museum of Modern Art
Center for the Arts Forum
Yerba Buena Gardens
Financial District
0 75 150 m
0 75 150 yards

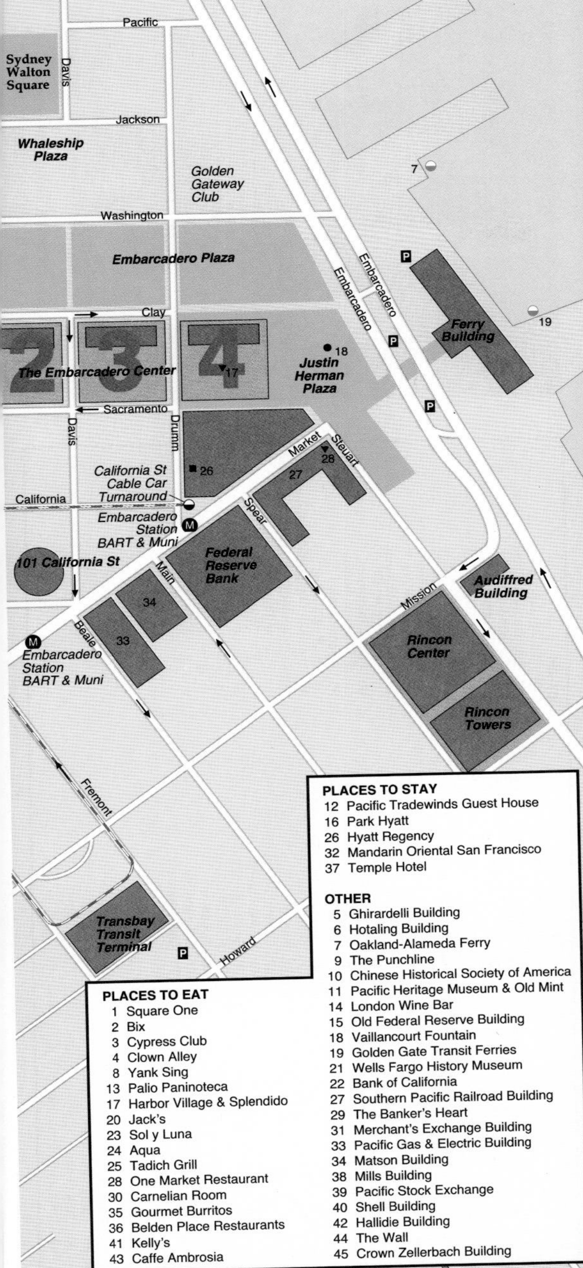
Pacific
Sydney Walton Square
Davis
Jackson
Whaleship Plaza
Golden Gateway Club
Washington
Embarcadero Plaza
Embarcadero
Embarcadero
Clay
The Embarcadero Center
17
18
Justin Herman Plaza
Ferry Building
7
19
Sacramento
Davis
Drumm
Market
Steuart
28
27
26
California St Cable Car Turnaround
California
Embarcadero Station BART & Muni
Spear
Federal Reserve Bank
101 California St
Main
34
Beale
33
Embarcadero Station BART & Muni
Mission
Audiffred Building
Rincon Center
Rincon Towers
Fremont
Transbay Transit Terminal
Howard
PLACES TO STAY
12 Pacific Tradewinds Guest House
16 Park Hyatt
26 Hyatt Regency
32 Mandarin Oriental San Francisco
37 Temple Hotel
OTHER
5 Ghirardelli Building
6 Hotaling Building
7 Oakland-Alameda Ferry
9 The Punchline
10 Chinese Historical Society of America
11 Pacific Heritage Museum & Old Mint
14 London Wine Bar
15 Old Federal Reserve Building
18 Vaillancourt Fountain
19 Golden Gate Transit Ferries
21 Wells Fargo History Museum
22 Bank of California
27 Southern Pacific Railroad Building
29 The Banker's Heart
31 Merchant's Exchange Building
33 Pacific Gas & Electric Building
34 Matson Building
38 Mills Building
39 Pacific Stock Exchange
40 Shell Building
42 Hallidie Building
44 The Wall
45 Crown Zellerbach Building
PLACES TO EAT
1 Square One
2 Bix
3 Cypress Club
4 Clown Alley
8 Yank Sing
13 Palio Paninoteca
17 Harbor Village & Splendido
20 Jack's
23 Sol y Luna
24 Aqua
25 Tadich Grill
28 One Market Restaurant
30 Carnelian Room
35 Gourmet Burritos
36 Belden Place Restaurants
41 Kelly's
43 Caffe Ambrosia

PLACES TO STAY

1 Aida Hotel
6 Mosser's Victorian Hotel
7 Marriott Hotel
9 Sheraton Palace Hotel
14 European Guest House
16 Hotel Britton
17 Best Western Carriage Inn
18 Best Western Americania
32 Griffon Hotel
33 Harbor Court Hotel
39 San Francisco International Student Center
53 Globe Hostel
70 San Francisco RV Park

PLACES TO EAT

2 Tu Lan
12 Yank Sing
15 Cafe do Brasil
19 Cadillac Bar & Grill
20 Chevy's
24 Caffe Museo
26 Eddie Rickenbacker's
34 Hamburger Mary's
37 Icon Byte Bar & Grill
41 Lulu
47 ¡Wa-Ha-Ka!
61 Ruby's
64 Fringale
65 South Park Cafe
66 Caffe Centro
72 Delancey St. Restaurant

CLUBS & BARS

27 Caribbean Zone
28 DV8
35 Holy Cow
36 Paradise Lounge
38 Cat's Grill & Alley Club
40 Rawhide
43 Kate O'Brien's
44 Ace Cafe
45 20 Tank Brewery
46 The Eagle
48 Slim's
49 DNA Lounge
50 The Stud
52 Up & Down Club
54 Julie's Supper Club
55 1015 Club
56 End Up
57 Covered Wagon Saloon
58 Sound Factory
59 Gordon Biersch Brewery
62 Hotel Utah Saloon
63 Trocadero
67 330 Ritch St
71 Club Townsend

OTHER

3 Old Mint Building
4 San Francisco Shopping Center
5 Cartoon Art Museum
8 St Patrick's Church
10 Rand McNally Map & Travel Store
11 Stacy's Bookstore
13 Five Fremont Center
21 Center for the Arts Forum
22 Center for the Arts Theater
23 San Francisco Museum of Modern Art (SFMOMA)
25 Pacific Telephone & Telegraph Building
29 Rincon Center
30 Audiffred Building
31 The Jewish Museum San Francisco
42 Ansel Adams Center for Photography
51 Phoenix Theater
60 Union 76 Tower
68 Jack London's Birthplace
69 Liberty Ship *Jeremiah O'Brien*

SCOTT SUMMERS

Pacific Telephone & Telegraph Building towers over SoMa's enclave of art.

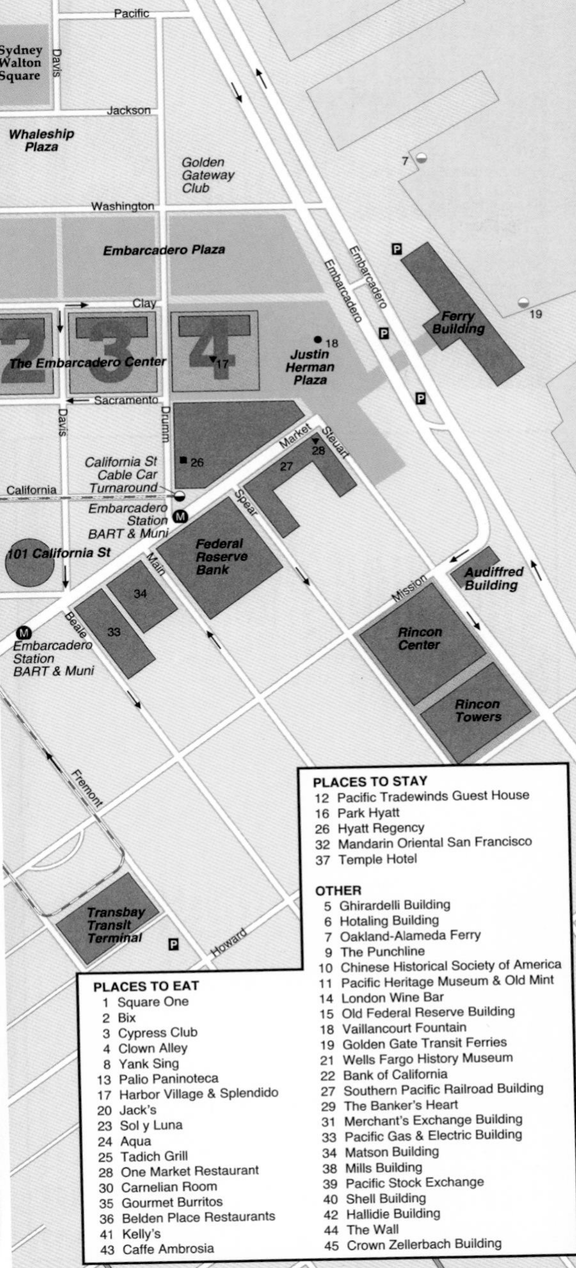
Pacific
Sydney Walton Square
Davis
Jackson
Whaleship Plaza
Golden Gateway Club
7
Washington
Embarcadero Plaza
Embarcadero
Embarcadero
Clay
2
3
4
The Embarcadero Center
17
18
Justin Herman Plaza
Ferry Building
19
Sacramento
Davis
Drumm
Market
Steuart
28
27
26
California St Cable Car Turnaround
California
Embarcadero Station BART & Muni
Spear
101 California St
Federal Reserve Bank
Main
34
Beale
33
Embarcadero Station BART & Muni
Mission
Audiffred Building
Rincon Center
Rincon Towers
Fremont
Transbay Transit Terminal
Howard
PLACES TO STAY
12 Pacific Tradewinds Guest House
16 Park Hyatt
26 Hyatt Regency
32 Mandarin Oriental San Francisco
37 Temple Hotel
OTHER
5 Ghirardelli Building
6 Hotaling Building
7 Oakland-Alameda Ferry
9 The Punchline
10 Chinese Historical Society of America
11 Pacific Heritage Museum & Old Mint
14 London Wine Bar
15 Old Federal Reserve Building
18 Vaillancourt Fountain
19 Golden Gate Transit Ferries
21 Wells Fargo History Museum
22 Bank of California
27 Southern Pacific Railroad Building
29 The Banker's Heart
31 Merchant's Exchange Building
33 Pacific Gas & Electric Building
34 Matson Building
38 Mills Building
39 Pacific Stock Exchange
40 Shell Building
42 Hallidie Building
44 The Wall
45 Crown Zellerbach Building
PLACES TO EAT
1 Square One
2 Bix
3 Cypress Club
4 Clown Alley
8 Yank Sing
13 Palio Paninoteca
17 Harbor Village & Splendido
20 Jack's
23 Sol y Luna
24 Aqua
25 Tadich Grill
28 One Market Restaurant
30 Carnelian Room
35 Gourmet Burritos
36 Belden Place Restaurants
41 Kelly's
43 Caffe Ambrosia

PLACES TO STAY

1 Aida Hotel
6 Mosser's Victorian Hotel
7 Marriott Hotel
9 Sheraton Palace Hotel
14 European Guest House
16 Hotel Britton
17 Best Western Carriage Inn
18 Best Western Americania
32 Griffon Hotel
33 Harbor Court Hotel
39 San Francisco International Student Center
53 Globe Hostel
70 San Francisco RV Park

PLACES TO EAT

2 Tu Lan
12 Yank Sing
15 Cafe do Brasil
19 Cadillac Bar & Grill
20 Chevy's
24 Caffe Museo
26 Eddie Rickenbacker's
34 Hamburger Mary's
37 Icon Byte Bar & Grill
41 Lulu
47 ¡Wa-Ha-Ka!
61 Ruby's
64 Fringale
65 South Park Cafe
66 Caffe Centro
72 Delancey St. Restaurant

CLUBS & BARS

27 Caribbean Zone
28 DV8
35 Holy Cow
36 Paradise Lounge
38 Cat's Grill & Alley Club
40 Rawhide
43 Kate O'Brien's
44 Ace Cafe
45 20 Tank Brewery
46 The Eagle
48 Slim's
49 DNA Lounge
50 The Stud
52 Up & Down Club
54 Julie's Supper Club
55 1015 Club
56 End Up
57 Covered Wagon Saloon
58 Sound Factory
59 Gordon Biersch Brewery
62 Hotel Utah Saloon
63 Trocadero
67 330 Ritch St
71 Club Townsend

OTHER

3 Old Mint Building
4 San Francisco Shopping Center
5 Cartoon Art Museum
8 St Patrick's Church
10 Rand McNally Map & Travel Store
11 Stacy's Bookstore
13 Five Fremont Center
21 Center for the Arts Forum
22 Center for the Arts Theater
23 San Francisco Museum of Modern Art (SFMOMA)
25 Pacific Telephone & Telegraph Building
29 Rincon Center
30 Audiffred Building
31 The Jewish Museum San Francisco
42 Ansel Adams Center for Photography
51 Phoenix Theater
60 Union 76 Tower
68 Jack London's Birthplace
69 Liberty Ship *Jeremiah O'Brien*

SCOTT SUMMERS

Pacific Telephone & Telegraph Building towers over SoMa's enclave of art.

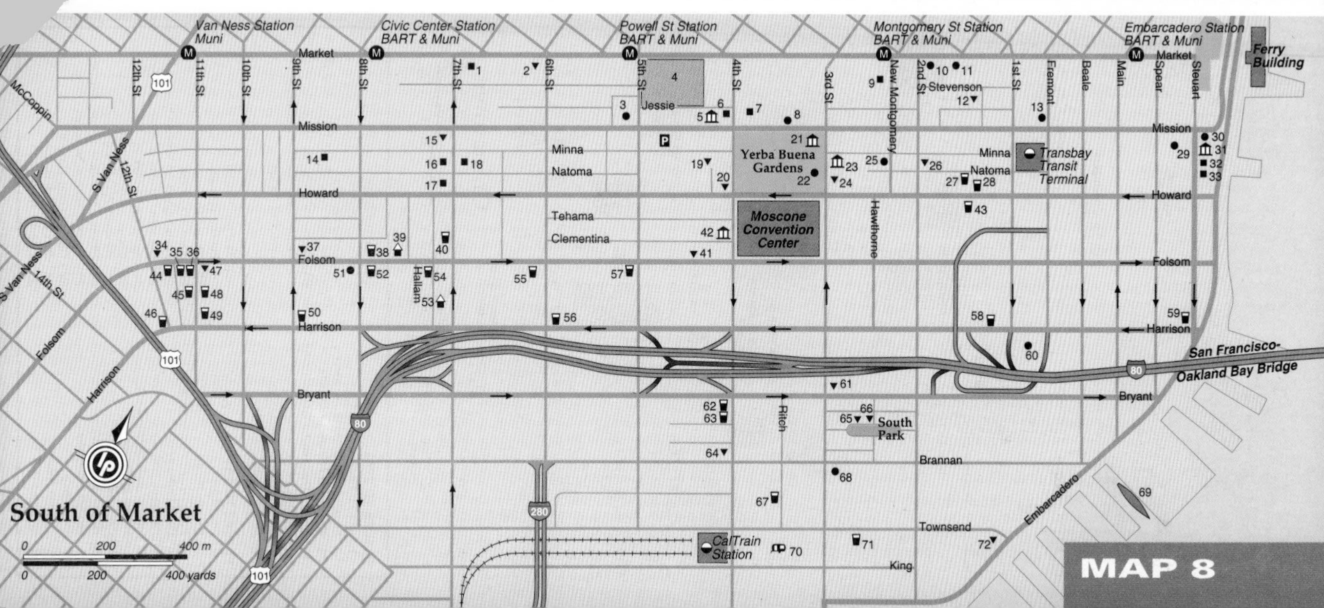
MAP 8
South of Market
Van Ness Station Muni
Civic Center Station BART & Muni
Powell St Station BART & Muni
Montgomery St Station BART & Muni
Embarcadero Station BART & Muni
Ferry Building
Market
Mission
Minna
Natoma
Howard
Tehama
Clementina
Folsom
Harrison
Bryant
Brannan
Townsend
King
Jessie
Stevenson
Hallam
Hawthorne
Ritch
12th St
11th St
10th St
9th St
8th St
7th St
6th St
5th St
4th St
3rd St
New Montgomery
2nd St
1st St
Fremont
Beale
Main
Spear
Steuart
McCoppin
S Van Ness
14th St
Embarcadero
Yerba Buena Gardens
Moscone Convention Center
Transbay Transit Terminal
South Park
CalTrain Station
San Francisco-Oakland Bay Bridge
0 200 400 m
0 200 400 yards

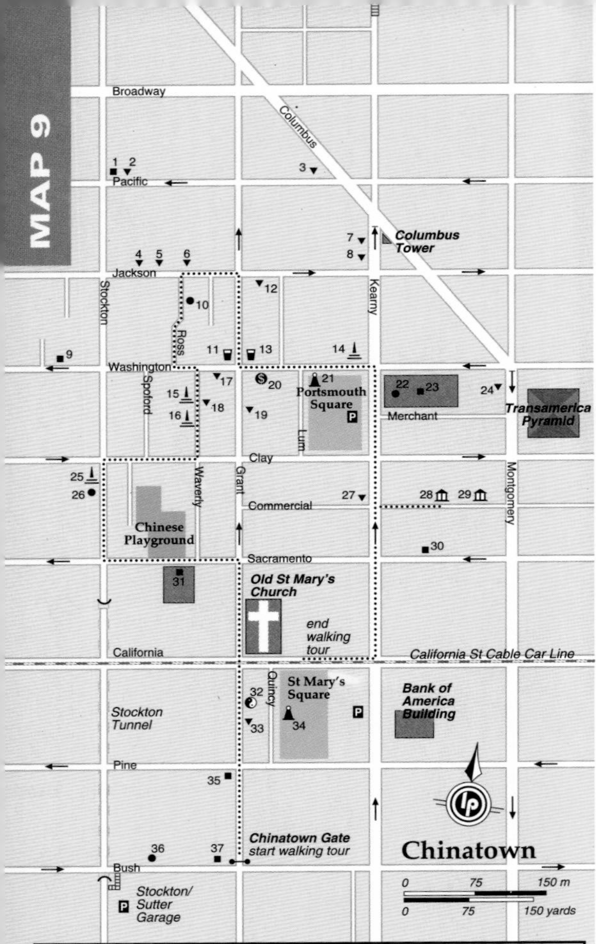

Broadway
Columbus
Pacific
Jackson
Washington
Clay
Commercial
Sacramento
California
Pine
Bush
Stockton
Ross
Spofford
Waverly
Grant
Quincy
Lum
Kearny
Merchant
Montgomery
Columbus Tower
Portsmouth Square
Transamerica Pyramid
Chinese Playground
Old St Mary's Church
end walking tour
California St Cable Car Line
St Mary's Square
Bank of America Building
Stockton Tunnel
Chinatown Gate
start walking tour
Stockton/ Sutter Garage

Chinatown

0 75 150 m
0 75 150 yards

PLACES TO STAY
1 Obrero Hotel
9 Gum Moon Women's Residence
23 Holiday Inn Financial District
30 Pacific Tradewinds Guest House
31 YMCA Chinatown
35 Grant Plaza
37 Astoria Hotel

PLACES TO EAT
2 New Asia
3 Brandy Ho's
4 Feng Haung Pastry Shop, Garden Bakery
5 Delicious Dim Sum
6 Yung Kee Rice Noodle Co, House of Dim Sum
7 Chef Jia's
8 House of Nanking
12 Woey Loey Goey Cafe
17 Sam Wo's
18 The Pot Sticker
19 Empress of China
24 Tommy Toy's
27 R&G Lounge
33 Lotus Garden

OTHER
10 Golden Gate Cookie Company
11 Buddha Lounge
13 Li Po's
14 Buddha's Universal Church
15 Tin Hou Temple
16 Norras Temple
18 Jeng Sen Temple
20 Bank of Canton
21 Robert Louis Stevenson Memorial
22 Chinese Cultural Center
25 Kong Chow Temple
26 Chinese Consolidated Benevolent Building
28 Chinese Historical Society Museum
29 Pacific Heritage Museum
32 Ching Chung Temple
34 Sun Yat-Sen Statue
36 Council Travel

RICK GERHARTER

Still life in Chinatown

TONY WHEELER

Grant St. in Chinatown

TONY WHEELER

The columns of the Palace of Fine Arts, found in the Marina

TOM SMALLMAN

You can ride the cable car through Russian Hill to Fisherman's Wharf.

RICK GERHARTER

Still life in Chinatown

TONY WHEELER

Grant St. in Chinatown

TONY WHEELER

The columns of the Palace of Fine Arts, found in the Marina

TOM SMALLMAN

You can ride the cable car through Russian Hill to Fisherman's Wharf.

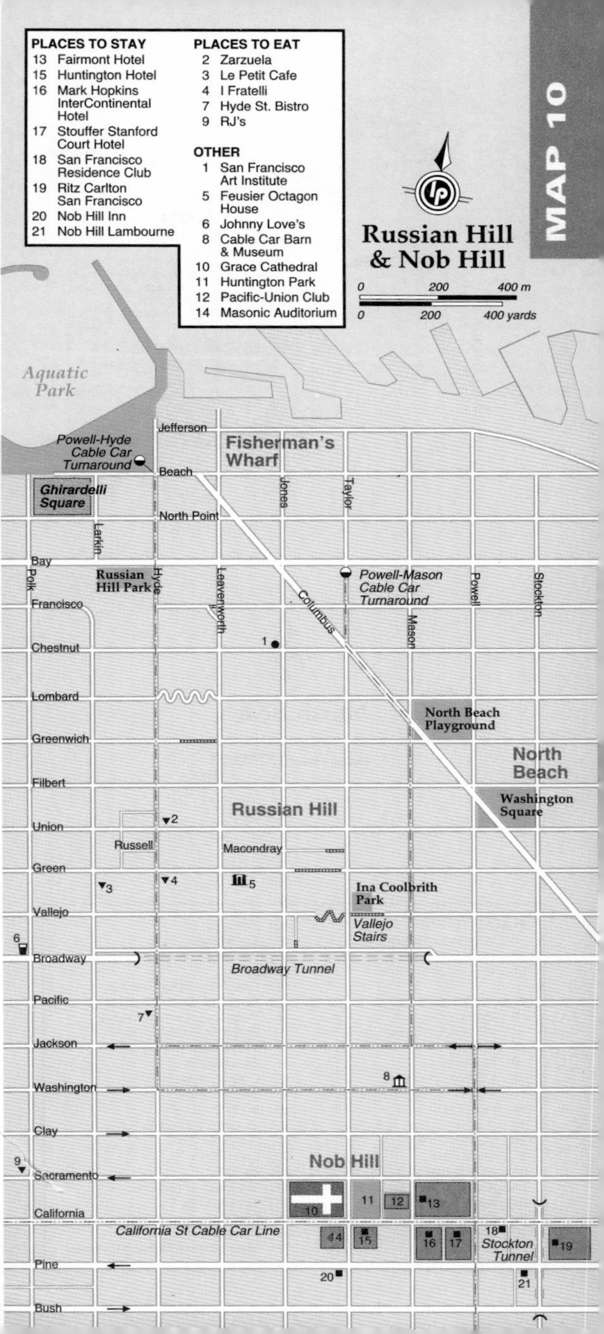

PLACES TO STAY
13 Fairmont Hotel
15 Huntington Hotel
16 Mark Hopkins InterContinental Hotel
17 Stouffer Stanford Court Hotel
18 San Francisco Residence Club
19 Ritz Carlton San Francisco
20 Nob Hill Inn
21 Nob Hill Lambourne

PLACES TO EAT
2 Zarzuela
3 Le Petit Cafe
4 I Fratelli
7 Hyde St. Bistro
9 RJ's

OTHER
1 San Francisco Art Institute
5 Feusier Octagon House
6 Johnny Love's
8 Cable Car Barn & Museum
10 Grace Cathedral
11 Huntington Park
12 Pacific-Union Club
14 Masonic Auditorium

Russian Hill & Nob Hill

0 200 400 m
0 200 400 yards

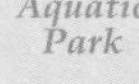

Jefferson
Powell-Hyde Cable Car Turnaround
Fisherman's Wharf
Beach
Ghirardelli Square
Jones
Taylor
North Point
Larkin
Bay
Polk
Russian Hill Park
Hyde
Leavenworth
Powell-Mason Cable Car Turnaround
Powell
Stockton
Francisco
Columbus
Mason
Chestnut
Lombard
North Beach Playground
Greenwich
North Beach
Filbert
Russian Hill
Washington Square
Union
Russell
Macondray
Green
Ina Coolbrith Park
Vallejo
Vallejo Stairs
Broadway
Broadway Tunnel
Pacific
Jackson
Washington
Clay
Nob Hill
Sacramento
California
California St Cable Car Line
Stockton Tunnel
Pine
Bush

MAP 11

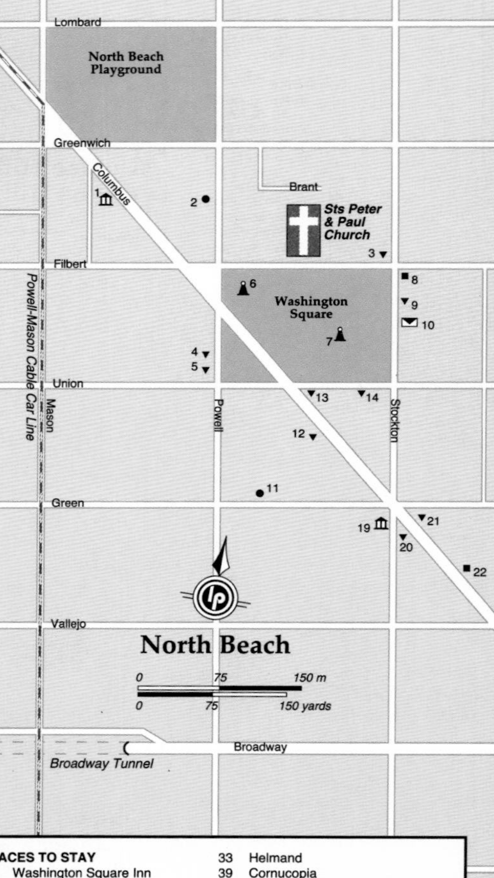

PLACES TO STAY
8 Washington Square Inn
22 Hotel Bohéme
31 Green Tortoise Hostel

PLACES TO EAT
3 Mama's Grill
4 Washington Square Bar & Grill
5 Anthony's
9 Moose's
12 L'Osteria del Forno
13 Mario's Bohemian Cigar Store
14 Fior D'Italia
15 North Beach Pizza
20 US Restaurant
21 Stella Pastry
24 Mo's Burger
25 North Beach Pizza Too
27 Basta Pasta
29 The Stinking Rose
30 Condor Bistro
32 Brandy Ho's
33 Helmand
39 Cornucopia

OTHER
1 Lyle Tuttle Tattoo Museum
2 Rock Posters & Collectibles
6 Volunteer Fireman's Statue
7 Benjamin Franklin Statue
10 Post Office
11 Club Fugazi
16 Quantity Postcards
17 Savoy Tivoli
18 North End Caffe
19 Museum of North Beach
23 Gathering Caffe
26 Cafe Trieste
28 Saloon
34 City Lights Bookstore
35 Vesuvio Cafe
36 Specs'
37 Tosca Cafe
38 San Francisco Brewing Company

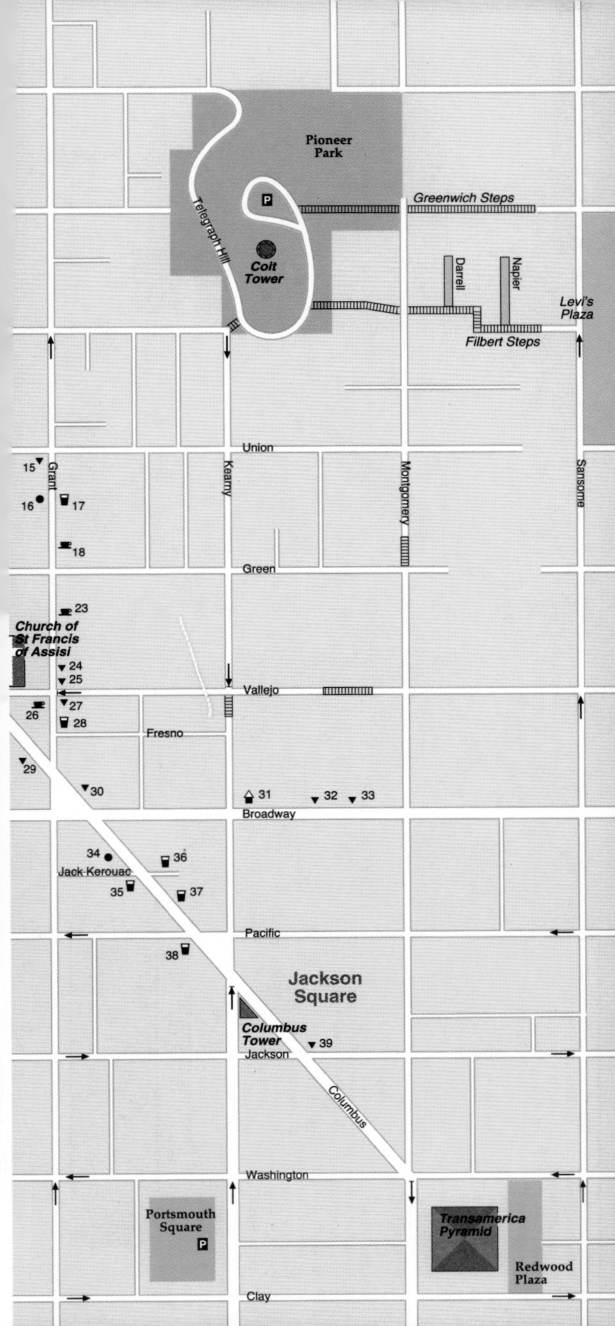

Pioneer Park
Greenwich Steps
Telegraph Hill
Coit Tower
Darrell
Napier
Levi's Plaza
Filbert Steps
Union
Grant
Kearny
Montgomery
Sansome
Green
Church of St Francis of Assisi
Vallejo
Fresno
Broadway
Jack Kerouac
Pacific
Jackson Square
Columbus Tower
Jackson
Columbus
Washington
Portsmouth Square
Transamerica Pyramid
Redwood Plaza
Clay
15
16
17
18
23
24
25
26
27
28
29
30
31
32
33
34
35
36
37
38
39

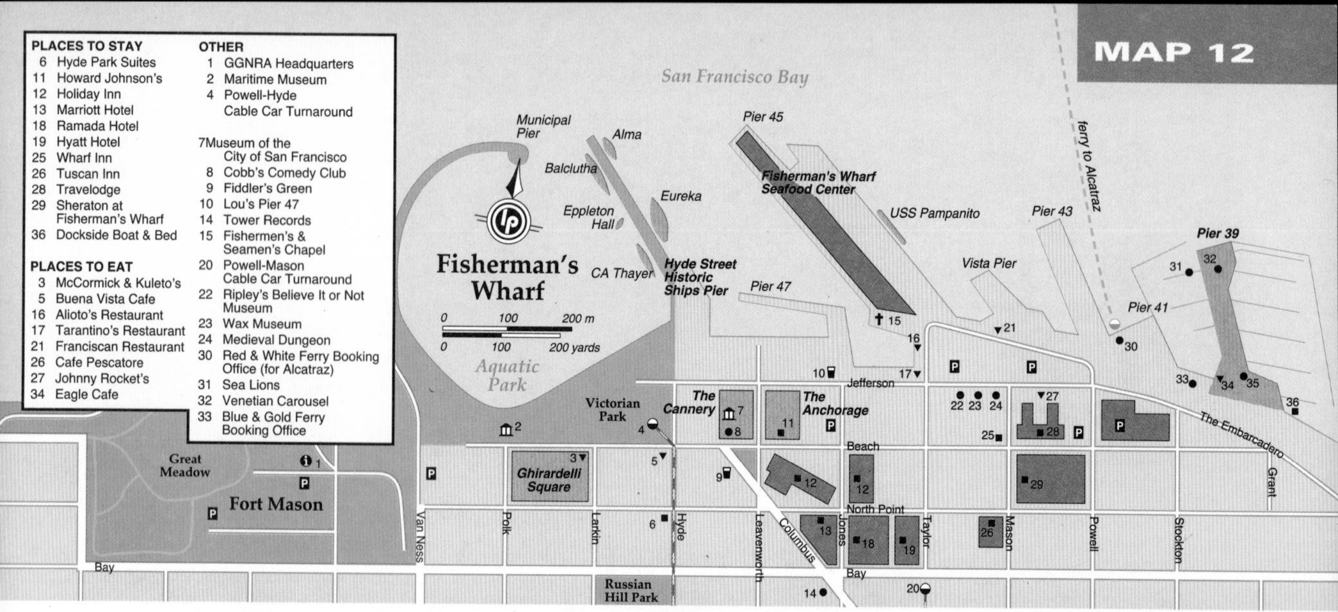

MAP 12

PLACES TO STAY

6 Hyde Park Suites
11 Howard Johnson's
12 Holiday Inn
13 Marriott Hotel
18 Ramada Hotel
19 Hyatt Hotel
25 Wharf Inn
26 Tuscan Inn
28 Travelodge
29 Sheraton at Fisherman's Wharf
36 Dockside Boat & Bed

PLACES TO EAT

3 McCormick & Kuleto's
5 Buena Vista Cafe
16 Alioto's Restaurant
17 Tarantino's Restaurant
21 Franciscan Restaurant
26 Cafe Pescatore
27 Johnny Rocket's
34 Eagle Cafe

OTHER

1 GGNRA Headquarters
2 Maritime Museum
4 Powell-Hyde Cable Car Turnaround
7Museum of the City of San Francisco
8 Cobb's Comedy Club
9 Fiddler's Green
10 Lou's Pier 47
14 Tower Records
15 Fishermen's & Seamen's Chapel
20 Powell-Mason Cable Car Turnaround
22 Ripley's Believe It or Not Museum
23 Wax Museum
24 Medieval Dungeon
30 Red & White Ferry Booking Office (for Alcatraz)
31 Sea Lions
32 Venetian Carousel
33 Blue & Gold Ferry Booking Office

Fisherman's Wharf

0 100 200 m
0 100 200 yards

San Francisco Bay
Municipal Pier
Alma
Balclutha
Eureka
Eppleton Hall
CA Thayer
Hyde Street Historic Ships Pier
Pier 45
Fisherman's Wharf Seafood Center
USS Pampanito
Pier 47
Vista Pier
Pier 43
ferry to Alcatraz
Pier 41
Pier 39
Aquatic Park
Victorian Park
The Cannery
The Anchorage
Ghirardelli Square
Great Meadow
Fort Mason
Russian Hill Park
Jefferson
Beach
North Point
Bay
The Embarcadero
Columbus
Van Ness
Polk
Larkin
Hyde
Leavenworth
Jones
Taylor
Mason
Powell
Stockton
Grant

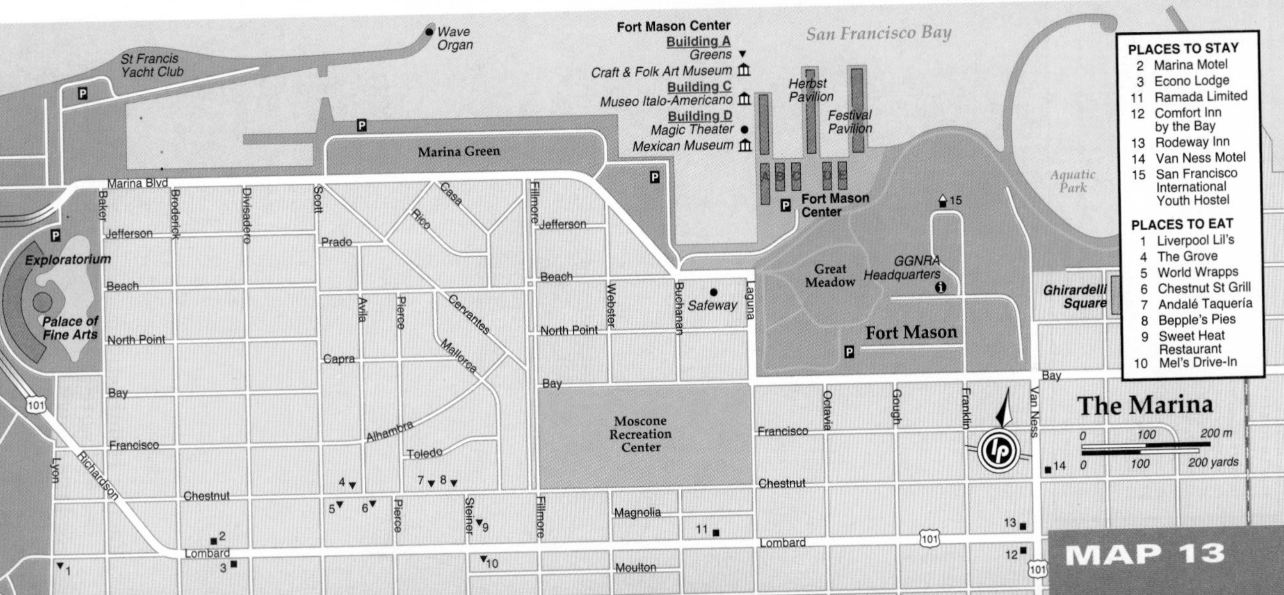
MAP 13
The Marina
PLACES TO STAY
2 Marina Motel
3 Econo Lodge
11 Ramada Limited
12 Comfort Inn by the Bay
13 Rodeway Inn
14 Van Ness Motel
15 San Francisco International Youth Hostel
PLACES TO EAT
1 Liverpool Lil's
4 The Grove
5 World Wrapps
6 Chestnut St Grill
7 Andalé Taquería
8 Bepple's Pies
9 Sweet Heat Restaurant
10 Mel's Drive-In
Fort Mason Center
Building A
Greens
Craft & Folk Art Museum
Building C
Museo Italo-Americano
Building D
Magic Theater
Mexican Museum
San Francisco Bay
Wave Organ
St Francis Yacht Club
Marina Green
Herbst Pavilion
Festival Pavilion
Fort Mason Center
Aquatic Park
Ghirardelli Square
Great Meadow
GGNRA Headquarters
Fort Mason
Safeway
Moscone Recreation Center
Exploratorium
Palace of Fine Arts
Marina Blvd
Baker
Broderick
Divisadero
Scott
Casa
Rico
Fillmore
Jefferson
Prado
Beach
Cervantes
Avila
Pierce
Webster
Buchanan
Laguna
North Point
Capra
Mallorca
Bay
Alhambra
Toledo
Francisco
Octavia
Gough
Franklin
Van Ness
Lyon
Richardson
Chestnut
Steiner
Magnolia
Lombard
Moulton
0 100 200 m
0 100 200 yards

MAP 14

PLACES TO STAY
14 Sherman House
16 Bed & Breakfast Inn
28 El Drisco Hotel
37 Mansions Hotel
48 Best Western Miyako Inn
49 Queen Anne Hotel
50 Majestic Hotel
61 Miyako Hotel

PLACES TO EAT
4 Plump Jack
5 Pane e Vino
7 Yoshida Ya
8 Prego
10 Perry's
11 Bepples Pies
13 Doidge's Kitchen
15 Amici's East Coast Pizzeria
17 Pasand Madras Cuisine
26 Golden Turtle
30 Jackson Fillmore
32 Pauli's Cafe
36 Hillcrest Bar & Cafe
38 Hard Rock Cafe
39 Elite Cafe
40 Pacific Heights Bar & Grill
42 Chestnut Cafe
43 Godzilla Sushi
44 Osome
45 Toraya Sushi Bar & Grill
46 Neecha
47 Pizza Inferno
51 Sanppo
52 Iroha
64 Tommy's Joynt

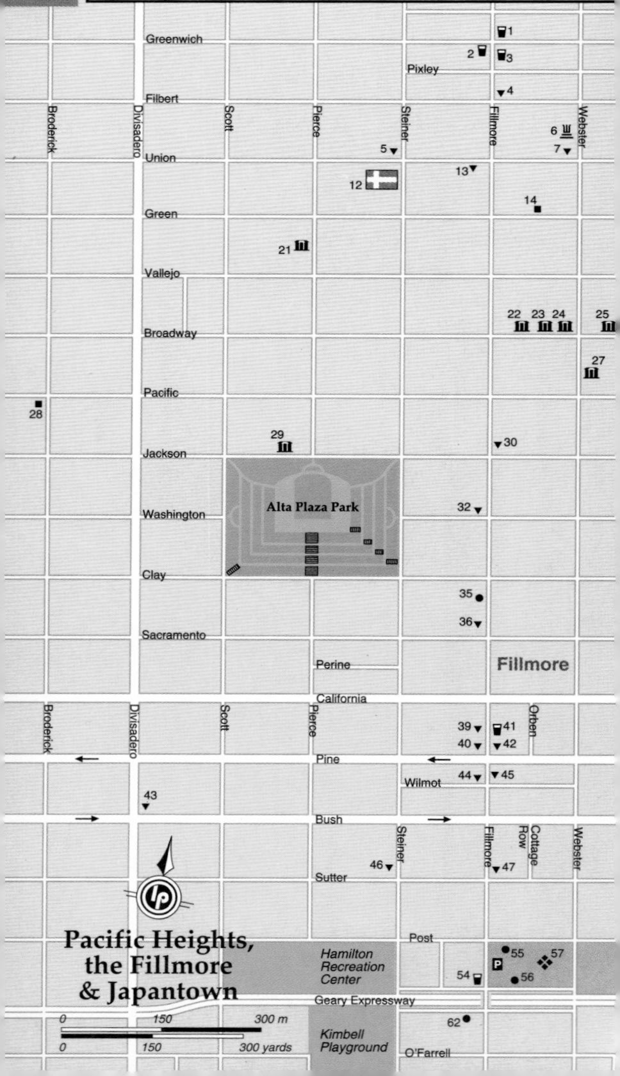

Pacific Heights, the Fillmore & Japantown

OTHER

1 Golden Gate Grill
2 Balboa Cafe
3 Baja Cantina
6 Vedanta Temple Building
9 Union Ale House
12 Church of St. Mary the Virgin
18 Octagon House
19 Holy Trinity Russian Orthodox Cathedral
20 Alhambra Theater
21 Casebolt House
22 Hammond Mansion
23 Second Flood Mansion
24 Grant Mansion
25 First Flood Mansion
27 Bourn House
29 Gibbs House
31 Whittier House
33 Spreckels Mansion
34 Haas-Lilienthal House
35 Clay Theater
41 Harry's Bar
53 Galaxy Cinema
54 Jack's Bar
55 Kabuki 8 Theater
56 Kabuki Hot Spring
57 Kinokuniya Building
58 Kintetsu Restaurant Mall (Isobune, Mifune, Benihana of Tokyo)
59 Peace Pagoda
60 Tasamak Plaza
62 Fillmore Auditorium
63 St. Mary's Cathedral

Filbert
Buchanan
Laguna
Octavia
Gough
Franklin
Van Ness
Polk
Union
Charlton
101
Green
Pacific Heights
Vallejo
Broadway
Pacific
Jackson
Washington
Lafayette Park
Clay
Sacramento
California
California St Cable Car Turnaround
Pine
Bush
Sutter
Buchanan Mall
Japantown
Post
Japan Center
Geary
O'Farrell

MAP 15

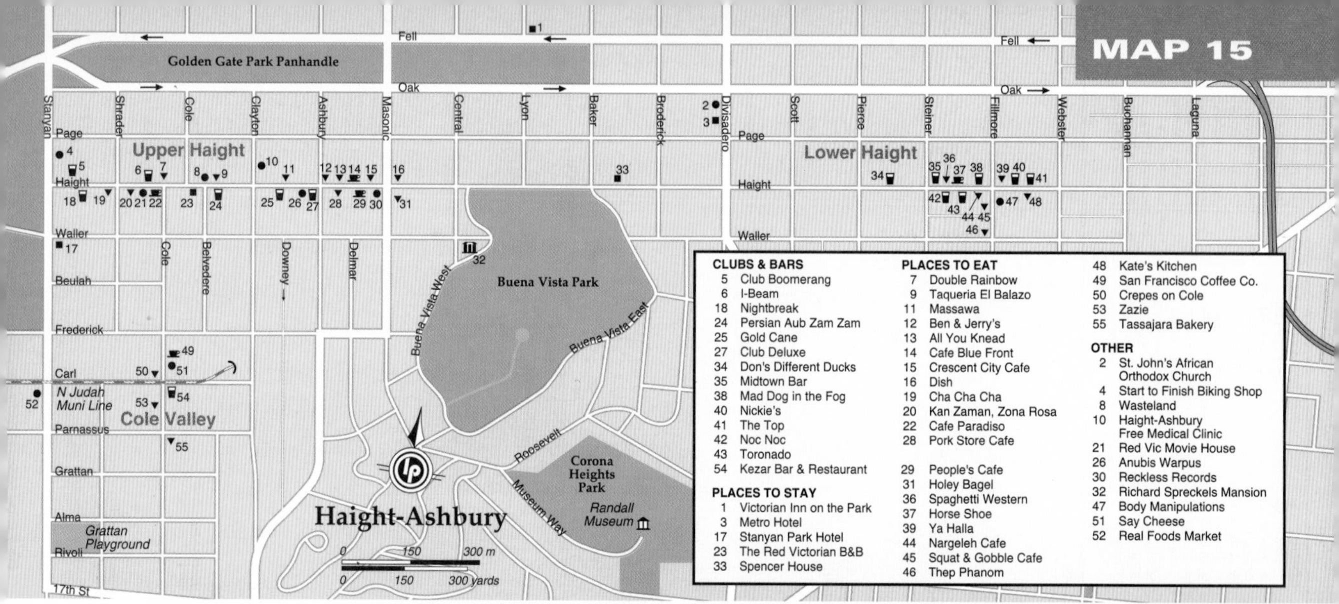

Haight-Ashbury

CLUBS & BARS

5 Club Boomerang
6 I-Beam
18 Nightbreak
24 Persian Aub Zam Zam
25 Gold Cane
27 Club Deluxe
34 Don's Different Ducks
35 Midtown Bar
38 Mad Dog in the Fog
40 Nickie's
41 The Top
42 Noc Noc
43 Toronado
54 Kezar Bar & Restaurant

PLACES TO STAY

1 Victorian Inn on the Park
3 Metro Hotel
17 Stanyan Park Hotel
23 The Red Victorian B&B
33 Spencer House

PLACES TO EAT

7 Double Rainbow
9 Taqueria El Balazo
11 Massawa
12 Ben & Jerry's
13 All You Knead
14 Cafe Blue Front
15 Crescent City Cafe
16 Dish
19 Cha Cha Cha
20 Kan Zaman, Zona Rosa
22 Cafe Paradiso
28 Pork Store Cafe
29 People's Cafe
31 Holey Bagel
36 Spaghetti Western
37 Horse Shoe
39 Ya Halla
44 Nargeleh Cafe
45 Squat & Gobble Cafe
46 Thep Phanom
48 Kate's Kitchen
49 San Francisco Coffee Co.
50 Crepes on Cole
53 Zazie
55 Tassajara Bakery

OTHER

2 St. John's African Orthodox Church
4 Start to Finish Biking Shop
8 Wasteland
10 Haight-Ashbury Free Medical Clinic
21 Red Vic Movie House
26 Anubis Warpus
30 Reckless Records
32 Richard Spreckels Mansion
47 Body Manipulations
51 Say Cheese
52 Real Foods Market

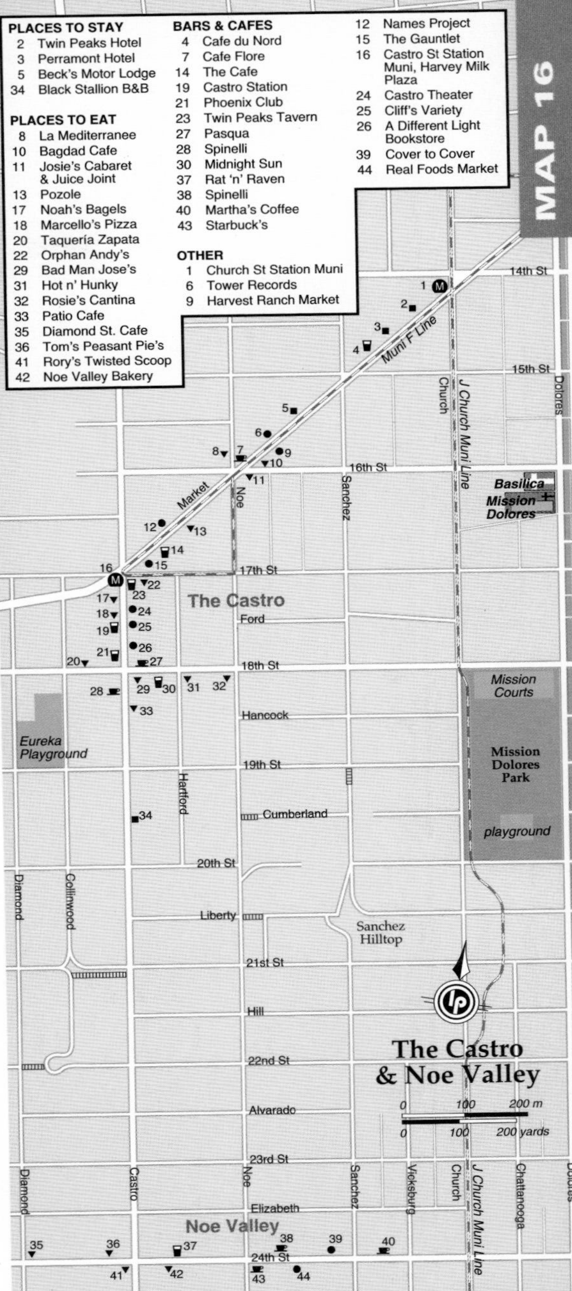
MAP 16
PLACES TO STAY
2 Twin Peaks Hotel
3 Perramont Hotel
5 Beck's Motor Lodge
34 Black Stallion B&B
PLACES TO EAT
8 La Mediterranee
10 Bagdad Cafe
11 Josie's Cabaret & Juice Joint
13 Pozole
17 Noah's Bagels
18 Marcello's Pizza
20 Taquería Zapata
22 Orphan Andy's
29 Bad Man Jose's
31 Hot n' Hunky
32 Rosie's Cantina
33 Patio Cafe
35 Diamond St. Cafe
36 Tom's Peasant Pie's
41 Rory's Twisted Scoop
42 Noe Valley Bakery
BARS & CAFES
4 Cafe du Nord
7 Cafe Flore
14 The Cafe
19 Castro Station
21 Phoenix Club
23 Twin Peaks Tavern
27 Pasqua
28 Spinelli
30 Midnight Sun
37 Rat 'n' Raven
38 Spinelli
40 Martha's Coffee
43 Starbuck's
OTHER
1 Church St Station Muni
6 Tower Records
9 Harvest Ranch Market
12 Names Project
15 The Gauntlet
16 Castro St Station Muni, Harvey Milk Plaza
24 Castro Theater
25 Cliff's Variety
26 A Different Light Bookstore
39 Cover to Cover
44 Real Foods Market
14th St
15th St
16th St
17th St
18th St
19th St
20th St
21st St
22nd St
23rd St
24th St
Muni F Line
Market
Noe
Sanchez
Church
J Church Muni Line
Dolores
Basilica Mission Dolores
The Castro
Ford
Hancock
Cumberland
Liberty
Hill
Alvarado
Elizabeth
Hartford
Diamond
Collinwood
Castro
Vicksburg
Chattanooga
Eureka Playground
Mission Courts
Mission Dolores Park
playground
Sanchez Hilltop
Noe Valley
The Castro & Noe Valley
0 100 200 m
0 100 200 yards

MAP 17

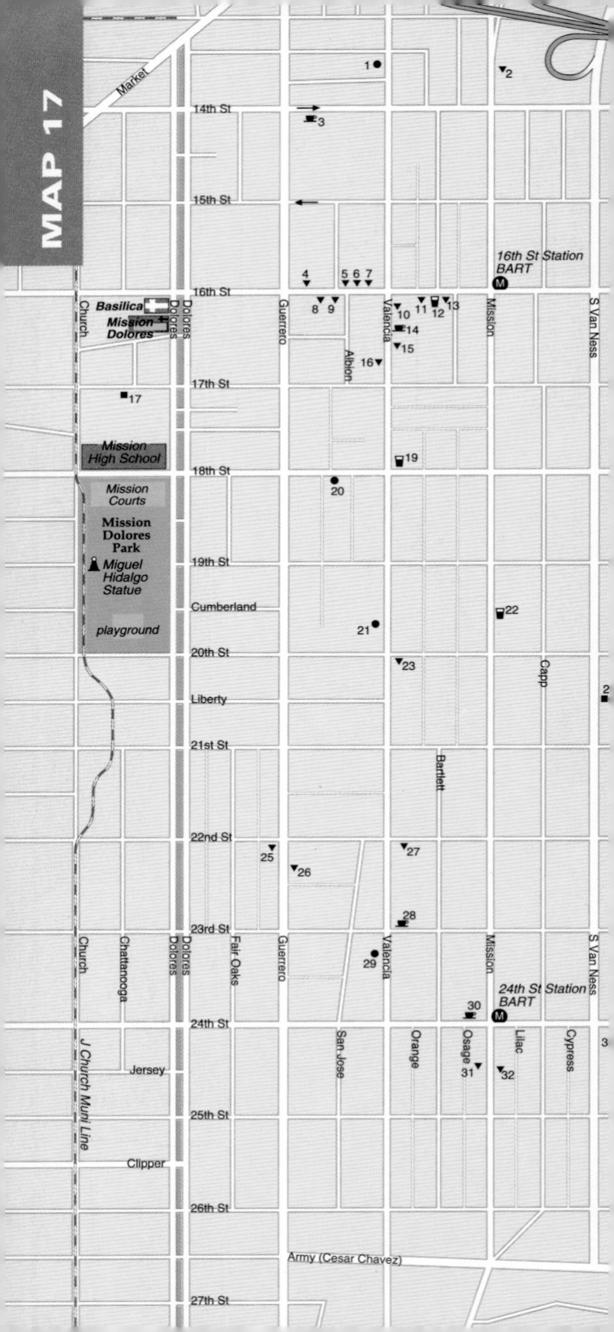

Market
14th St
15th St
16th St Station BART
16th St
Church
Basilica
Mission Dolores
Dolores
Dolores
Guerrero
Albion
Valencia
Mission
S Van Ness
17th St
Mission High School
18th St
Mission Courts
Mission Dolores Park
Miguel Hidalgo Statue
playground
19th St
Cumberland
20th St
Capp
Liberty
21st St
Bartlett
22nd St
23rd St
Church
Chattanooga
Dolores
Dolores
Fair Oaks
Guerrero
Valencia
Mission
S Van Ness
24th St Station BART
24th St
San Jose
Orange
Osage
Lilac
Cypress
Jersey
J Church Muni Line
25th St
Clipper
26th St
Army (Cesar Chavez)
27th St
1
2
3
4
5
6
7
8
9
10
11
12
13
14
15
16
17
19
20
21
22
23
25
26
27
28
29
30
31
32

The Mission

PLACES TO STAY
17 Dolores Park Inn
24 Inn San Francisco

PLACES TO EAT
2 Woodward's Garden
4 Pastaio
5 Aunt Mary's
6 Cafe Picaro
7 Ti Couz
8 Cafe Macondo
9 Truly Mediterranean
10 Taquería La Cumbre
11 Panchitas
13 Taquería Pancho Villa
15 Cafe Istanbul
16 Puerto Alegre
23 La Rondalla
25 Flying Saucer
26 Le Trou
27 Esperpento
31 La Taquería San Jose
32 La Tacqueria
33 El Nuevo Fruitlandia

OTHER
1 Levi Strauss Factory
3 Red Dora's Bearded Lady Cafe & Gallery
12 Esta Noche
14 Muddy Waters
18 Rite Spot
19 Elbo Room
20 Women's Building, Dovre Club
21 Modern Times Bookshop
22 Original McCarthy's
28 Radio Valencia Cafe
29 Good Vibrations
30 Cafe La Boheme

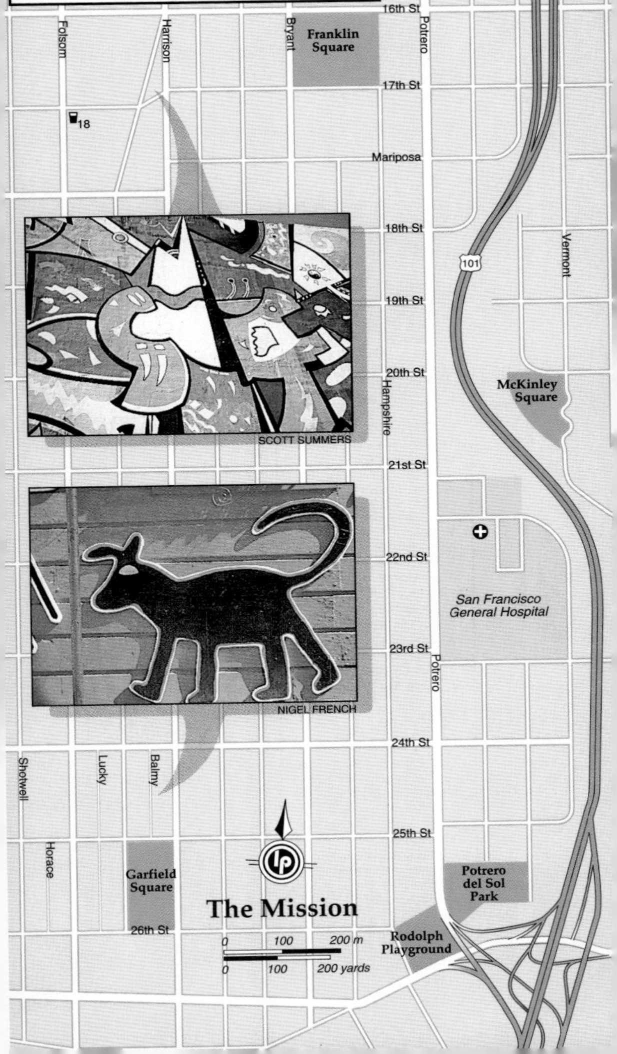

16th St
17th St
Mariposa
18th St
19th St
20th St
21st St
22nd St
23rd St
24th St
25th St
26th St
Folsom
Harrison
Bryant
Potrero
Hampshire
Vermont
Shotwell
Lucky
Balmy
Horace
Franklin Square
McKinley Square
San Francisco General Hospital
Garfield Square
Potrero del Sol Park
Rodolph Playground
101
18

SCOTT SUMMERS

NIGEL FRENCH

0 100 200 m
0 100 200 yards

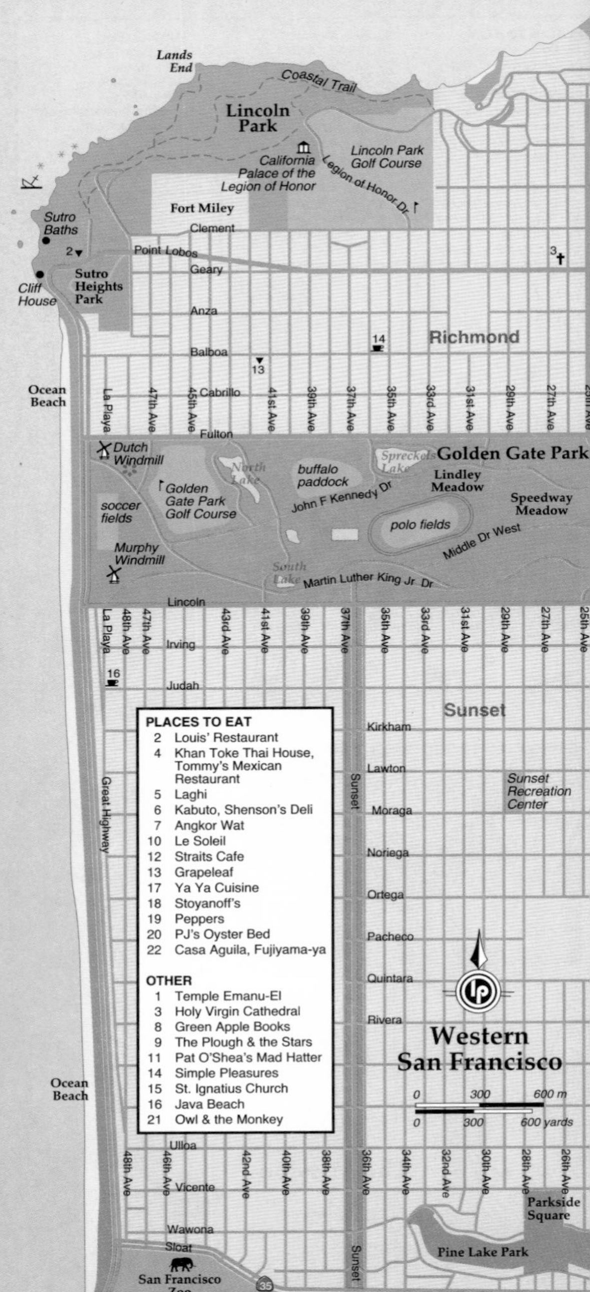
Western
San Francisco
Lands End
Coastal Trail
Lincoln Park
California Palace of the Legion of Honor
Lincoln Park Golf Course
Legion of Honor Dr
Fort Miley
Sutro Baths
Cliff House
Sutro Heights Park
Clement
Point Lobos
Geary
Anza
Balboa
Cabrillo
Fulton
Richmond
Ocean Beach
La Playa
47th Ave
45th Ave
41st Ave
39th Ave
37th Ave
35th Ave
33rd Ave
31st Ave
29th Ave
27th Ave
Golden Gate Park
Dutch Windmill
North Lake
buffalo paddock
Spreckels Lake
Lindley Meadow
Speedway Meadow
Golden Gate Park Golf Course
soccer fields
John F Kennedy Dr
polo fields
Middle Dr West
Murphy Windmill
South Lake
Martin Luther King Jr Dr
Lincoln
48th Ave
43rd Ave
25th Ave
Irving
Judah
Sunset
Kirkham
Lawton
Moraga
Noriega
Ortega
Pacheco
Quintara
Rivera
Great Highway
Sunset Recreation Center
PLACES TO EAT
2 Louis' Restaurant
4 Khan Toke Thai House, Tommy's Mexican Restaurant
5 Laghi
6 Kabuto, Shenson's Deli
7 Angkor Wat
10 Le Soleil
12 Straits Cafe
13 Grapeleaf
17 Ya Ya Cuisine
18 Stoyanoff's
19 Peppers
20 PJ's Oyster Bed
22 Casa Aguila, Fujiyama-ya
OTHER
1 Temple Emanu-El
3 Holy Virgin Cathedral
8 Green Apple Books
9 The Plough & the Stars
11 Pat O'Shea's Mad Hatter
14 Simple Pleasures
15 St. Ignatius Church
16 Java Beach
21 Owl & the Monkey
0 300 600 m
0 300 600 yards
Ulloa
Vicente
Wawona
Sloat
46th Ave
42nd Ave
40th Ave
38th Ave
36th Ave
34th Ave
32nd Ave
30th Ave
28th Ave
26th Ave
Parkside Square
Pine Lake Park
San Francisco Zoo
35